SOCIAL WORK THEORY IN PRACTICE

Sara Miller McCune founded SAGE Publishing in 1965 to support the dissemination of usable knowledge and educate a global community. SAGE publishes more than 1000 journals and over 800 new books each year, spanning a wide range of subject areas. Our growing selection of library products includes archives, data, case studies and video. SAGE remains majority owned by our founder and after her lifetime will become owned by a charitable trust that secures the company's continued independence.

Los Angeles | London | New Delhi | Singapore | Washington DC | Melbourne

SOCIAL WORK THEORY IN PRACTICE

PHILIP HESLOP & CATHRYN MEREDITH

Los Angeles | London | New Delhi
Singapore | Washington DC | Melbourne

Los Angeles | London | New Delhi
Singapore | Washington DC | Melbourne

SAGE Publications Ltd
1 Oliver's Yard
55 City Road
London EC1Y 1SP

SAGE Publications Inc.
2455 Teller Road
Thousand Oaks, California 91320

SAGE Publications India Pvt Ltd
B 1/I 1 Mohan Cooperative Industrial Area
Mathura Road
New Delhi 110 044

SAGE Publications Asia-Pacific Pte Ltd
3 Church Street
#10-04 Samsung Hub
Singapore 049483

© Philip Heslop and Cathryn Meredith 2021

First published 2021

Apart from any fair dealing for the purposes of research or private study, or criticism or review, as permitted under the Copyright, Designs and Patents Act, 1988, this publication may be reproduced, stored or transmitted in any form, or by any means, only with the prior permission in writing of the publishers, or in the case of reprographic reproduction, in accordance with the terms of licences issued by the Copyright Licensing Agency. Enquiries concerning reproduction outside those terms should be sent to the publishers.

Editor: Kate Keers
Assistant editor: Ruth Lilly
Production editor: Martin Fox
Copyeditor: Jane Fricker
Proofreader: Derek Markham
Indexer: Martin Hargreaves
Marketing manager: Camille Richmond
Cover design: Wendy Scott
Typeset by: C&M Digitals (P) Ltd, Chennai, India
Printed in the UK

Library of Congress Control Number: 2020937812

British Library Cataloguing in Publication data

A catalogue record for this book is available from the British Library

ISBN 978-1-5264-9237-1
ISBN 978-1-5264-9236-4 (pbk)

At SAGE we take sustainability seriously. Most of our products are printed in the UK using responsibly sourced papers and boards. When we print overseas we ensure sustainable papers are used as measured by the PREPS grading system. We undertake an annual audit to monitor our sustainability.

This book is dedicated to our much-loved friend, colleague, and office roommate, Rosanne Cooper. Rosanne was full of warmth and humour, and truly passionate about social work practice and education. She had an unparalleled ability to come up with a pragmatic solution for absolutely any situation. We miss her terribly.

CONTENTS

ABOUT THE AUTHORS

Philip Heslop (Phil)

I have been a social worker since 1992 and chose social work as a profession to challenge inequality and discrimination. I have worked mainly in childcare social work, and from 1995, specifically in fostering and adoption. I have worked in statutory, voluntary and independent social work and have worked in all four countries of the UK. I developed a specialism working with male carers, as well as caring for children on the autism spectrum. I have held a wide range of practice, training, reviewing and management roles. I am qualified to teach adults and children, have been an NVQ assessor and am a Fellow of the Higher Education Academy. I joined Northumbria University's teaching team in 2013 where I teach across all social work programmes. I am particularly interested in why people need social work support, how practitioners engage people they work with and compassionate people-based practice.

Cathryn Meredith (Cat)

I qualified as a social worker in 2001, and went on to practise in a variety of mental health settings. I became an Approved Social Worker (ASW) and later an Approved Mental Health Professional (AMHP). I developed a special interest in working with people diagnosed with emotionally unstable personality disorder, although I don't subscribe to this label. I qualified as a Best Interests Assessor (BIA), and went on to become a local authority Mental Capacity Act lead. From 2013 until its closure, I was a College of Social Work accredited Expert Safeguarding Adults Practitioner. I began teaching and researching at Northumbria University in 2013, focusing particularly on social work with adults, human rights and mental health. I am a Fellow of the Higher Education Academy and I am currently completing a PhD, which explores the personalisation of safeguarding when people are experiencing dementia.

ACKNOWLEDGEMENTS

Philip ~ To Cath and my two granddaughters, Grace Binney and Lucy Heslop, along with Joe, Simon, Siobhan, Scott and Kayleigh. Thank you.

Cathryn ~ To my fantastic family, Stew, Mia and Jean, and all of my friends in the Rona Room. Thank you for getting me through!

INTRODUCTION

In our earlier book, *Social Work: From Assessment to Intervention*, we set out our view that social workers are concerned with working with people – often during very difficult times – to make sense of complex and difficult situations and understand how to navigate towards solutions. Whether we use it intentionally or instinctively, formally or informally, theory is what guides this sense making. The decisions that we reach about how to intervene with people who are in need or at risk are informed by our theoretical knowledge and how we theorise – attempt to explain – their situations. The decisions that we make as social workers can have an enormous impact on people's lives, so it is crucial that they are informed by more than assumption and good intentions. In this book, we aim to introduce theoretical knowledge in an accessible way, demonstrating its relevance to social work and exploring its application in practice. Whether you are beginning your qualifying training, are in the early years of practice, or are a more experienced social worker attending to your continuing professional development (CPD), this book will equip you with the underpinning theoretical knowledge you need to practise with people – communally and organisationally.

Social work: Theory in practice

Social work's relationship with theory is undeniable yet contentious; debates have long persisted about where the balance between theory and practice lies. In the UK, the introduction of fast-track, practice-based models of social work education appears to have further polarised opinion. In 2013, the year that the first Frontline cohort began, two reviews of social work education were commissioned. Professor David Croisdale-Appleby was invited to review social work education from the perspective of adult social care, whilst Sir Martin Narey was invited to undertake a concurrent review considering the children's workforce. The reports of the two reviews presented very different stances on the relationship between theory and social work practice. Martin Narey's *Making the Education of Social Workers Consistently Effective* (2014) suggested that theory had, perhaps, been overemphasised in social work education. He cited his conversation with a Director of Children's Services who told him, 'Universities have been allowed to provide too much theory, too much sociology and not enough about spotting things in a family which are wrong' (p. 30), and reported what the chair of the Victoria Climbié inquiry, Lord Laming, had said of social work education: 'I suspect it has been captured by academics more comfortable with theory than preparation to practice' (p. 38). David

Croisdale-Appleby's report, *Re-visioning Social Work Education* (2014), however, saw theory as intrinsic to social work education and practice:

> social work education is an extraordinarily complex subject because it draws upon a wide range of other academic disciplines, and synthesises from those disciplines its own chosen set of beliefs, precepts, ideologies, doctrines and authority. As a profession, social work requires its practitioners to understand intricate and often seemingly impenetrable behaviours and situations, whilst not having the same level of objective scientific support for their analysis and conclusions to assist them and upon which to rely as have, for example medical and other clinical practitioners or expert witnesses with forensic science expertise. Rather, social workers have to rely on their understanding of social work theory, their knowledge of lives of disadvantaged and vulnerable people and their own mental processes and judgement ... So the task for social work education is to equip practitioners with the theoretical knowledge and practical capability to do high quality work which is characterised in this way. It requires education in which both theory-informing practice and practice-informing-theory are inexorably linked. (p. 15)

Readers will not be surprised to hear that the authors of this book are firmly team Croisdale-Appleby! We do not see a fight between theory and practice; we believe that the two are symbiotic. However, we are very aware that students find it difficult to navigate the conflicting messages that they are given about theory in social work, and we also recognise that they can experience tension and disconnect between the theory they are taught and the experience of *doing* social work.

We continue to encounter many social workers who subscribe to what Neil Thompson (2010) terms *the fallacy of theoryless practice*. They firmly assert an anti-intellectual stance and argue that social work is premised on intuition and practice wisdom. Mullaly sums this up perfectly, noting that many

> social workers either turn cold or rebel at the mere mention of theory. Theory is viewed as esoteric, abstract, and something people discuss in universities. Practice, on the other hand, is seen as common sense, concrete, and occurring in the real world. (1997, p. 99)

We consider this a dangerous stance. To accept current practices, received wisdom and prevailing ideas as common sense, rather than understanding that they are theoretically driven, is to practise uncritically. Uncritical social workers enact power without thinking about power structures, therefore accept the status quo, rather than challenging it. Conversely, many social work educators present theoretical knowledge in an inaccessible, exclusionary or unhelpful way. Theory is talked about *a lot* in social work, and this can feel overwhelming when you are starting out and concepts are new and unfamiliar. The vastness of the theoretical knowledge base and the multitude of competing/contradictory perspectives are daunting, and the language of theory can seem impenetrable. Unfamiliar terminology may be used unintentionally, or it may represent conscious intellectual elitism; either way, it can reinforce ideas that theory is a higher order, academic activity, far removed from the very practical, interpersonal skills of social work.

It is easy to see why many people entering the social work profession become confused by debates which seem to artificially and reductively pit theory and practice against each other. During the course of our teaching, we have come to recognise a phenomenon amongst our students – on both qualifying and post-qualifying programmes – that Professor of Education Pat Thompson refers to as *theory-fright* (Thompson, 2018). Just as stage-fright can leave an actor unable to adequately perform their role, theory-fright can impede and limit social work practice. Left unchecked, theory-fright goes on to result in anti-intellectualism, theory avoidance, theory denial, assertions of theoryless practice and an overall uncritical approach.

Theory-fright

If the terms used to discuss theory aren't explained or defined, then there is an assumption that they are understood. But what if you *don't* understand what the lecturer or author means? Theory is so strongly emphasised in social work education, literature, policy and discourse, that students can feel too embarrassed to stop the lecturer and ask for clarification – what if everyone else in the room knows exactly what they mean? *Surely the lecturer would explain this term if it was anything other than blindingly obvious, wouldn't she? I must be stupid.* The more the undefined term is used, the more inadequate the student feels and the less engaged they become. The student associates theory with the negative emotions that they are experiencing and decides they will just never get it. Theory-fright has set in.

Others might have an excellent grasp of theory in the classroom, but struggle to relate their knowledge to their practice. Imagine a student on the first day of placement is given a desk next to a social worker who immediately says, 'forget all of that theory nonsense from university, this is the real world'. The student shadows members of the team and sees *what* they do, but the pace is so busy, there is no time to ask them *why*. Supervision sessions are rushed and theory is never discussed, only case management. A placement review is coming up where the student will be expected to talk about how theory has been applied in practice. The student feels confused, unprepared and anxious. Theory-fright has set in.

Our motivation in writing this book is to save you from theory-fright by providing an accessible entry point. We want to promote your confidence in understanding theory and how it can be incorporated in social work practice by providing uncomplicated descriptions, definitions, insights and examples of a wide range of theoretical perspectives and constructs. Our strong commitment is to challenge anti-intellectualism by demystifying theoretical knowledge and helping you to see that theory is everywhere in social work. Don't avoid it, embrace it!

Structure of the text

As social work educators, we understand that learning is more effective when knowledge is contextualised, allowing consideration of how it relates to and can be incorporated into practice situations. To give life and context to the learning offered, we have populated this book with case studies involving fictional social workers who share an office as they reflect on their interactions with individuals and families experiencing a broad range of social issues. The characters embody different practice experience, theoretical perspectives and approaches relevant to contemporary social work.

Through them we explore mechanisms for professional development and notice how practice changes and develops over time. There is enormous pressure on social workers to 'get things right', but we do not develop an ability to do this simply by qualifying to practise. Social workers never stop professionally developing; our practice and our thinking evolve over time in response to our experiences. We also share examples from the authors' own practice to humanise and model how reflection supports professional development. All chapters include learning exercises to support you to reflect on your developing understanding of theory and explore how it can be applied.

The book is structured in two parts:

Part I Theory: Explaining the world and understanding our practice

These chapters are thematically grouped, with each explaining a range of related theories and considering how they connect to social work.

Chapter 1: Understanding theory in practice

This chapter establishes a foundation on which subsequent chapters will build by setting out general parameters of theory. We explore what it is and is not, recognising it as a 'fuzzy' concept that can be both formal and informal, explicit and intuitive. We consider how social work's relationship with theory has evolved and why social work is a theory-driven profession.

Chapter 2: Foundations of theory in social work

Social work draws theory from a wide range of fields; however, some disciplines have been so influential on social work that they can be considered *foundational* to how our profession has evolved, how social services are organised and delivered, and how we practise as social workers. In this chapter, we explore core theoretical tenets of religion, philosophy, psychology and sociology to offer context for theories from these fields which are explored in subsequent chapters.

Chapter 3: Economics, politics and the organisational delivery of social work

Social work is a public service shaped and directed by the economic, political and organisational context in which it takes place. This chapter considers how economic and political theories influence each other and result in social policy: considering, for example, how neoliberalism has reduced the welfare state and responsibilised citizens, how New Public Management and managerialism have reduced social workers' individual autonomy, and how austerity has increased demand for social work whilst simultaneously withdrawing resources.

Chapter 4: Critical and radical theories

This chapter focuses on theories which take a critical approach to explore society and challenge received wisdom. We introduce Gramsci's notions of hegemony, exploring how power relations and accepted cultural norms directly influence our practice as social workers. We consider theories of modernism, postmodernism and post-traditionalism, and some of the prominent theorists associated with them. The final part of the chapter specifically explores radical and critical models of social work which can help us empower the people we work with, challenge inequality, and take progressive action.

Chapter 5: Theories of human development

Social workers need knowledge of how humans behave, develop and change across the life course. In this chapter we present a selection of theories which consider humans' behavioural, psychological, cognitive and social development from birth through to end of life. We explore staged theories of development as well as theories that help us to understand how people learn. Ageing is introduced as a social construct, as well as a biological process, and we examine how society creates normative assumptions of how people should behave at particular points in their life, which can contribute to ageism.

Chapter 6: Theories of systems and relationships

Systemic and relationship-based practice are increasingly popular social work approaches. In this chapter, we begin by exploring what systems are and general principles about how they behave, before focusing on theories which help us to understand and make sense of *social* systems. We consider relationships and interconnections between people, groups and society through key theoretical approaches which frequently underpin contemporary social work discourses, such as ecology, complexity, intersectionality and attachment. Arguably the system that social work encounters the most frequently is the family, therefore this chapter explores what family means and how it is established in the 21st century.

Chapter 7: Theories of risk and vulnerability

This chapter considers how risk has come to dominate contemporary society, influencing models of safeguarding which have shifted social work from focusing on people's needs, to focusing on people's safety. Moving beyond locating problems in individuals, we consider how stigma, inequality and discrimination create vulnerabilities which place people at risk. We present knowledge of a range of theories relating to needs around which services are usually organised (physical and mental health needs, disability, learning disability, dementia, etc.), as well as considering how poverty and socioeconomic factors perpetuate inequality.

Part II Practice: Using theory in our work with people

Scaffolding on the foundation of knowledge established in Part I, each chapter in Part II focuses on a particular area of social work practice. The practice context is established by summarising key considerations, legislation and policy, and case studies demonstrate how theories from Part I are applied.

Chapter 8: Applying theory in practice

We want theoretical knowledge to be something that you embrace as a key part of your practice, but we know that is not easy! In this chapter we consider the mechanisms you can harness to meaningfully incorporate theory into your practice. We explore praxis, critical reflection, theoretical and conceptual frameworks, theorising and hypothesising, and consider how theory can be incorporated into supervision – and why sadly, it often is not.

Chapter 9: Children and their families

This chapter sets out how legislation and policy shape the practice context of social work with children and their families. It considers the rights of both children and parents, and explores how theory manifests in three children and families practice scenarios:

- Trish undertakes a safeguarding assessment in response to an urgent situation
- Martin and Akram visit a young person for a looked after child review
- Karen assesses a mother's parenting capacity and makes recommendations

Chapter 10: Foster and kinship care

The vast majority of *looked after children* are in foster or kinship care placements. This chapter looks at the range of circumstances which can lead to children being fostered, the different types of placements they might experience, and how foster and kinship carers are assessed and supported. Theory is explored through three fostering practice scenarios:

- Judith responds to a young person going missing from placement
- Akram supports kinship carers
- Martin assesses prospective foster carers

Chapter 11: Offenders

This chapter considers the link between social factors and offending behaviour, and the multiple ways in which social work responds to offenders. It explores specialist roles social workers may undertake in Youth Offending Teams or Liaison and Diversion Services, and recognises that people who offend have social needs and are entitled to have them met in the same way as anyone else. Three practice scenarios explore how theory informs social work with offenders:

- Martin case manages a young offender who has been involved in *county lines*
- Judith assesses the needs of an offender
- Akram acts as an Appropriate Adult

Chapter 12: Physical disabilities

Society is largely designed for bodies which function in a particular way, and so people whose physicality does not match this assumption are disabled by it. This chapter looks at how people with a diverse range of physical presentations are disabled and disadvantaged by both government policy and societal attitudes, and establishes social work's role in challenging this. Three practice scenarios consider how theory can help social workers to understand the needs and experiences of people with disabilities:

- Martin and Akram undertake a Care Act assessment of Kendra, who has multiple sclerosis
- Akram reflects on his assessment of a family whose son uses a wheelchair
- Trish considers her identity as a deaf woman and reflects on her colleague Karen's adjustment to physical disability

Chapter 13: Mental distress

Needs relating to mental wellbeing are so prevalent that we encounter them whatever the focus of our social work practice. This chapter considers how mental distress has historically been viewed as a health issue, but is increasingly recognised to be a response to social factors. It establishes that social workers have a key role in promoting mental wellbeing and responding to difficulties. Theory is applied in three practice scenarios:

- Judith supports Kian, a young man diagnosed with schizophrenia
- Lloyd responds to a safeguarding alert about a vulnerable person
- Lloyd helps Akram to prepare for an assessment of Barry, who has depression

Chapter 14: Learning disabilities and autism

People with learning disabilities and autism have been subjected to stigma, abuse and inequality throughout history. This chapter examines three recent examples of this: the tragic and unnecessary death of Connor Sparrowhawk; the inhumane incarceration of Bethany; and the Whorlton Hall abuse scandal. Theory is used in three different practice situations:

- Karen has contact with Marie, a parent with autism
- Martin visits George, who has a learning disability
- Lloyd writes a blog post about assessing mental capacity

Chapter 15: Older people

All across the world, people are living longer. Unfortunately, our ageing society is also an ageist society, which assumes that older people have less to offer than the young. This chapter explores how negative stereotypes are perpetuated and recognises the need for policies, services and practices which value older people, represent their true diversity and aspire for people of all ages to live full, active and satisfying lives. Theory is incorporated in three practice scenarios:

- Trish begins a safeguarding enquiry after a hospital raises concerns about Geri
- Ali investigates a complaint about a hospital discharge
- Dianne undertakes a carer's assessment

THE SOCIAL WORKERS

This book is rooted in practice, and we have populated it with case studies involving social workers located in a busy local authority team. They undertake a broad range of work which in real life would straddle many different teams. The character case studies enable us to explore a range of different practice experience, theoretical perspectives and approaches to understand situations and identify possible courses of action. As well as interacting with people and families experiencing a wide range of social issues, the social workers interact with each other, allowing us to explore mechanisms for professional support and development including reflection and formal and informal supervision.

ALI has been a qualified social worker for over 20 years and is now a team manager. He is very knowledgeable about theory, but generally views anti-oppressive practice as his overall ethos and approach.

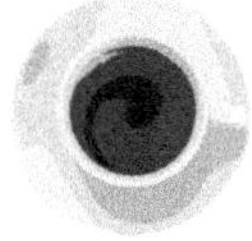

KAREN is a very experienced senior practitioner. Her practice is theoretically informed, measured, considerate and eclectic. She has recently experienced life changing circumstances.

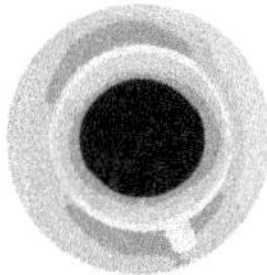

DIANNE has been a social worker for 15 years. She is somewhat sceptical about theory, believing that social work is largely intuitive and based upon common sense. She is Akram's practice educator.

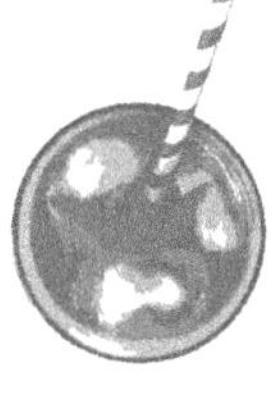

JUDITH is a social, political and environmental activist who is proud to have been a frontline social worker for over 35 years. She is radical, anarchic, anti-establishment and outspoken about her belief that public sector workers should be servants, not masters.

MARTIN has been qualified for four years and recently went on an intensive systemic practice training course. It helped him to understand and think differently about some of his own relationships and early life experiences and he is now a passionate advocate of the approach.

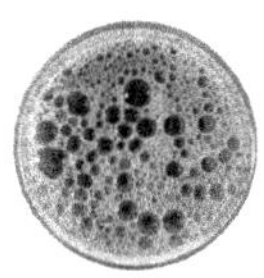

TRISH is a deaf woman. She has been qualified for three years and is drawn to logical and scientific approaches, such as structured assessment tools and decision trees. Trish believes that effective social work is based upon strict adherence to legislation, policy and procedure.

LLOYD is a newly qualified social worker, undertaking his assessed and supported year in employement (ASYE). He is passionate about rights-based practice, views himself as quite academic and takes a critical, intellectual stance. Lloyd writes a regular social work blog and has a large social media following.

AKRAM is a student social worker on his final placement with Dianne as his practice educator. Akram really enjoys working with people but he is worried about how he will meet requirements around demonstrating his application of theory to practice. He has really struggled to grasp theoretical concepts in teaching and has a high level of theory-fright.

PART I

THEORY: EXPLAINING THE WORLD AND UNDERSTANDING OUR PRACTICE

1 UNDERSTANDING THEORY IN PRACTICE

Introduction

This chapter is our starting point: a place to examine what theory is and is not, to recognise its often-ambiguous nature and to consider how it relates to social work. We will help you think through your existing understanding of theory, and recognise how it influences your sense making – sometimes explicitly, but most often implicitly.

What is theory?

A standard definition of theory is:

> a supposition or a system of ideas intended to explain something, especially one based on general principles independent of the thing to be explained [or] an idea used to account for a situation or justify a course of action. (*Oxford Dictionary*, 2019)

Exercise 1.1

In the beginning, what existed? This question poses many possibilities and the way you think about it will depend on how you see the world. In considering this question, you will draw on your own unique combination of existing knowledge, beliefs and understandings, and in using these to attempt to answer the question, you are theorising; each possibility is a theoretical construct.

Humankind has been theorising the nature of existence... well, as long as we have existed! Was the way that you interpreted and responded to the question based on your particular religious or scientific perspectives? Perhaps it was a combination of both. Religion and science continue to present the main theoretical explanations of existence. In science, this is variously referred to as *Theory of Everything*, *Final Theory*, *Ultimate Theory* or *Master Theory*. Stephen Hawking's book *A Brief History of Time* has sold more than 10 million copies and has been translated into over 35 languages, indicating a huge global interest in scientific explanations of our universe. Religion remains popular: 84% of the global population identifies with a particular faith, and religious affiliation is rising everywhere other than Western Europe and North America (Pew Research Center, 2017). Whilst organised religion is less fashionable in Western societies, many people who do not identify with a specific faith acknowledge some form of spirituality. It is clear that religious and spiritual theories of existence are pervasive. Some people accommodate scientific theories within their religious belief (or vice versa), for example, believing that god was responsible for the big bang that was responsible for the universe.

Exercise 1.2

Let's consider another example – something a little more straightforward than the nature of existence! Throw up a pen, watch it drop and land. What is happening here, and why? We can theorise to explain this phenomenon. We know the pen will hit the ground because logic and experience tell us this is what will happen and most of us have at least a basic understanding of the theory of gravity. A physicist will have a more sophisticated understanding and may use theory to devise mathematical formulae predicting and describing the pen's route through the air by taking into account factors such as density, speed, velocity, trajectory, landing point, etc. Now, do you think that a dog watching the pen being thrown understands what's happening? Almost certainly not in the same way as humans do, but then, not all humans understand what is happening to the pen in the same way as the physicist does. Dogs catch sticks – maybe the dog watching the pen will catch it before it lands. The dog does not know about gravity and is not making mathematical calculations, but may still catch the pen. Is the dog theorising or just chasing and catching? This is all theoretical conjecture.

What theory is not

Theory is not *truth*. It is an interpretive tool which helps us to develop an understanding, but it does not give us absolute or definitive answers. People perceive the truth differently and can hold entirely different perspectives and opinions on the same situation without either being wrong or right, so who is to decide what is true? Nor is theory constant. It evolves over time and shifts in response to culture. New theories emerge to challenge existing ones and ideas which we once viewed as fact become defunct. Perhaps these factors are reflected in the commonly used phrase, 'it's just a theory'.

A fuzzy concept

Earlier, we appeared to offer a concrete definition of theory, but dictionary definitions are by nature simplifications. Theories are only a means to understand or explain *to some extent* what is happening; they are *fuzzy concepts*. Fuzziness occurs when the boundaries and application of information are not clear-cut and can vary considerably according to context. Understanding fuzziness helps us appreciate that theory is less concrete than it at first seems. The term fuzzy logic was first coined in the 1960s by Lotfi Zadeh of the University of California at Berkeley, in relation to computers and the notion that nothing is precisely true or false because different variables create partial truths. Is a 30-year-old young? Youth is a fuzzy concept because there is no single value which defines it. Someone who is 60 may well consider the 30-year-old young, whilst someone who is 15 very likely will not, rendering the same person simultaneously young and old! We have no agreed boundaries for the concept of youth, and it has many possible definitions depending on the context. It is useful for us to think of theory in the same way in order to realise it is a generalised, perspective-bound way of explaining phenomena, rather than a definite universal truth based on objective reality (or truism).

Exercise 1.3

Do you believe in aliens? Some people do not, whilst others believe that they have encountered, or even been abducted by aliens. Many more people accept that it is highly unlikely that the Earth is the only planet supporting life, therefore it is inevitable that aliens exist in some form, somewhere in the wide expanse of the universe. It is possible for two people to both believe that aliens exist, but for entirely different reasons. Silly though this alien discussion appears, it demonstrates that true and false are not the same as the sides of a coin. A coin has only two variables: heads or tails. If tossed, it will land on either heads or tails and we can reasonably predict (everything being equal) a 50% probability of either heads or tails. Life is more complex than this. We cannot think about whether aliens exist in the same binary terms as we can heads or tails, so any answer to this question can only really elicit partial truths. Humans employ fuzzy logic to make sense of our lives, situations and experiences. But then, this is just a theory!

Theory and social work

We have started to consider what is meant by theory, but what do we mean by *social work theory*? How do we even agree the parameters of social work theory when the very nature of social work is theoretically contested? It's helpful to start by rejecting the idea that a theory has to originate within social work in order to be a social work theory. We often find that when students are discussing how theory was applied to social work practice, what they are actually referencing are the methods and approaches (for example, anti-oppressive practice, task-centred, strengths-based, etc.) that guided their intervention. But before we intervene to navigate towards solutions, we need to situate the individual experience of the person we are working with in the broader political and social structures of the world. We need to consider not just the external, observable elements of people's lives, but also their internal, psychological worlds. Social work is informed by countless theories across a multitude of disciplines. In our earlier book, *Social Work: From Assessment to Intervention*, we referred to it as 'a magpie profession because we are not captivated by a single theory; rather we adopt different approaches that we apply in diverse contexts' (Heslop and Meredith, 2019, p. 115).

It is also helpful to recognise that as social workers *we use theory all of the time* – whether we intend to or not. Beckett and Horner (2016) differentiate between *formal* theories which have a recognisable proponent or theoretician, and *informal* theories, which cannot be attributed to a recognisable theoretician, but nonetheless inform how social workers assess, form opinions and decide on interventions. Beckett and Horner (2016) cite Payne's (2014) explanation that formal theory is written, debated academically and within the profession, whilst informal theory consists of wider societal ideas and/or practitioner's experience; they highlight the advantages of applying formal and informal theory together. A wealth of literature considers informal theories in the form of practitioner decision-making and reflexivity (Fook and Gardner, 2007; Taylor and White, 2000). Maclean and Harrison (2015) suggest that informal theories represent knowledge from experience and practice wisdom. Many social work academics (such as Doel and Shardlow, 1998; Munro, 2011) recognise and promote the importance of practice wisdom, though it has no identifiable theoretician.

Social work as a theory-driven profession

If we think about the central tasks of social work as supporting individuals, families and communities through difficulties and safeguarding vulnerable people of all ages from harm, it is difficult to imagine any historical society without something akin to social workers. People helped others long before anything like a state, as we now know it, emerged. But there is much speculation and debate about when and where social work began to be an organised response with specific objectives *beyond* the basic human need to help others. Doel (2012) explains that social work is a modern profession with its roots in antiquity, and has both reformist and radical roots. Its role in mediating between the state and the individual is highly contested (Parton, 1996/2000). The nature of social work is not fixed; people view it differently and their views alter over time (Oko, 2011) and are influenced by geographical, cultural and historical contexts. It is therefore no wonder that social work has evolved from and continues to embrace many different theories:

> social work is an age old phenomenon. The seeds of the origin of social work could be traced from global ideologies which include humanism, rationalism, welfarism, liberalism, democracy, secularism and utilitarianism. (Thomas, 2010, Preface)

What we now consider social work practice traces its roots to the Industrial Revolution. Whilst the Industrial Revolution sparked huge leaps in technological and scientific advancements, the great migrations to urban areas throughout the Western world led to increased social problems and in turn social activism (see Chapter 3). In England, the 1834 Victorian Poor Laws established workhouses where destitute people could work in harsh conditions in return for shelter and food. The workhouse system ignited debates about the deserving/undeserving nature of poverty and the success or otherwise of offering universal relief. Public opinion vacillated between contempt and sympathy for the poor, and Victorian philanthropists emerged to set up charities to help people experiencing hardship and poverty. The relationship between charitable relief and workhouse support was ill-defined, and led to concerns about whether support fostered dependency which perpetuated poverty. In 1869, the government published a policy statement (the *Goschen Minute*) on the 'necessity for co-operation between the London Boards of Guardians [who managed Poor Law relief and workhouse provision] and London charities' (*The Spectator*, 1869). This statement delineated the support available to poor people, emphasising that the Guardians were to assist only the 'totally destitute', whilst charities could provide help before people reached this point. It also instructed both Guardians and charities to record and list assistance being provided to people in order to prevent overlap.

From the mid-19th century onwards, various Christian societies organised the visiting of poor people – sometimes weekly – in a practice known as district, or household, visiting. Visiting was a voluntary, religiously motivated practice based on the belief – or theory – that destitution could be alleviated through spiritual welfare.

> The simple doctrine that informed district visiting for much of its history was that impoverished and benighted souls could be saved by the agency of another human being, who cared enough about them to be interested in their survival and spiritual well-being. (Prochaska, 2006, pp. 66–7)

Visits included Christian discussion and practical support in the form of clothes, blankets and food. Prochaska (2006) argues this practice of district visiting was the forerunner of the social casework model developed by the Charity Organisation Societies (COS), founded in England in 1869 (Wilson et al., 2011). The casework approach was first developed by Mrs Ellen Ranyard through the *Bible & Domestic Female Mission* in Glasgow in 1857, whose working-class women voluntarily visited poor people. Members of the COS adopted this approach and termed it a form of scientific casework or 'scientific charity', so as to separate out the 'undeserving' from the 'deserving' poor. Theoretically speaking, casework was established to determine whether or not impoverished people deserved support, and if so, what form this should take. However, whilst the COS had given social work a structured approach in both the UK and USA, American educational reformer Abraham Flexner, writing in 1915, challenged its professional status, arguing that it lacked a teachable method, specialist skills, knowledge or theory (Gitterman, 2014).

Visiting was ultimately superseded by state social services funded through compulsory taxation following the Beveridge Report (1942) and the Second World War (1939–44). The birth of the British welfare state in the post-war period extended people's rights to social services and created further demand for social work. In his work on Christianity and social service in modern Britain, Prochaska (2006) suggests religion and secularism competed on how best to provide social care, with the former arguing for voluntary support based on religious values and the latter on compulsory contributions and collectivist state-provided services. However, it can be argued that theory was incorporated into social work functions on a relatively ad hoc basis, given that there was no statutory requirement for social workers to have specific training until the Local Authority Social Services Act 1970 and the creation of the Central Council for Education and Training in Social Work (CCETSW).

In the 1970s CCETSW began to establish social work as an academic discipline. Social work education drew – and continues to draw – from theories associated with related social science disciplines, such as psychology, social policy, sociology and law, but also incorporated ideas from the disparate fields of philosophy, mechanics, business, geography and beyond. Religion, meanwhile, is an influence on many social work ideas and individual practitioners. Healy (2014) suggests that many social work theories have been developed for specific contexts – 'theories for practice are intended to offer a range of options for understanding and responding to particular concerns' (p. 9). Theoretical approaches offer the lens to interpret the world and influence practice direction and choice.

Garrett (2018) argues that contemporary UK social work operates within four conflicting theoretical perspectives, which each 'give rise to distinctive approaches to social work' (p. 3). These are:

- **Therapeutic perspectives** – social issues are addressed by working with individuals through approaches such as psychoanalysis, counselling, coaching and mentoring.
- **Socialist-collectivist perspectives** – social issues are seen as the result of structural inequalities and are addressed through collective social action. Most associated with radical social work.
- **Individual-reformist perspectives** – social issues are addressed through gradual social change using approaches such as anti-oppressive practice and relationship-based social work.
- **Managerialist-technocratic perspectives** – social work is a business providing services to customers with a diverse range of social needs. Standardised processes are believed to produce consistency and performance is managed through targets and outcomes.

Through theories for practice, social workers can exercise different possibilities of understanding people's needs and the purpose of their own practice. Healy (2014) provides a dynamic approach to theory and models of practice, classifying contemporary social work theory into five categories:

- **Systems theories** – rather than individual capacity, relationships, social networks and interconnectedness are the focus (see Chapter 6).
- **Problem-solving theories** – focus, unsurprisingly, on solving problems, and include task-centred approaches, crisis intervention and motivational interviewing.
- **Strengths and solution-focused theories** – look to strengths, solutions and the future rather than focusing on the problem.
- **Modern critical social work theories** – take a critical stance to social structuring, related to radical, Marxist, structural, feminist, anti-racist, anti-oppressive and anti-discriminatory social work (see Chapter 4).
- **Postmodern social work theories** – developing from the 1990s, these theories have grown in influence in social work practice. Key concepts in postmodern social work include discourse, subjectivity, power, deconstruction and narrative (see Chapter 4).

Theories are therefore the means to organise and present understandings and interpretations. They are explanations and mechanisms to communicate how we experience phenomena and the world we inhabit. This is true for social work, professionally, and workers individually.

Theory or evidence-based practice?

The highly influential Munro Review recognised that one of the principles of an effective child protection system was 'Good professional practice is informed by knowledge of the latest theory and research' (2011, p. 23). However, since the late 20th century, theorising the application of research in social work policy and practice has become increasingly conceptualised as evidence-based practice:

> Evidence-based practice in social work makes practice decisions utilizing a variety of different sources of scientifically credible evidence, in conjunction with the social worker's clinical skills, and the client's preferences. (McNeece and Thyer, 2004, p. 10)

The shift of focus from theory to evidence can be seen in the key professional guidance frameworks. In the guidance on using the *Professional Capabilities Framework* (British Association of Social Workers [BASW], 2018a), the term *theory* appears only once, whilst *evidence* appears 13 times, four of these as part of the term *evidence-informed practice*. Is theory part of this evidence, or distinct from it? The *Knowledge and Skills Statement for Social Workers in Adult Services* (Department of Health, 2015) refers to evidence five times, but theory only once, whilst the equivalent statement of *Knowledge and Skills for Child and Family Social Work* (Department for Education, 2014) mentions theory twice and evidence six times. Both of these Knowledge and Skills Statements require social workers to have 'a critical understanding of the difference between theory, research, evidence and expertise' (Department for Education, 2014, p. 3; Department of Health, 2015, p. 5). With the greatest respect to the Chief Social Workers, we feel that this is easier said than done! Galpin et al. (2019) argue that notions of evidence-based/evidence-informed practice are so poorly defined within the Professional Capabilities Framework and the Knowledge and Skills Statements that they may actually present a barrier to practitioners engaging with research.

Howe (2009) considers what constitutes good social work and best practice, and identifies that many theories and approaches compete with and cancel each other out, '[we] could go around in circles describing how each theory in turn is intent on shooting another until there is no theory left standing' (Howe, 2009, p. 197). He describes how proponents of evidence-based practice use it to guide which services and interventions will have the most effective outcomes, ruling some theories in and others out on the basis of research evidence or the lack thereof. Lishman (2018) believes that promoting evidence-based practice ensures social workers keep up to date with current theory and research, rather than relying on outdated knowledge or choosing a course of action based solely on past experience. It is critical that students and practitioners have access to up-to-date and relevant research, because what is seen to work today may well be rejected tomorrow and vice versa. Healy (2012) suggests that the gathering and utilisation of evidence through research leads to a dynamic and responsive profession as well as innovative practices that can be shared professionally. This opportunity to replicate successful practice is a clear strength of evidence-based practice and specialist electronic databases such as the Social Care Institute for Excellence (SCIE) have purposefully been established to distribute knowledge.

It seems obvious to suggest social workers should use evidence to inform their practice, however, Wilson et al. (2011) explain evidence-based practice is more complicated than it first may seem and has become a *contested terrain*. Evidence-based practice originated in medicine to enable clinicians to objectively draw from a scientific and empirical knowledge base, evaluating the impact and efficacy of their interventions against predefined, organisational objectives (Lishman, 2018), but is this a good fit with the subjective, messy, emotional nature of social work? Social need and social work practice are so under-researched that some argue we actually have precious little evidence of what is effective (Healy, 2014). What we do have is drawn from overwhelmingly qualitative methodologies which are radically different to medicine's clinical and logical approaches; human relationships simply cannot be measured in the same way as pharmacological treatment outcomes. Shaw (2007) identifies social work research as unique and distinct from other disciplines because of its emancipatory positioning which challenges inequality and oppression. Since 2017, the Department for Education has funded the What Works Centre for Children's Social Care, which aims to develop the evidence base for social policy and social work with children and families. In 2019, 14 leading academics co-signed an open letter expressing concerns that some of the centre's research was 'Curtailing rights in the name of evidence' (Turner, 2019).

Evidence-based practice is outcome orientated – it considers the evidence to select the best response to meet the desired outcome – but who defines the outcomes that are desired and why? Very often the outcomes to social problems are set at national and local policy levels, by government and employers; these outcomes will frequently be very different from those an individual or family would choose for themselves. Research is never wholly objective and when it focuses on how best to achieve outcomes determined by policy, the resulting evidence is built on the presupposition that these outcomes are the 'right' ones. Sheldin argues that in this way, evidence-based practice often becomes a top-down managerial tool for securing compliance of practitioners (Sheldin, 2001, in Corby, 2006, p. 33). We believe that practitioners develop expertise – at least in part – through knowledge and synthesis of theory. Research always incorporates theory, and theory is both based upon and used to provide evidence, but we can apply theory much more broadly (and yet more selectively) than evidence-based practice, by tailoring it to the individual situation rather than using it to secure a predetermined outcome.

Theories, models, methods and approaches

The terms *theory, model, method and approach* are often used interchangeably to describe specific tools of social work practice, but in fact they are independent concepts which influence each other. Teater (2014) argues that the actions the social worker will take, or the selection of a method, is dependent on the practitioner's theoretical understanding of a current situation or behaviour. Our worldview (theory) will have some influence over our practice (models, methods, approaches), but it is not the only influence. A social worker may disagree with austerity measures, but follow agency policy on the allocation of services, or personally disapprove of substance use but continue to professionally support a person using substances.

As we have explained *theory* is fuzzy; this fuzziness also extends to practice models, methods and approaches. While acknowledging the fuzziness of these concepts we also recognise this is not wholly helpful to students and therefore throughout this book, when we refer to one of these terms, we understand it in the following ways:

Theories – we have discussed theory earlier in this chapter, noting its fuzzy nature and defining it as a means to describe, explain and predict the world or a particular phenomenon we encounter within it

Models – ways to visualise, demonstrate or apply theory

Methods – the recipe of tools, techniques and processes we use to intervene

Approaches – overarching way of working which employs a range of theories, models and methods

Martin

Martin is working with Sam, who is nearing the end of his time in a residential rehabilitation unit addressing his addiction to drugs and alcohol. Sam is sober and feeling positive, but knows that he will find things more difficult when he leaves the unit, and wants Martin's support to plan for this. Martin strongly identifies as a systemic practitioner, so this is his overall **approach**. He believes that Bronfenbrenner's ecological systems **theory** is a useful way of understanding how Sam's addiction connects to his relationships and environment. He decides to employ a strengths-based **model**. Martin uses an ecomap, combined with appreciative inquiry as the **methods** through which to explore potential resources that Sam can draw from when he leaves the unit. In completing the ecomap, Sam identifies strengths that he had not previously considered, and he and Martin discuss how these can be used as part of his plan to maintain sobriety.

Essentially, theory helps us to understand what is happening, why, and may offer predictions of potential outcomes which help us to know whether or not action needs to be taken. Once this is established, models, methods and approaches guide what action is taken and how. We are mindful that although we have offered these definitions, the multifaceted nature of social work theory and practice means that there are times throughout this book where we are also guilty of using them interchangeably!

Which theory?

Any blanket will keep you warm, but you may well have a preferred blanket, and many children won't sleep without their *special* blanket. In the same way, many social workers have a strong preference for a particular theory and feel a sense of security in explaining and responding to everything through its lens. We are all human and inevitably find that some theories resonate with us personally more than others. Whilst we respect this view – at times we have certainly been guilty of it ourselves – we believe that it is important to be familiar with a range of theories. One of social work's great strengths is its multifaceted approach; this allows us to select and apply those theories which fit the individual situation, instead of trying to fit the individual situation to the theory. Some theories work better than others in particular situations, but no theory can provide a one size fits all solution and there is no benefit in applying a theory if it is not helpful to the person or family that you are working with. Overstating one theory's potential for application by valuing it to the exclusion of all others (*pet theory syndrome*) is as problematic as avoiding theory all together.

Author's experience Cat

I marked an assignment in which a student reflected on applying theory during her practice placement. She described working with a family whose daughter was physically disabled and not currently attending school. The local school could not afford the adaptations necessary for her to be able to access classrooms and facilities, and the only other option currently being offered by the local authority was a residential school some distance away. The family did not want to be separated. The student gave an excellent overview of attachment theory. She referenced its original theorist, John Bowlby, and demonstrated how his theory was developed by Mary Ainsworth, whose work was in turn extended by Main and Solomon. She incorporated recent articles from social work journals to demonstrate how attachment theory is incorporated into contemporary social work practice. The student's nuanced theoretical knowledge was clearly evidenced – it just wasn't really relevant to this family's situation.

In a tutorial, I asked why she had given such disproportionate focus to attachment theory. I explained how she could have used political and economic theories, social and medical models of disability, theories of stigma and discrimination to explore the exclusion that the family was experiencing. The student explained that she felt that in lectures attachment theory had been presented as fundamental to all social work practice with children, and as her practice educator specialised in attachment theory it had been referenced a great deal during supervision. Attachment theory is useful in many situations, but doggedly and exclusively applying it here was not. It resulted in an undue focus on the parent–child relationship, inadvertently implying that the parents, rather than structural inequality, were causing the situation.

Conclusion

We have set out general parameters of theory and recognised how and why social work is a theory-driven profession. Social work policy and professional literature have made a semantic shift from theory to evidence-based practice over the past two decades. We believe that theory *is* the evidence base for social work practice. Social work is by necessity a messy, qualitative profession, because it deals with people and relationships, both of which are erratic and unpredictable. Social work cannot – and should not – hope to sit neatly with quantitative, scientific knowledge in the way that medicine can, but effective social workers can employ skilful eclecticism to weave together different theories and create unique, individual understandings. This is the foundation on which subsequent chapters will build as we consider specific theories and their application.

2 FOUNDATIONS OF THEORY IN SOCIAL WORK

Introduction

We have noted that social work practice draws from theories which have arisen in many other disciplines. This is a book about using theory in social work practice, and it is neither possible, nor desirable to detail every single theory from every single discipline. Some fields, however, have been so influential on social work they can be considered *foundational* to how our profession has evolved and developed, how social services are organised and delivered, and how we practise as social workers. Subsequent chapters will explore theory predominantly arising from philosophy, psychology and sociology, and so here we outline their core theoretical tenets to offer context for what is to come. All of these disciplines have been influenced by religion, and so that is our starting point.

Religion

Religion, spirituality and mysticism have influenced society since our most ancient times. In multicultural, 21st century UK, very few social work agencies are openly aligned with specific religions, but religion and spirituality play a central role in the lives and identities of many people, families and communities with whom we work (Hodge, 2015). Many social workers follow a particular faith, and this influences their values and approach to practice. Whether or not you subscribe to a form of spirituality on an individual level, the relationship between religion and the profession of social work is undeniable; nationally and internationally, most forms of organised social work were instigated by individuals and organisations with religious convictions.

Defining religion is problematic. The term is most commonly used to refer to an agreed system of beliefs (or theory!) about a god or creator held jointly by a community. Most religions, therefore, involve some form of organising body which sanctions belief. Overarching, organised religions are readily identifiable, and most people know the fundamental tenets of Judaism, Christianity, Buddhism, Islam, etc. However, it is important to recognise that these broad faiths actually comprise an enormous diversity of beliefs. Religions are like trees; they grow, develop and branch off. Christianity evolved from Judaism and so these two distinct movements share some beliefs whilst having very opposing stances on others. Religions contain near endless denominations: Jews may be affiliated to Reform, Masorti or Orthodox Judaism; Christians may be Catholic, Protestant, Evangelical, Mormon; Buddhists may be Mahayana, Theravada, Vajrayana; Muslims may be Sunni or Shia. These examples are in no way exhaustive, and beyond such denominations exist further subdivisions or branches which denote differences – whether large or small – all the way down to individual sites of worship and personal expressions of faith. People may have the same religion in name, but theorise, conceptualise, practise and experience their faiths very differently.

A survey on belief and religious affiliation by Humanists UK (2011) concluded that nearly two-thirds of people who belong to a religion do not regard themselves as 'religious' (Humanists UK, 2011). This is a strong indication that people often identify with a religion for cultural and social reasons even though they do not personally agree with all the beliefs held by that religious body. It seems being religious is more complicated than just being associated with a religion, as affiliation and belief are two different things. The concept of spirituality adds another dimension: many people are more comfortable with a personal notion of spirituality than a specific religion or religious practice. Church attendance has dropped over recent decades, but the market in books and podcasts on spirituality is thriving. Specifically to social work, Gray and Lovat (2008) state that mysticism and the unseen is as important to many people as concrete and observable reality. They further suggest that social work and social workers are motivated by influences that are more religious and spiritual than is generally assumed in a pragmatic profession.

Philosophy

The literal translation of the Greek word philosophy is *love of knowledge*. We use the word to describe an ancient academic discipline as well as a theory or attitude that acts as a guiding principle for behaviour. As you can imagine for such an ancient discipline, there have been many philosophical schools and theories and as philosophy is so vast that its endless branches are often grouped into core fields. There is much debate about how to do this, but as a basic suggestion:

Aesthetics is concerned with the nature of personal truths, beauty, art and taste.

Logic is concerned with rational thought, reasoning and argument.

Epistemology is concerned with the nature of knowledge and knowing.

Metaphysics is concerned with existence, religion and the nature of reality.

Ethics is concerned with values, morality, right and wrong, good and evil.

Philosophy originally described any form of inquiry or body of knowledge, but as civilisations developed, distinct territories emerged. Mathematics and natural philosophy (science) proved to have such wide application that they became separate disciplines in their own right (Vuletic, 2018), and science evolved into the domains of natural science (biology, chemistry, physics, astronomy) and social science (anthropology, economics, politics, sociology, psychology, etc.). There is significant debate about whether or not social work can or should be considered a social science.

Philosophy influences all disciplines which have evolved from it, and modern philosophy is concerned with questions which cannot be cohesively addressed through maths or science alone, such as the fundamental nature of knowledge, reality and existence. Two key concepts are ontology and epistemology.

Ontology – the nature of the world and what we can know about it

Ontology philosophically considers whether things exist and how existence is understood. Different ontological approaches examine how we understand the nature of our physical, psychological and social worlds and the concept of reality. Whether we realise it or not, we all hold an ontological position which influences how we perceive, examine and interpret experiences.

Epistemology – the philosophy or theory of knowing

Epistemology draws a distinction between opinion and justified belief by considering *how* we know what we know. All theoretical and empirical approaches presuppose, explicitly or implicitly, some epistemological position or other. For example, a feminist epistemology would argue that in assessing someone's situation, a social worker should not practise in a detached way which seeks to separate reason from emotion.

Exercise 2.1

Let's try and make sense of all that. Imagine that you are in a room with a table. Let's ask the ontological question – does the table exist? Now let's ask the epistemological question – what are the rules for *demonstrating* whether the table exists? The table has physical properties which you can interact with – you can see and touch the table; if you knock on it, you can hear the sound that it makes; depending on its composition, you can smell its wood, metal or plastic; if you feel so inclined, you can even taste the table! Your epistemological stance is that you can confirm the existence of the table by interacting with its physical properties.

Now let's think about black holes. If black holes exist, they are physical objects, but no one has ever seen or physically interacted with one, so *can* they exist (ontological question)? We can theorise that black holes exist even though we can't see them, because we can observe their effect on other objects such as stars. So, we can demonstrate the ontological existence of black holes through a relational epistemological approach.

In social work, the vast majority of the time we are dealing with social/psychological concepts – for example, love, attachment, rejection, risk, need, resilience, professionalism. We definitely can't see any of these constructs or interact with them on a sensory level, so how can we demonstrate whether or not they exist? Here our epistemological approach is based upon reported or observed experiences which we register against our own lexicon of experience (including our theoretical knowledge), and subjectively describe.

Ontological and epistemological debates emanating from philosophy pervade all theories and different theorists adopt different stances or *paradigms*. A paradigm is a worldview, or a set of assumptions about how things work. Silverman (2005, p. 97) describes a paradigm as a 'framework for how we look at reality' and this often designates a typical pattern, example, prototype or model which we replicate, repeat or follow. Philosopher and historian of science Thomas Kuhn's work (1970) highlights the lack of consensus around a single paradigm or means to understand knowledge. Three main paradigms guide the social sciences:

Positivism/post-positivism methods from the natural sciences are applied to the study of people and society, usually through quantitative methods. Positivism assumes that empirical evidence about social life can be objectively collected and measured, then generalised to make statements about the behaviour of society as a whole. Post-positivism accepts that objectivity can never be guaranteed, because practitioners' beliefs will influence their approach to information gathering and interpretation.

Interpretivism believes that people and their social interactions are so complex that it is impossible to acquire measurable facts about them. It supports qualitative methods of listening, observing and attempting to understand the subjective meanings people make of their world. Interpretive approaches acknowledge practitioners' own values and subjectivity.

Critical theory draws significantly from feminist and Marxist theories' focus on the inequalities and power differentials that exist in society. Critical theorists reject the notions that scientific methods can be applied to understand social situations, arguing that positivist approaches reinforce power differentials and are morally questionable. Critical theory believes that any attempt to understand society is a political activity which must question and critique established practices and institutions in order to identify inequality, and seek to bring about change.

Identifying and understanding the personal philosophy that underpins our professional approach is an important part of our social work practice: these fundamental and deeply held beliefs determine the weight that we give to different types of information and knowledge when undertaking assessments and making professional decisions.

Trish

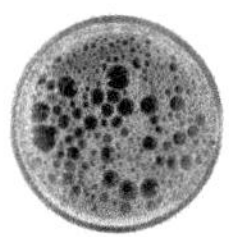

As a deaf woman and a single parent, Trish had experienced a great deal of prejudice and discrimination. Trish's own experience and viewpoint evidence to her that the world is unfair; this for her is a rational truth. As a social work student, Trish was drawn to scientific means to understand practice situations, such as decision trees, standardised checklists and rating scales. She reasoned that she had experienced bias all her life and therefore it was critically important to her that her own bias and opinions should not influence assessments. Trish believes that scientific methods can dispel bias and if handled correctly, challenge discrimination. Her personal philosophy is to seek to practice empirically and apply a scientific means to assessments and interventions.

Exercise 2.2

Reflect on how Trish has arrived at her personal philosophy.

Can you identify your own and what has influenced it?

Is evidence more reliable when it is gathered through a tried and trusted method, or through an interpretive element? Why do you think this and is this always the case, or does your view change depending on the situation?

Psychology

Psychology is the scientific study of the mind and behaviour. It has applications in many different fields, for example, education, sports, forensics, but we are probably most familiar with it in its clinical form, where it is used to assess and treat mental distress through specific therapeutic approaches (cognitive behavioural therapy, dialectical behavioural therapy, systemic family therapy, psychoanalysis, etc.). This association with mental distress often causes confusion between psychology and psychiatry, a branch of medicine which primarily relies on pharmacological treatments. Like all disciplines, psychology has changed and evolved over time, shaped by the perspectives of different theorists to incorporate multiple paradigms collected within schools which we shall explore in turn below. Historically, psychologists would be associated with a single school, however many contemporary psychologists take a much more eclectic stance, drawing from theories and concepts across two or more different schools.

Structuralism and functionalism

Psychology is considered to have originated with Wilhelm Wundt (1832–1920), who set up the first psychology laboratory in Germany in 1879. He and his student Edward Titchener developed structuralism, which sought to understand human behaviour by breaking mental processes down into their most basic components and analysing these through introspection (conscious examination of thoughts and emotions). Functionalist psychology was formed in order to oppose structuralism, and many feel that it is too ill-defined to be considered a school of psychology in its own right (Hothersall, 2003). While structuralists sought to map mental processes, functionalists were concerned with their roles and purpose. Functionalist psychology is distinct from sociological functionalism, which we will discuss later in this chapter.

Gestalt

The German word Gestalt loosely translates as *one from many*. This school of psychology was developed in the early 20th century by Austro-Hungarian psychologist Max Wertheimer, alongside German psychologists Wolfgang Köhler and Kurt Koffka. Building on earlier theories from philosophers such as David Hume and Immanuel Kant, they used ideas around perception to develop an alternative to structuralism. Simply put, Gestalt psychologists believed that the whole is greater than the sum of its parts, therefore psychology should examine the entirety of an experience, rather than individual components. Problems are viewed as a whole and Wertheimer considered that they may be solved through productive thinking (quick, improvised responses), or reproductive thinking (applying previous experience and knowledge). It is important to make a distinction between Gestalt *psychology* and Gestalt *therapy* which was popularised by the German psychiatrist and psychoanalyst Fritz Perls. Whilst Perls originally drew from principles of Gestalt psychology, his therapeutic model radically deviated from it.

Behaviourism

Behaviourism or behavioural psychology is based on the idea that behaviour is a series of learned responses to environmental stimuli: we act in the way that we are conditioned to behave. The work of some behaviourists has been so influential that their work has become part of popular culture. Although the term classical conditioning may be unfamiliar, it is very likely that you know about Pavlov's dogs. Russian behavioural psychologist Ivan Pavlov rang a bell every time the dogs in his laboratory were fed. This conditioned the dogs to associate the bell with food, until eventually they salivated upon hearing it, even when no food was given. Similarly, you may not have heard of Burrhus Skinner's work on operant conditioning, but you are probably familiar with the ideas of negative and positive reinforcement which developed from it.

Psychodynamic psychology

Psychodynamic psychology is the systematic study of factors which underlie our behaviours and emotions, particularly our early life experiences and our conscious and subconscious motivations. The term was first used by Austrian neurologist Sigmund Freud (1856–1939), to encapsulate mental processes as flows of psychological energy (Bowlby, 1997). In his personality theory, Freud (1923: 1962 edition) presented the mind as the *psyche*, comprising three distinct components which interact with each other:

the *id* – instinctual desires

the *superego* – moral conscience

the *ego* – the realistic mediator between the id and the superego.

Freud collaborated closely with Swiss psychiatrist Carl Jung for many years before disagreements led to division. Freud's daughter, Anna, became a highly esteemed psychological theorist in her own right and was one of the founders of psychoanalytic child psychology. Anna Freud's work influenced British psychologist and psychiatrist John Bowlby, whose work on attachment is explored in Chapter 6.

Humanism

Humanism focuses on the importance of the individual's interpretation of social reality (Ingleby, 2010), suggesting that if people recognise their strengths, they can harness them to achieve their potential – this is known as self-actualisation. Humanism is most closely associated with the work of two theorists whose ideas continue to have an enormous impact on social work practice, Abraham Maslow and Carl Rogers. Maslow felt that the psychodynamic and behavioural schools treated people as bags of symptoms and that psychology should instead focus on people's positive aspects (Hoffman, 1988). Maslow is best known for his 1943 Hierarchy of Needs, a prioritised model of stages through which people ascend in order to achieve self-actualisation (see Figure 2.1).

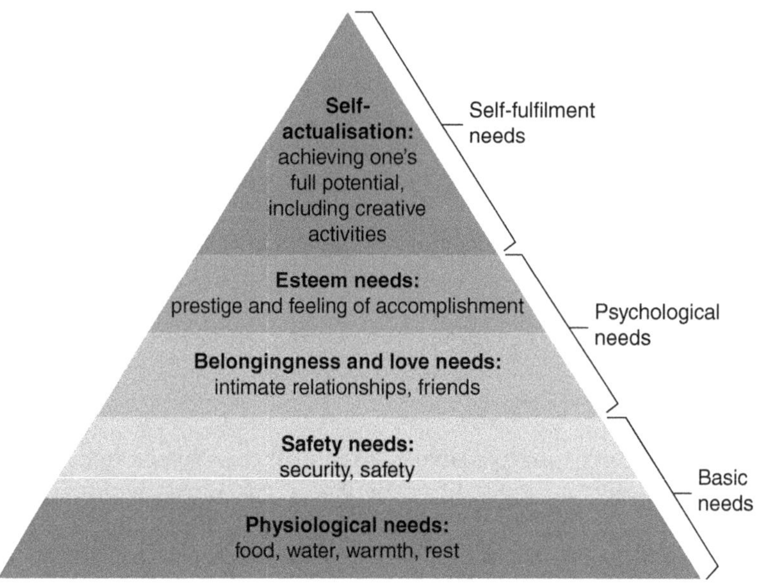

Figure 2.1 Maslow's Hierarchy of Needs

Carl Rogers concurred with Maslow and extended his ideas to develop *client-centred therapy*, the three core conditions of which are:

1. **Congruence** – therapists should relate to clients openly, not hide behind a professional or personal facade.
2. **Unconditional positive regard** – the therapist must accept their client for whom they are and show genuine willingness to listen without interruption, judgement or opinion.
3. **Empathy** – the therapist must demonstrate their wish to understand and appreciate the client's perspective (Rogers, 1951).

By placing expectations on the professional, rather than solely the client's behaviour, Rogers revolutionised therapeutic psychological approaches. His influence can be seen in common social work approaches such as person-centred practice, strengths-based practice and the exchange model of assessment.

Cognitive psychology

Cognitive psychology focuses on mental processes such as how we think, perceive, process, remember and learn. The cognitive revolution of the 1950s followed criticisms that behaviourism failed to address how internal processes impacted on behaviour. Essentially, cognitive psychology explores the mental processes that occur in the space between a stimulus and a response (Ingleby, 2010). The main theorists associated with this school are the Swiss psychologist Jean Piaget (1896–1980) and the Soviet psychologist Lev Vygotsky (1896–1934), both of whom we will consider in Chapter 5.

Sociology

Social work is very much related to sociology, a social science which employs methods from the physical sciences to study and understand society, social relationships and culture. There have been many sociological movements and schools of thought, but from its early days, sociology has been associated with positivism, which holds that the most valid form of knowledge is scientific knowledge. Auguste Comte (1798–1857) championed sociology as a positive science for society, but it is Frenchman Emile Durkheim (1858–1917) who is considered to have established sociology as an academic discipline. Durkheim is considered to be one of sociology's three *founding fathers*, with Marx and Weber, although the three differed in many areas. Durkheim promoted positivism, arguing for a scientific methodology to sociological research. In contrast, Karl Marx (1818–83) took a stance of anti-positivism, favouring a dialectical (multiple, contradictory perspectives) approach and advocating for critical analysis rather than the scientific accumulation of facts. Max Weber (1864–1920) was also an anti-positivist and a strong proponent of studying social action through observation and interpretation. Weber saw change occurring in a rational fashion; as we gain ever increasing insight and knowledge, we are better able to explain. He demonstrated this through the steady rationalisation of human thought from our ancient belief in multiple gods (polytheism) to one god (monotheism) and ultimately a godless (atheist) modernity. Weber's classification of professions as social structures that are artificially created, rather than organically developed, is highly influential on how social work has considered its own identity, bureaucracy, agency and power.

Sociology continues to be influenced by the natural sciences and the belief that social relationships can be understood in much the same way as biological structures. However, a more interpretive approach recognises that social relationships are not necessarily governed by logic. Sociologists are divided by quantitative (broadly positivist) and qualitative (broadly interpretivist) approaches to research. Qualitative research has often been considered to be less robust and scientific than quantitative studies, and so has sought to justify its basically interpretive approach by developing ways to validate qualitative data. In the 1920s and 1930s, Weber's work influenced the Chicago School's development of the methodological approach of ethnography. Originally referred to as fieldwork, ethnography is the observation of people in their own environments in order to produce an interpretive, written account of their culture. This observational method of study resulted in the emergence and increasing acceptance of qualitative methodologies in mainstream research. In the 1960s Strauss and Glaser developed grounded theory to codify qualitative data often derived from interviews. Whilst debates around whether qualitative or quantitative data – or even a mixture of the two – rage, the simple truth is that both involve some facts and some interpretation. Research can only ever represent those involved in being studied, a sample of the population rather than the whole. The methodology, means and tools used to gather and understand data are always hostage to the bias and interpretation of the researcher(s).

Practice experience Phil

As a sociology student in the early 1980s I was made aware of the importance of both theory and practice. Having attended a single-sex school, outside of my own family I was relatively unaware of women's issues and societal experiences. It was not until my late teens that I learnt from seminar discussions about how groups are marginalised, and my eyes were opened to other people's experiences. I recognised how theoretically, society seemed politically and socially fragmented and there was a wide and unfair gulf between different sections. I was angry that children experienced poverty in a wealthy country. This divide in society was amplified during the Miners' Strike (1984–5) with many people taking sides either for or against Margaret Thatcher's Conservative Party government. Born and bred in Northeast England, I directly experienced the region's post-industrial hardship, but it was through studying theory that I was able to join the dots and see how many people (including my own family and friends) experienced social, economic and personal disadvantage. I graduated from university at a time when the country was experiencing mass unemployment and, unable to find work, became involved in a Trades Union Congress (TUC) group, the Tyneside Unemployed Workers' Movement. The combination of my personal experiences and the theoretical understanding I had developed whilst studying sociology made social work an obvious career choice; it presented the opportunity for me to work with people experiencing difficulties and challenge oppression.

Sociology has four main overarching theoretical perspectives:

Functionalism considers the relationship and interdependency between all social groups

Conflict theory considers the inequalities of society (discussed below within Marxism

Symbolic interaction considers how individuals interact with one another (discussed below within social constructionism)

Feminism, which initially considered gender inequality, but evolved to consider *all* forms of inequality.

We explore aspects of these theoretical perspectives which are most relevant to social work practice below.

Functionalism

Sociologically, functionalism broadly reflects on the natural order and function of society and social relationships. Emile Durkheim founded functionalism in liberal France, arguing that societies evolve through ever more complicated social institutions. For Durkheim, social institutions such as family, culture and politics are organised in a way that forms a whole society in a similar manner to how the human body represents a complex array of smaller biological organisms. Durkheim held that people operate through complex and unequal relationships between diverse social institutions, which evolve to become naturally ordered, with those best placed to exercise decision-making arising to positions of power. Although Durkheim recognised change occurring and creating disorder, he believed that basic institutions evolve in response in order to restore the natural function of society.

Structural functionalists such as Talcott Parsons (1902–78) proposed that the industrial revolution saw the land-based, rural workforce restructure into a more mobile, labouring class in order to meet the needs of industrial capitalist society. Parsons held that the very nature of family changed as labour moved from countryside agriculture, to large, urban factories. Workers in factories were men, and when men migrated to factory locations, their wives and children followed, leaving their extended families behind. As a result of this, nuclear families developed, comprising only mother, father and children. In essence, Parsons presented the heterosexual nuclear family as the natural reproductive organ of industrialised capitalism, a family form which replaced agriculturally orientated, multigenerational extended families. The structural functionalist explanation of family was very much the main sociological perspective for much of the 20th century (Newman, 1999) and an important component of systems theory (see Chapter 6). Cunningham and Cunningham (2014) explain that a functionalist perspective in social work tends to focus on the smooth running of society against the influence of behaviour which deviates from social order. This leads to a conclusion that problems are located within individuals and therefore when individuals dysfunction, it is they who need to change, rather than the institutions around them.

Marxism

The German philosopher Karl Marx (1818–83) has had a mixed press, to say the least! In some quarters he is eulogised and credited with almost mythical powers of intellect and persuasion;

in others he is demonised as an inhuman monster. As with almost everything, perspective is important. Marx and Marxism are historically associated with the concept of *production*, whereby to survive, humans produce food and clothing and other essential items through hunting, farming or manufacture. Society is arranged to ensure the productive processes within economic epochs (e.g. feudal or capitalist) resulting in economic social classes who are dependent upon their position in relation to production (Marx, 1983 edn). The arrangement of the production-based society ensures that one minority class dominates through ownership of the means of production, whilst the majority (politically and economically inferior) class is the producing or working class – referred to as the proletariat in capitalist society, and peasants in feudal society. Marx's subsequent description of conflict and antagonism between the classes is due to the majority of human social relationships owing their position to this economic distribution of production and diverging class interests. Essential to classical Marxism is the position that the state is in place to maintain the class status quo and quell unrest from the producing mass class (Lenin, 1977 edn). In relation to family formation, Marx's close collaborator Frederic Engels (1820–95) presented the family as being merely the systemic construct of economic production, reproduction and class oppression (Engels and Barrett, 1986 edn).

While Marxist theory is highly regarded by its proponents, the tendency to attribute everything to an economic causation and class struggle has limited its scope. The delegation of social relationships into epochal hierarchies confines too much to the dustbin of history, and categorising pre-industrial modes of human organisation as primitive is too reductionist and simplistic. Human organisation is, by its very nature, diverse and complex. Marxism developed the dialectical comprehension of society whereby change occurs through a process of thesis, antithesis and synthesis. In this way Marxism seeks to explain large social revolutionary change along with smaller scale social phenomena involving family and social structures. A central tenet of Marxism has been the promotion of class-based strife and the conceptualisation of the inevitable proletarian revolution. Whilst the Russian, Chinese and Cuban revolutions provide examples of this, for the majority of the world, the proletarian revolution has not happened. This lack of class upheaval has caused some consternation amongst generations of social scientists who would normally be attracted to class revolution and revolutionary world changing acts.

The Hungarian Marxist Georg Lukács (1885–1971), who was both a proponent and critic of Stalinism (state-based Soviet communism), argued that people/workers are reified into commodities and objects which render them passive rather than class conscious. He felt the proletariat possessed the means to become conscious and recognise the contradictions in class relations, and went on to influence the neo-Marxists from the Frankfurt School and the New Left in the 1960s and 1970s. The Frankfurt School, and Herbert Marcuse, critiqued capitalism and (and Soviet communism) as developing one-dimensional philosophical technological forms of social repression. For Marcuse (1898–1979) the working class had not evolved in accordance with classic Marxism due to the advent of new forms of social control through false needs which integrated individuals into the existing system of production through consumption and mass media based advertisements (Marcuse, 1964/2002). Individuals are seen to conform to the status quo through a lack of critical evaluation or opposition to the system. Marcuse did, though, see progressive representation in minority groups, outsiders and radical intelligentsia (for instance, the literature of Samuel Beckett). More recently Louis Althusser (1918–90) developed a Marxism based upon structuralism and the recognition of the importance of ideology and politics alongside economic progress (Althusser, 2007) and in the United Kingdom, Stuart Hall (1932–2014) stressed the part of cultural dimensions and media interpretations (Hall, 1999). Marxism has influenced aspects of social work, particularly more radical and community-orientated social work. While functionalism seeks to locate an individual into the system, Marxism espouses challenge to the system.

Feminism

Feminism is a theoretical critique based upon the inequalities women encounter within a paternal society which conceptualises humanity as divided by gender and reinforces this through a variety of linguistic, social and psychological constructs (Cranny-Francis et al., 2003). It is fairly commonly accepted that society has been structured by gendered relations and women have held unequal positions in society. The UK has had two women Prime Ministers, but most people – whatever their political persuasion – recognise that Thatcher and May have received different treatment to the dozens of men who have held the same position. Feminism responds to the unequal, discriminatory and oppressive treatment experienced by women both personally and structurally. The feminist critique has fundamentally altered societal perceptions, and feminist sociology has influenced our understanding of relationships and social structuring (Hearn et al., 1998). The nature and source of women's oppression has been much debated; is it male-orientated, perpetuated by state interests, or both (Hearn et al., 1998)? Sylvia Walby (b. 1953) proposed six structures of patriarchy: household production; patriarchal relations in paid work; patriarchal relations in the state; male violence; patriarchal relations in sexuality; and patriarchal relations in cultural institutions (Walby, 1997).

Feminism is usually thought of in three distinct waves. First-wave feminism originated at the Seneca Falls Conference (1850) as a critique of male sexual and political hegemony (see Chapter 4) and a political agenda based on women's suffrage (David, 2008; Walby, 1997). This impetus for social change fluctuated and the movement initially stalled in the early 20th century, but regained momentum following the Second World War. Second-wave feminism (often referred to as the Women's Liberation or Women's Lib movement) originated in the 1960s, with a strong focus on inequality, sexuality and family life. Third-wave feminism, which began in the 1990s, is concerned with individuality and identity. As with sociology in general, different trends have emerged from liberal to Marxist and radical feminism (Tong, 1989). Feminist sociology embraces a range of diverse, theoretically based inequalities (David, 2008) and whilst initially developed to describe women's oppression and promote their equality (Tong, 1989), feminism has progressed from advocating solely for women, to broader notions of anti-oppressive practice (in social work) and general human rights (Dominelli, 1996). The emergence of feminism has encouraged men's studies, which promote the discussion of masculinity and fatherhood (Connell, 1995; Hearn et al., 1998; Lamb and Tamis-Lemonda, 2004).

In the 1960s, cultural anthropologist Margaret Mead (1901–78) spent time living with remote New Guinea tribes and observed that they conceptualised gender very differently to Western society. Her seminal 1963 study, *Sex and Temperament in Three Primitive Societies,* is often used to support the stance that gender is a social construct (see discussion of constructionism later in this chapter). It has been speculated that as gender is a social construct, it can take many, varied forms; some claim there are as many genders as there are people on the planet. American gender theorist and philosopher Judith Butler (b. 1956) has theorised extensively on gender and significantly influenced feminism, gender studies and queer theory (which is concerned with critical perspectives on gender and sexualities). She is best known for writing *Gender Trouble: Feminism and the Subversion of Identity* (1990), in which she suggested that feminism had mistakenly assumed that all women have common characteristics and therefore continued to divide humans into binary constructs of male and female. She argues this gender-based division inadvertently neglects individual agency and identity, and proposes that masculinity and femininity are on a continuum that allows for personal agency and individual identity. Butler suggests that gender and sexuality are constructed around both social norms and personal agency, allowing for diverse, alternative and flexible identities which individuals *perform*. Gender is therefore something we *do*, rather than something we *are*.

Butler's work on performance and performativity is highly relevant to social work not only because of its relationship to gender and sexuality, but because it can also be extended to consider performances *beyond* gender and sexuality. We can speculate how individuals unconsciously conform to expected roles – even when they consciously seek to challenge them. Consider how conceptualising a 'service user' conjures images of expected behaviours and attitudes for both the person referred to as service user as well as the professional referring to them. These can be described as performances that conform to their expected role. Similarly, we can speculate how professionals such as social workers perform their role within accepted professional and cultural boundaries. Feminist discourses have therefore extended beyond woman's equality and have encouraged thinking about diversity, inclusivity and non-hierarchical-based social work practice.

Social constructionism

We develop an understanding of the world by socially sharing our experiences within it and through this process, our *reality* is formed. We might talk to someone, see something on TV, read about something in a book or on the internet, hear a song: all of these are means of sharing and communicating to explain and understand our experiences. We are largely unaware of ourselves undertaking this process, and we tend to assume that everyone shares the same reality as we do... until something comes along and challenges that view. When this happens, we either reject whatever the new information suggests and carry on as before, or we incorporate the new information to construct a new version of reality, and run with that:

> At its simplest, social construction refers to an element of life that may seem perfectly 'natural' and as always having been that way, but actually turns out to be something that has emerged out of social, cultural and historical processes and events ... Actions, perceptions, thoughts and even feelings are all in their own ways framed and shaped by the society in which we live. (Yuill and Gibson, 2011, p. 10)

Exercise 2.3

Think back to a time when you believed in the tooth fairy, or the Easter bunny. That was your reality and you assumed that it was everyone else's, although now you know that it was not. How was your belief challenged? Did you accept new evidence and change your view easily, or did you resist at first?

Conceptualising a socially constructed world is a fairly new idea which emerged from symbolic interactionism and phenomenology in the mid-twentieth century. Austrian-American Sociologists Berger and Luckmann's *The Social Construction of Reality* (1966) challenged the understanding of reality as an entity, and argued the social order is constructed by the interaction of individuals and groups over time. In the digital age, social constructionism has fast gained traction, with technology increasingly forcing us to question what, if anything, is objectively real. The film franchise *The Matrix* popularised the notion of a computer-generated reality in which humans existed, completely unaware that their physical self was elsewhere. We have grown used to virtual and augmented reality. Social media has given rise to the practice of catfishing, where someone intentionally presents themselves as a different person in order to deceive another.

Appreciating the world is socially constructed has influenced social work directly, through communication theories and systemic practice as well as other sociological movements like postmodernism. Yuill and Gibson (2011) argue that social constructionism is an important sociological concept for social workers because it offers insight into what we see and understand: it forces social workers to appreciate there are different perspectives. This is crucial because we seek to independently assess people and enshrine diversity regardless of personal opinion and agency remit. Most people recognise that traditionally gendered relations based on men as breadwinners and women as homemakers are socially constructed and sociological approaches to families have developed a more flexible, dynamic and less traditional understanding of gender (Giddens, 1994). However, for Judith Butler (1990) the social construction of gender is more than personal agency and sexual difference; unconscious societal forces also define gender and the impact of this reaches beyond personal relationships and identities. Social work was (and many would argue still is) traditionally viewed as *women's work*, and struggled to acquire professional status because it was held in lower esteem than roles more commonly associated with men. Hegemonic social constructions of gender often remain active way beyond their conscious acceptance (Dominelli, 1996, 2002b).

Additionally, social constructionism allows for diverse practice reflecting different constructions of social work, its purpose and nature (Oko, 2011). For instance, it has been suggested that social work combines two distinct sociological approaches: community-based social work promotes challenging power at the political level, while case-management social work is much more concerned with promoting change through individual psychological processes (Hatton, 2015). Notwithstanding individual practice preferences, UK-based social work has shifted its focus away from a radical or emancipatory activity and moved towards a profession seen to be responsible for promoting the social fabric and order (Gilbert and Powell, 2010; Lee, 2014). Social work is a construct which evolves in response to social, political, cultural and economic forces.

Conclusion

Theories and ideas from religion, philosophy, psychology and sociology provided the foundation of the social work profession, and we encourage you to recognise the overlapping nature of theory across and even within disciplines. In contemporary practice we regularly use theory and ideas from these disciplines to help us understand, explain and respond to situations. We don't need to understand these fields in their entirety (if such understanding is even possible) to apply some of the theories within them, but it is helpful for us to understand that ideas are constructed through particular lenses. A theory arising from religion will seek to explain human behaviour differently from a theory arising from psychology because the two disciplines are built upon different principles and evidence bases. It is significant to recognise how many of the theories this chapter highlights as foundational to social work are the ideas of white men. This perspective, therefore, dominates our profession and our practice through an unspoken default position which implicitly disadvantages women, people of colour and other minority groups.

3 ECONOMICS, POLITICS AND THE ORGANISATIONAL DELIVERY OF SOCIAL WORK

Introduction

Social work is a public service which adapts, evolves and changes in response to political, economic and organisational contexts. Most people agree that there is a need for social services of some sort, but debates persist around to what extent and how they should be funded and managed. In this chapter we consider two key mechanisms of societal structure, economics and politics. We explore how they contribute to theoretically driven policies – specifically considering austerity, responsibilisation and troubled families – and shape the way social work is organised to respond.

Economics and social work

Economics is concerned with the production, consumption and distribution of goods and services, and the money that these processes generate and allocate. Economic perspectives influence all aspects of society from the personal to the political, including the way in which social work is funded and practised. Social workers are employed and paid to provide social services, but when we begin to think about *how* services should be funded, *by whom* and *for what*, things become contentious and contested. During the 2016 UK referendum on European Union (EU) membership, the pro-Brexit campaign notoriously covered a bus with a poster stating 'We send the EU £350 million a week. Let's fund our NHS instead.' Everyone knows what the NHS does, it is a much more tangible institution than the EU, so the economic choice the bus apparently presented was persuasive; unfortunately, it was also disingenuous. Most people believe that funding social care is important, but this does not necessarily mean that they want to pay more council tax, or divert monies away from another service that they or their family might need.

Classical and Keynesian economics

Classical economics developed in Britain during the 18th and 19th centuries and is most associated with Adam Smith (1723–90) and John Stuart Mill (1806–73). These economists saw the marketplace as a naturally self-regulating institution which adjusts production in line with demand, and therefore does not require government interference. Such theories are variously described as classical economics, market capitalism, free-market economics and laissez-faire capitalism. They proved highly influential in Britain during the Industrial Revolution, which generated wealth and made the fortunes of many. As canals and railways made the world more accessible, new markets opened up to fresh consumers and many products became nationally (and internationally) available for the first time. The market for Scottish whisky, for instance, boomed as it became globally available, and more whisky was produced to meet the rising demand. Times changed figuratively and literally; for the first time ever, clocks were standardised across Britain to enable trains transporting goods to run on scheduled timetables.

Production costs and wages responded to market demand, but the market is not sentimental or concerned with human conditions. Cities grew and transport infrastructure developed, but alongside this, considerable social inequality and poverty also grew (see Chapter 1). A skilled worker could be made redundant overnight as labour responded to fluctuating market demand, or machinery replaced their role. This left families facing uncertain futures, and frequently destitution and poverty. As markets fluctuated and industries closed overnight, it became clear that fortunes could be lost as easily as they had been made. Classical economic thinking fell out of favour when the mass unemployment and considerable human hardship of the 1930s Great Depression necessitated government regulation to alleviate poverty.

Influenced by these events, John Maynard Keynes (1883–1946) argued for a different economic approach. He reasoned that allowing the market to self-regulate led to unpredictability, but controlling economies through large, government-sponsored schemes which were not as prone to market demands could make them more predictable. Keynesian economics proved popular with political leaders who favoured government-run projects developed to alleviate unemployment, poverty and economic uncertainty, and influenced the decision to nationalise many industries after the Second World War. In the United Kingdom, cross-party consensus politics on the benefits of state-run services and industries led to the NHS and coincided with considerable growth in social services and the welfare state, which became a blueprint for many other countries (Turbett, 2014).

The welfare state – consensus

In the UK, social work has been intertwined with welfarism and, particularly up until the late 1970s, the welfare state (Hardy, 2016). Social work isn't easy; we must choose our practice on the spectrum of advocating to meet needs and the allocation of services. Individual practitioners invariably sit at different points of this spectrum determined by their own political and economic ideologies. In her excellent book on understanding and using theory in social work, Juliette Oko (2011) reflects on consensus, conflict and interpretive theories. She describes consensus and conflict theories as alternative structuralist approaches (see Chapter 2): consensus is the adoption of shared beliefs and socialisation; conflict is a more critical view of society. The welfare state is often reductively presented as the institutions it came to be associated with – the NHS, social services and the welfare benefits system. What the welfare state actually represented was the UK society's consensus on welfare that recognised the need for its citizens to have universal access to health care, housing and economic security. This consensus formed the basis for industrial relations as trade unions negotiated with management on workplace conditions, practices and remuneration. Retrospectively, it also seems that social workers shared a consensus with the people they worked with to aim for a better, brighter and fairer future.

Neoliberalism and the welfare state – conflict?

Neoliberalism is a term for economics characterised by principles of free-market trade, deregulation of financial markets, privatisation, individualisation, and a shift away from the welfare state. The concept has received a fairly mixed press, and your particular view is likely to be closely related to where you fall on the political spectrum. Supporters of neoliberalism view it as a pure form of capitalism and a return to classical economics which promotes individual choice and freedom. Detractors see it as privileging profit at the expense of abandoning the disadvantaged. The exact origins of the term neoliberal are unclear, but it is recorded to have been used at a Paris conference which economist Friedrich Hayek (1899–1992) attended in 1938, and was later applied to 1970s Chilean economics, when the Pinochet dictatorship was described as an essential temporary solution to restore effective market rule.

Keynesian economics dominated until *stagflation*: the high unemployment and high inflation which hit in the 1970s. Through stagflation, economies were seen to be out of control with ever-rising inflation as governments spent increasingly more money with little impact on unemployment. During this time, economists like Friedrich Hayek and Milton Freedman, and politicians such as UK Prime Minister Margaret Thatcher and US President Ronald Reagan argued for a return to market-based classical economics which would prioritise cutting inflation over promoting full employment. The welfare state came under increasing scrutiny. It had been 'a form of centre-left compromise, where governments would invest and regulate business to protect workers from fluctuations in the market, thus keeping, for example, unemployment low' (Fenton, 2019, p. 24), but now was increasingly criticised for facilitating state interference in its citizens' lives and fostering their dependency.

The political left traditionally seeks equality through the redistribution of wealth through taxation, state ownership or cooperatives. Right-wing orientated liberals traditionally argue for equality of opportunity and freedom of choice through market-based economics and policies. Conservative politicians like Margaret Thatcher, Ian Duncan Smith and Michael Gove have all argued that it is more *socially just* for people to benefit from the results of their work, than to forcibly redistribute wealth and resources in the name of equality. Fenton (2019) argues that radical social work (see Chapter 4) has influenced the values of the entire profession, centring them on the principle of *social justice*. Many argue that social work's commitment to social justice makes it incompatible with neoliberalism. However, it is important to recognise that social justice itself is fairly contested as a term and people with left-wing ideologies tend to define social justice differently to those with right-wing ideologies.

Exercise 3.1

What do you see as the difference between the terms *socially just* and *social justice*?

Is it more important to aim for *equality* by targeting services at disadvantaged individuals and groups, or to ensure *equality of opportunity* for all?

Whatever your own stance on neoliberalism, it is fair to consider that radicalism has influenced social work's values, while economic prudence (neoliberalism) has influenced its organisation and delivery. Margaret Thatcher's Conservative government (1979–90) adopted neoliberal economic policy which shifted emphasis from equality to equality of opportunity. This had an enormous effect on the organisation of social services (Deacon and MacDonald, 2017), which were increasingly rationed and regulated in line with market forces. Thatcher government policies paved the way for further neoliberalisation under the New Labour government (1997–2010), and the austerity and responsibilisation agendas of both the Coalition (2010–15) and Conservative governments (2015–).

Progressive neoliberalism developed in the USA and was a significant influence on the UK's New Labour government, where it led to the deregulation of institutions such as banks, and the opening up of industries to competition, which could include community groups. Cummins (2020) argues that terms used by progressive neoliberalism – autonomy, independence, choice, rights, etc. – have been unquestioningly incorporated into social policy and social work practice, particularly in community care and mental health. But although these terms appear positive, Cummins suggests that social and economic policies which employ them have increased inequality, reduced welfare payments and cut services, leading to higher rates of mental health distress. Social problems are misrepresented or misperceived as failings of community care, rather than traced back to a lack of economic investment, and used to justify legislation which further restricts personal and civil liberties (Cummins, 2020). The election of Donald Trump as president of the United States of America is seen by some as a rejection of progressive neoliberalism and progressive discourses (Brenner and Fraser, 2017), as his *America First* policy is premised on anti-neoliberal stances such as restricting immigration and restricting international free trade.

Politics

Politically, the UK is made up of four countries – England, Scotland, Wales and Northern Ireland (called the United Kingdom of Great Britain and Northern Ireland, often shortened to the UK). It is governed by a parliamentary democracy headed by the reigning monarch. As a unitary state, the UK is governed through Parliament, comprising the House of Commons, with elected Members of Parliament (MPs) and the unelected House of Lords. There are devolved governments with elected members in the Scottish Parliament, the National Assembly for Wales and the Northern Ireland Assembly. The UK Parliament has traditionally involved two large parties – Labour and Conservative – who have each formed single party governments. The smaller Liberal Democrats Party formed a coalition government with the Conservative Party between 2010 and 2015. The Labour, Conservative and Liberal Democrat parties are all UK wide except for Northern Ireland. There are distinct national parties in each of the three devolved national parliaments/assemblies, however the Scottish National Party is the third largest political party in the UK Parliament.

Traditionally, political parties have been located on a political spectrum and seen to lean towards left, centre or right (see Table 3.1). This notion of a left–right spectrum originates from the French Revolution when supporters of the revolution were described as being to the president's left and supporters of the king to his right. Those on the left are generally considered to be progressive, those on the right traditionalist, and those in the centre moderate. The ideologies of political parties shift along the political spectrum. For example, whilst the Labour Party is traditionally seen as left-wing, Tony Blair's Labour government promoted a centre-left political stance. Nationalism has also added complexity to political positions. Traditionally nationalism when associated with protecting national supremacy is seen as right wing (e.g. the UK Independence Party, UKIP), but when viewed from a national minority perspective is more left leaning (e.g. the Welsh Nationalist Party, Plaid Cymru).

Table 3.1 Traditional political party affiliations

Traditionally Left-wing Leaning Political Parties	Traditionally Centre Leaning Political Parties	Traditionally Right-wing Leaning Political Parties
Labour Party – UK wide (except Northern Ireland)	Liberal Democrats – UK wide (except Northern Ireland)	Conservative (and Unionist) Party – UK wide (except Northern Ireland)
The Scottish National Party (SNP) – Scotland	Alliance Party of Northern Ireland – Northern Ireland	Democratic Unionist Party (DUP) – Northern Ireland
Sinn Fein – Northern Ireland		Ulster Unionist Party – Northern Ireland
Plaid Cymru – Wales		The Brexit Party – UK wide
The Green Party – UK wide		UK Independence Party (UKIP) – UK wide
Socialist and Democratic Unionist Party – Northern Ireland		

Our professional associations, such as the British Association of Social Workers (BASW) and the International Federation of Social Workers (IFSW), enshrine social justice and challenging inequality as central values of social work. Some people interpret these values politically, others do not.

Exercise 3.2

Is social work a political activity? This is an enormously divisive question and your answer depends very much on how you define politics – to some of course it is, and to others of course it is not. Reflect on *why* you think that it is or isn't.

How we perceive and approach our social work practice enters the political arena at both a personal and a public level through notions of equality (for instance, feminism and gendered structures in society) as well as social policy. In classroom debates, we find that the reason many people reject notions of social work as a political act is because they oppose the alignment of the profession with a specific political party. Deacon and MacDonald state: 'While it is not a professional requirement that social work practitioners be politically motivated, some would certainly argue that they should be' (2017, p. 163). Maas-Lowit (2018) suggests: 'Politics is about the use of forms of power that enable people to negotiate in order to obtain their needs' (p. 48). This definition acknowledges that many people in society lack access to levers of power, and is (at least in part) consistent with the reasons many people give for choosing a career in social work.

Traditionally, UK social work has been associated with left-leaning politics. In its early formation years, it was closely aligned with the socialist Fabian Society and rose to prominence when Attlee's Labour government (1945–51) created the welfare state in the aftermath of the Second World War. But social work practice in the 2020s would be unrecognisable to a social worker from the 1960s. Many feel that it is false or hypocritical to continue to claim that social work is a socialist activity when contemporary social workers can be viewed as paid officers within a profession which exercises powers of social control, determining who is and isn't eligible to receive support. Others will argue with equal validity that a system can only be changed from the inside. Party politics and political ideology exert a strong influence on practice. Social workers are responsible for implementing policy created by political parties, whether or not those parties and policies align with their personal beliefs. From a postmodern perspective (see Chapter 4), Fook (2016) argues that: 'Political neutrality may not, in fact, be possible' (p. 16).

Ali and Trish

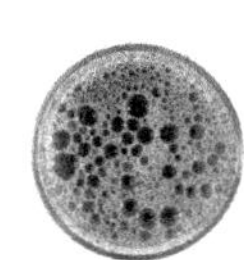

Politically, Ali has always viewed himself as a Labour Party supporter. He has become increasingly concerned by how public services seem to fail many people. He is upset by the number of homeless people he encounters in the town centre, particularly as many of them seem to be young care leavers. Ali wants nothing more than raised taxes and a return to a large and supportive welfare state. He believes in collective action through trade unions and has always voted Labour.

Trish has had a lot of adversity in her life and is very proud that as a young, lone mum she managed to complete a demanding three-year degree and qualify as a social worker. She believes that everyone can improve their circumstances if they work hard. She believes social policy must be economically focused and the state should take a reduced role in citizens' lives to encourage people to take more personal responsibility for improving their own situations. She believes that the prudent social policy endorsed by the Conservative Party will result in economic prosperity for everyone.

Exercise 3.3

How do you think that Ali and Trish's political views might impact on their social work practice? Whose views do you feel most aligned with and why?

Policy

Politics influences economics and vice versa. Political and economic ideologies are premised on theories about how society is or should be organised, what its priorities are or should be, how groups and individuals within it behave or should behave. Governments set public policy and enact legislation which establishes how the country responds to political, economic and social issues. In this section, we explore three contemporary, theoretically interlinked policies which significantly impact social work.

Responsibilisation

Social work has always operated at the interface of choice and control. On the one hand, we seek to promote individual autonomy, but on the other, we must protect people from harm. As public servants, are we accountable to employers, individuals using services, the local community or society as a whole? The notion of individual responsibility is closely linked with neoliberalism in both accountability for action (there must be consequences for doing something 'wrong') and self-support (families should 'look after their own' rather than rely on the state). Neoliberalism endorses equality of opportunity and rewards success, but it also secures that those who are less successful or fall on hard times do not benefit from welfare provision because it considers this to foster dependency. Raitakari et al. (2019) define responsibilisation as:

> the advanced liberal mode of governmentality, which aims to strengthen citizens' abilities to self-governance through various techniques that include the intertwined elements of surveillance and empowerment. (Raitakari et al., 2019, p. 264)

Newman and Clarke (2009) reflect on the reconstruction of contemporary citizenship within a market-based state, and identify several trends:

- **empowered citizen** – free from bureaucracy
- **worker-citizen** – unemployment is discouraged
- **contracted citizen** – contracted across a range of state policies, such as education, parenting, etc.
- **responsible citizen** – greater autonomy over support and needs
- **conditional citizen** – toughened and restricted eligibility procedures for services
- **active citizen** – advocating for activities, such as volunteering

Responsible citizens, they conclude, are those who 'will take greater degrees of responsibility for their own care and welfare, and for that of their families' (Newman and Clarke, 2009: 164). Within this context, resilience becomes not just a strength-based objective but also a mechanism to legitimise reduced support. Newman and Clarke (2009) suggest reforms continue to promote decentralisation and responsibilisation. They highlight, for example, initiatives premised on behaviour-changing strategies, such as cognitive behavioural therapy (CBT) or parenting classes. Such initiatives are seen as cost-effective because they can be delivered cheaply and promote personal responsibility which reduces and discourages the need for ongoing service involvement. Liebenberg et al. (2015) found responsibilisation has become part of the mindset of many social workers: whereas historically they were likely to link youth offending or mental health problems to structural factors like unemployment and poverty (society's responsibility), contemporary social workers were much more likely to consider them to be the product of lifestyle choices (the individual's responsibility).

Austerity

Austerity is about living with unnecessary things, limiting or rationing resources and tolerating subsequent discomfort. In 2010, the Coalition government formed between the Conservatives and the Liberal Democrats introduced a programme of austerity intended to reduce the budget deficit. Over the subsequent decade, more than £30 billion of spending reductions were made across public services including welfare benefits, housing subsidies and social care services. To some, the austerity programme was a necessary response to the 2008 *Credit Crunch*, the worst global financial crisis since the Great Depression of the 1930s. To others, austerity was a political opportunity to refashion UK social policy and dismantle the welfare state. Whatever your perspective on the underlying motivation for the austerity programme, its impact on social work is irrefutable.

There has always been a limit to public spending. Budgets are often imagined as cakes sliced into different sized portions, but this is an artificial and ill-fitting model. A cake has to be made, and just as the baker must consider ratios and selection of ingredients, so national and local governments must consider what funds are allocated to social care budgets. The publicly available cake represents only one of multiple possible cakes which could be made. In this analogy, the Coalition government made a cake which protected NHS funding, but cut social care budgets, and some would argue that this encourages a perception that whilst health is an essential, universal need, social care is, at least in part, expendable.

In 2010, the United Nations Special Rapporteur on extreme poverty and human rights visited the UK to consider the impact of the austerity:

> The results? 14 million people, a fifth of the population, live in poverty. Four million of these are more than 50% below the poverty line, and 1.5 million are destitute, unable to afford basic essentials. The widely respected Institute for Fiscal Studies predicts a 7% rise in child poverty between 2015 and 2022, and various sources predict child poverty rates of as high as 40%. For almost one in every two children to be poor in twenty-first century Britain is not just a disgrace, but a social calamity and an economic disaster, all rolled into one. (Alston, 2018, p. 1)

BASW (n.d.) argues that social workers should critically consider the impact of poverty on individuals, families and communities. Poverty is an adversity that affects people in multiple ways and can be compounded or caused by the actions of the state and state representatives. Social workers have legal duties and powers which can be used to intervene to rectify injustices and prevent risk, but our role as state representatives is a conflicting one. The boundaries of our involvement are frequently denoted by the limits on public funding of services. In some situations, social workers are cast as 'protectors of the public purse' who, in applying eligibility thresholds and gatekeeping services, may directly or indirectly contribute to poverty. In other situations, social workers alleviate adversity and poverty by facilitating access to or advocating for services. During enforced austerity social work has been forced to respond to increased demand with fewer resources. Despite this, we must not lose sight of the potential long-term impact of decisions which seem cost-effective in the short-term.

'Troubled Families' – people with problems or problem people?

Children from the economically poorest communities are most likely to have social work involvement, and therefore social work enters the private space of poor people much more than affluent people. Does this mean that abuse and neglect only occur in poor families? Certainly not. However, it certainly seems to indicate that something directs a social work mandate towards one section of society and away from another. Throughout its history, social work practice has responded to poverty and worked with notions of deserving/undeserving poor. Ralston and Gayle explain, 'The general notion, that there is a section of undeserving poor who should receive punishment or correction, is a central concept in neo-liberal politics' (2017, p. 1). Lambert and Crossley (2017) suggest that a wide spectrum of policies have located 'troubles' or 'problems' in the family itself, without regard to social or economic considerations. They argue that the negative language contained in policies, e.g. *unemployable, social problem group, problem family, cycle of deprivation, underclass*, and more recently, *troubled*, is a pathologising discourse.

The New Labour government's Social Exclusion Task Force led to *Family Intervention Projects* (FIPs) working with 120,000 families identified as 'at risk' because they experienced five out of seven of the following problems: parental unemployment; maternal mental health; parental disability; poor housing; poverty; overcrowded living conditions; parents without educational qualification. The Coalition government's *Troubled Families Programme* (TFP) was partially based upon a reappraisal (Casey, 2012) of the Social Exclusion Task Force's work. The TFP is focused on disrupting perceived intergenerational patterns (see Chapters 6 and 7) in the most troubled families in the UK by targeting:

- worklessness
- poor school attendance
- mental and physical health problems
- crime and antisocial behaviour
- domestic violence and abuse
- children who are classified as in need of help and protection (Ministry of Housing, Communities and Local Government, 2019)

TFP aimed to provide coordinated, early intervention which would responsibilise these families and reduce the need for multiple different and costly services to react to their social needs and behaviours. This aim appeared to be underpinned by the idea that the social work profession wasn't doing its task very well, as evidenced when the programme's director, Louise Casey, bluntly told the *Daily Telegraph*:

> We are not running some cuddly social workers programme … we should be talking about things like shame and guilt … we have lost the ability to be judgmental because we worry about being seen as nasty to poor people. (20 July 2012)

Proponents of the Troubled Families Programme argue that it seeks to strengthen families and communities, building resilience and skills to prevent children entering the looked after child system (Family Action, n.d.). The government's review of the programme stated: 'The Troubled Families Programme (2015–2020) is working to achieve significant and sustained progress with up to 400,000 families with multiple, high-cost problems by 2020' (Ministry of Housing, Communities and Local Government, 2019, p. 7). This emphasis on the financial, rather than the social costs is telling. In creating the TFP, the Conservative government subscribed to the theory that 'troubled' families do not contribute to society's economic productivity because of 'worklessness' – the lack of desire to work, rather than the inability to gain work (unemployment). Alongside their failure to conform and contribute, 'troubled' families are viewed to present too high a financial burden on society through the cost of welfare benefits, health and social care services and criminal justice involvement. However, the *National Evaluation of the Troubled Families Programme* (Ministry of Housing, Communities and Local Government, 2019) found that most of the families targeted by TFP were not involved in crime or antisocial behaviour, rather they were poor with very high levels of mental and physical illnesses and disability. The Troubled Families policy appears to castigate those who do not conform to notions of community responsibility without recognising that the playing field is not level; some people have higher support needs than others. Moreover, political and economic policies play a significant role in constructing their circumstances.

Keating (2016) recognises that social policy and social work are interlinked, and social workers have to balance the tension between legislative (state) responsibility, people who use services, organisational demands and professional standards. He argues for:

> a closer alignment between the aims of social policy and the value base of social work by refocusing on human rights and social justice … an emphasis on social relationships, a focus on those who 'lose out' or are invisible and to intervene where required. In this way we should be able to support those in greatest need, redress social inequality and promote social justice. (p. 175)

Management theory and social work

Over the last four decades, theories and principles derived from business management have been increasingly presented as complementary to contemporary social work practice. Management theories have completely reorganised social care services, although many are critical of a shift to models which are focused on cost and outcomes, rather than professionally based. When Social Service Departments were first established in the post-war period, management approaches were influenced by two broad theoretical perspectives – *Taylorism* and *Mayoism*. Frederick Taylor (1856–1915) was a foreman in an American steel company who became fascinated by creating a more efficient and productive workforce. He applied scientific methods to analyse the component parts of each employee's work in order to eliminate unnecessary tasks, reduce waste and improve speed and efficiency. His approach was promoted as the *theory of scientific management* and applied very broadly, becoming highly influential. Elton Mayo (1880–1949) was an Australian psychologist who is generally regarded as the father of human relations. His book *The Human Problems of an Industrial Civilization* (1933) concluded that people's work performance is dependent on two aspects – the content of their role and their social relationships in the workplace. He criticised purely scientific approaches to management, because they created conflict in organisations by promoting management 'logic of cost and efficiency' at the expense of worker 'logic of sentiment'. Good management, he therefore asserted, found a balance between the needs of the organisation and the needs of the workforce.

William Deming (1900–93) was an American engineer and professor of statistics who worked with the Union of Japanese Scientists and Engineers after the Second World War. Deming trained hundreds of members of the Japanese workforce – including Akio Morita, who co-founded Sony – in business planning and concepts of quality control. Deming's ideas contributed to Japan's remarkable rise to become the second-largest economy in the world. Deming theorised that effective management requires a *System of Profound Knowledge*, comprising four lenses:

- **Appreciation of a system** – understanding the overall processes and all of its component parts – suppliers, producers and customers (see Chapter 6).
- **Knowledge of variation** – using statistical measures to determine the quality of the product and the range and causes of variation in quality.
- **Epistemological knowledge** – understanding how knowledge can be explained and the limits of what can be known (see Chapter 2).
- **Psychological knowledge** – understanding of concepts of human nature (see Chapter 2) (Deming, 1993).

Japan's meteoric economic rise drew Western attention to Deming's work, and in the 1980s it was used to underpin the model of *Top Quality Management* (TQM). The TQM model applies standardised approaches across entire organisations in order to drive up quality and efficacy (Figure 3.1).

With highly competitive global markets, the Keynesian economic principles upon which the welfare state depended were increasingly called into question. There was a growing view that public services should be managed economically through business-like principles and models such as TQM.

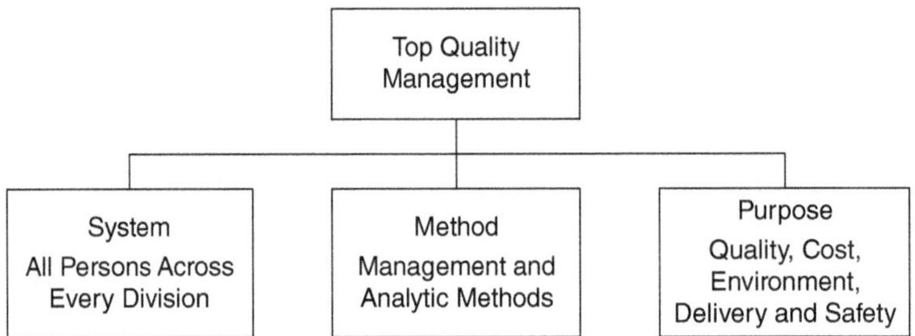

Figure 3.1 Top Quality Management model

New Public Management/managerialism

New Public Management (NPM) is a term used to describe a shift of direction in the management of public services which started in the 1980s, premised on core business principles often summed up as *the three E's* – economy, efficiency and effectiveness – and *the three M's* – markets, managers and measurement (Dunleavy and Hood, 1994; Hood, 1995). In the UK, Margaret Thatcher's Conservative government reimagined people using public services as customers who should be able to choose from a range of options. More choice in the social care marketplace, they argued, would create competition that would drive up standards whilst keeping costs low (Harlow, 2003). Until this point, the vast majority of social services were both funded and delivered by local authorities. NPM heralded the *purchaser/provider split*, whereby local authorities began to deliver fewer services in-house and instead purchase them from independent providers.

Successive Conservative governments continued the NPM approach to public services and the New Labour government echoed their neoliberal agenda, ushering in increased levels of bureaucratisation, modernisation, regulation and systems of information technology. They sought to raise standards and promote integrated interprofessional working models (Hardy, 2016) through social enterprise, and used private finance to fund public services. NPM is now seen as an historical phase, and the term *managerialism* is more commonly used to describe the operation of public services through business processes: 'One significant dimension of the reconstruction of the welfare state has been the process of managerialization: the shift towards managerial forms of organizational coordination' (Clarke et al., 2000, p. 6). Rogowski (2011a) identifies two related aspects of managerialism:

1 **Organisational coordination** – the ways of structuring organisations and constructing inter-organisational relationships, for instance moving from Social Service Departments to Children's Trusts.
2 **Management rather than professionally run services** – a mixed economy or market requires management oversight rather than professional intervention, for instance moving from social work (professionally led) to care management (procedurally led).

The modernisation agenda of NPM aligned the delivery of social services with business models for primarily economic reasons, however:

> the usefulness of business models in social service organisations has been debated and many scholars argue that public sector organisations differ too much from their private counterparts to make the continuing import of models worthwhile. (Tafvelin et al., 2014, p. 888)

Pamela Trevithick (2003) believes that managerialism underestimates the significance of emotions, fails to consider the impact of its policies and procedures on service users and practitioners, and fails to recognise that relationships are central to social work. Rogowski (2011b) agrees, and calls for relationship-based practice as a riposte to the ideological de-professionalisation managerialism effects through increasing bureaucratisation. Hardy (2016) suggests that the desire for improved services has come at the expense of professional discretion, autonomy and confidence. Contemporary social workers are faced with the difficult task of balancing professionally based values with procedurally based organisational requirements. Hingley-Jones and Ruch (2016) warn that managerialism has led to a point where we are not just practising in a climate of financial austerity, organisational cultures have become characterised by emotional austerity.

Social work managers and leaders

Managerialism saw social care services bureaucratised and structured into layers of line-management. This was in sharp contrast with the 1970s, when leadership was an overlooked element in social work education and social workers were generally reluctant to become managers. Before the advent of managerialism, social work managers were typically qualified social workers whose:

> approach tended to be guided by their social work experience, professional values and accumulated practice wisdom. Few, if any, had any specific management qualifications. Generally, they would have had professional allegiances with the workforce. (Scourfield, 2018, p. 36)

But post-NPM, rather than focusing on issues related to social work practice and community development, social work managers' roles became much more about controlling budgets and monitoring and measuring performance against organisational targets (Scourfield, 2018). As the skills of management became increasingly administrative, rather than experiential, it was no longer considered necessary for social services to be managed by people who had 'done the job'. A gulf opened between the aims and purpose of the social work profession and the aims and purpose of the employing agency.

Stanley and Russell (2014) recognise how managerialist discourses negatively influenced social work practice, with proceduralism and risk aversion narrowing the scope for innovative approaches. Baldwin (2004) held that managerialism's dominance could be tempered by practice leadership, and in her *Review of Child Protection* (2011), Professor Eileen Munro concurred. She identified that there was a disconnect between the realities of frontline social work and senior managers' understanding. She advocated for a new leadership role which could act as a bridge between social workers and senior managers: the *Principal Social Worker*. In Munro's model, Principal Social Workers would provide professional leadership by having the status and responsibility of a senior manager but still remain actively involved in frontline practice. She anticipated this role would ensure better communication and challenge between management and workforce through:

- providing an authentic voice for frontline social work staff
- remaining in practice to understand first-hand about what helps, what hinders
- working alongside senior management highlighting practice issues and acting as 'a critical friend' to all levels of the organisation
- advancing ideas and debates to raise practice standards at every level of the organisation
- linking to the national practice agenda to raise the profile of social work

Munro's recommendation was for every local authority to have a Principal Children and Families Social Worker, but the role was also implemented for adults, and in 2016 the Care Act's statutory guidance was amended to direct that every local authority must have a Principal Social Worker for Adults. Marion Russell was the first Principal Social Worker (PSW) appointed following the Munro Review, and her experiences in trying to implement the role led her to explore it for her doctoral thesis (2019). She found that PSWs were frustrated from effecting significant change by resistant and closed systems of leadership. Most were not supported to maintain frontline practice, and many combined their role with other management responsibilities:

> [PSWs] described tensions and difficulties because of what continued to be linear, top-down approaches to change from senior managers ... some of the challenges in implementing Munro's vision of the role were because of financial, cultural and ideological constraints as well as government imperatives, Ofsted inspection requirements and council priorities. (Russell, 2019)

Sadly, Russell's findings seem to suggest that the PSW role is often diverted from the leadership it was intended to provide by being combined with managerial responsibility which aligns the role more with senior management than the social work workforce. Further than this, PSWs alone cannot fight the tide against managerialism which is reinforced at institutional and government levels.

Akram

Akram is worried about what opportunities his placement will give him to demonstrate **PCF 9, Professional Leadership**. He finds it really difficult to think of a situation where he, a student, will be in a position of authority over any of the qualified and experienced social workers on the team. Over his lunch break, he gets chatting to Lloyd, the most recently qualified member of the team about this. Lloyd tells Akram that he needs to differentiate between management and leadership. He directs Akram to a literature review on social work by Corby Peters (2018), which defines leadership as:

> a collection of organisational, relational, and individual behaviors that affect positive change in order to address client and societal challenges through emotional competence and the full acceptance, validation, and trust of all individuals as capable human beings. (p. 40)

Lloyd asks Akram whether Ali, the team manager, is the only person in the team who meets this definition. Akram thinks about it and replies no – he has seen every member of the team help people to achieve change. Lloyd tells Akram that whether someone is a student social worker or a service manager, leadership is a key part of their practice. It can be demonstrated through their approach to self-management, assessment, decision-making, interprofessional working, care planning, advocating for people's rights and promotion of best practice which seeks to support people positively.

Exercise 3.4

How do management and leadership differ in your experience?
When have you demonstrated leadership and how?

Proceduralism and outcomes-based planning

Applying principles from industry to the operation of social work meant standardising processes through practice frameworks and procedural guidance. Across all areas of social work practice, the drive for consistency through standardised operational procedures resulted in standardised documentation with assessments premised on a script or checklist. This reduced practitioner discretion and Harlow (2003) argues that this resulted in technicist practice where frontline social workers began to act as managers of people's situations, rather than agents of change. This was perhaps most keenly felt in adult services, where social workers were largely recast as *care managers*. Harlow (2003) explains that care managers coordinate, rather than provide services, and as such are much more concerned with minimising risk and maintaining stability than effecting change. She questions the ability of a care manager to genuinely advocate on behalf of people who use services when they are responsible for costing the interventions they receive. Doel notes that:

> Social work is a profession that is orientated towards process (how things are done, the quality), and it has had to come to grips with an increasing focus on outcome (what is the product, the quantity). (2012, p. 114)

Managerialism incorporated performance measures into the social work process, gauging success against predetermined outcomes (Hardy, 2016). Outcomes-based planning draws again from the field of business management through the concept of SMART modelling. George Doran (1981) offered SMART as mnemonic acronym for articulating management goals and objectives:

Specific – aims and objectives, roles and tasks

Measurable – outcomes and goals

Achievable – goals and outcomes to enhance success and improve motivation

Realistic and relevant – outcomes with focus on core issues

Timely and time limited – addressing current issues using a plan with a review date

Social work often takes place in the midst of chaotic and confusing situations. In some situations, SMART planning can help manage expectations and maintain focus. But in many social work situations, outcomes-based planning is contentious: can we meaningfully measure human outcomes? For example, what are the desirable outcomes for children looked after by local authorities? Should we aim for immediate safety, or a nurturing environment; maintaining family relationships, or educational achievement and employability? Is happiness a realistic aim and, if so, how do we measure such an individual experience? The organisation's desired outcome will often differ greatly from the individual's. Doel notes that:

> The managerialist approach prioritises procedures and targets over professional values and standards and it stresses compliance and rule-governed behaviour rather than critical analysis and reflection. Managerialist practice therefore values quantitative measures over qualitative ones. (Doel, 2012, p. 37)

In 2009, the Department of Health undertook a consultation on adult safeguarding processes and discovered that a great many people felt they had been disempowered by professionals who had worked towards agency outcomes, rather than those desired by the person at risk. The Care Act 2014 incorporates outcomes in two distinct ways:

Desired outcomes – the outcomes that the individual person wants to achieve determined by their personal interpretation of wellbeing.

Eligibility outcomes – prescribed outcomes against which people's needs are assessed to determine if they are eligible for care and support provided by the local authority.

Jones (1999) suggests that the bureaucratisation of social work through NPM, managerialism, proceduralism and outcomes-based planning has skewed the very purpose of social work, making us very much the servants of organisations rather than the servants of the public:

> In the contemporary welfare system, state social work agencies do not require highly informed or educated, research-aware social workers. These are now regarded as positively unhelpful qualities that make for questioning and criticism. Rather what is now demanded is agency loyalty, an ability to follow instruction, to complete procedures and assessments on time, to modify and placate client demand, to manage inadequate

budgets and to work in such ways that will not expose the agency to public ridicule. (Jones, 1999, cited in Harris, 2003, p. 119)

Conclusion

It is surprisingly easy to overlook the macro context of our practice when we are consumed by the day-to-day micro elements. Social work is demanding and challenging and we do what we can – often with very little by way of resources. But the legislation, policy, procedures and organisational structures that we practise within are not neutral. They are underpinned by economic and political ideologies of central and local government. Social work has the potential to be a transformative profession which supports the most vulnerable people in society, but it is never free from economic and political constraint. If we problematise the people that we work with, rather than identifying the problems they are experiencing, we have accepted our role as managers of the status quo rather than agents of change. As local authorities seek to deliver statutory services within ever-tighter budgets, services and lines of management seem to be endlessly restructured. It is important that within this changing environment, individual practitioners identify their own beliefs and values – whether or not they consider them to be political – and hold true to them as best they can.

4 CRITICAL AND RADICAL THEORIES

Introduction

This chapter focuses on theories which take a critical approach to explore society and challenge received wisdom. We begin by introducing the notion of hegemony, exploring how the ways in which we understand power relations and accepted cultural norms directly influence our practice as social workers. We move on to consider theories of modernism, postmodernism and post-traditionalism, and some of the prominent theorists associated with them, such as Michel Foucault, Anthony Giddens and Pierre Bourdieu. Paulo Freire's work on critical consciousness leads us on to specifically consider critical and radical models of social work – not as historical approaches, but as highly relevant sources of knowledge to help us challenge inequality and empower the people we work with.

Antonio Gramsci and hegemony

In Ancient Greece, hegemony was a term used to refer to the political, economic, or military predominance of one state over others. In philosophy and sociology, the term cultural hegemony is used to describe leadership through implied or accepted power which influences personal and social attitudes and structures. Essentially, hegemony is achieved when certain cultural practices invisibly reinforce power relations and dictate who should lead, whilst those being led accept the status quo and their subordinate position in a hierarchically structured society. The notion of invisible power has its roots partly in Marxist thinking about the pervasive power of ideology, values and beliefs in reproducing class relations (see Chapter 2).

Contemporary thinking around hegemony is derived from the work of Antonio Gramsci (1891–1937). Gramsci was an Italian Marxist philosopher and communist politician who was imprisoned by Mussolini's regime in 1926, and remained incarcerated until his death in 1937. While in prison he wrote numerous books, which were smuggled out and published, most notably his *Prison Notebooks*. In these, Gramsci theorised on notions of hegemony and the manufacture of consent, arguing that the capitalist state is made up of two overlapping spheres: a political society, which rules through force, and a civil society, which rules through consent. He theorised that power is constituted in the realm of ideas and knowledge by hegemonic controls expressed through consent rather than force.

Power is a crucial aspect of any organisational structure, and is exerted through approaches of leadership and management. In 1959, French and Raven (cited in Lawler and Bilson, 2010, pp. 44–6), identified five bases of power used by leaders – some positive, some negative:

Legitimate power – the person's role or status provides a mandate for them to make demands and expect others to comply, for example, a manager exercising authority over their staff.

Coercive power – the person ensures compliance through the use of ultimatums and threats of negative consequences.

Reward power – the person incentivises compliance. Reward power is the reverse of coercive power – the carrot rather than the stick.

Referent power – the person's individual traits, for example, charisma/credibility, mean that they are held in high regard and others are enthused to comply.

Expert power – the person's high level of skill/knowledge means that they are held in high regard and this encourages others to defer to and comply with them.

In 1965, Raven added a sixth base, which resonates strongly with current debates around manipulation of media and notions of *fake news*:

Informational power – the person controls the information needed by others in order to make them comply.

Ali

As a team manager, Ali has legitimate power to allocate work, but his team is overstretched at present due to sickness absence, and he knows that no one really has the capacity to take on more. The service manager sends a weekly email around the whole service (informational power) naming and shaming managers whose teams breach expected timescales (coercive power), whilst those who meet them are commended (reward power). Ali relies on the respect that his team has for him (referent power) and their belief in the support that he can provide (expert power) to persuade his staff to complete the required work within the expected timescales.

Exercise 4.1

What forms of power do people use to make you comply?
Which are most effective? Why?
What forms of power do you use to make others comply?
Which are more effective? Why?

Gramsci described the ruling classes as exerting invisible power by controlling the construction of ideology and cultural norms, which allows them to gain/retain predominance not by force, but by popular consent (Gramsci, 2003 edn). For instance, a monarchy-based society accepts that certain people are destined to rule through birth. Gramsci's conceptualisation of hegemony inspired the use of explicit strategies to contest societal norms which discriminate against or oppress people in order to achieve hegemonic legitimacy.

Author's experience Phil

After qualifying as a social worker, one of the first women I worked with explained to me that she had multiple children 'taken off me'. She told me that with her first two children, alcohol and 'the wrong partners' affected her parenting and she acknowledged that it was probably best for her children to be placed with other carers. However, she felt differently about her third child, telling me that 'I had changed by then, but no one believed me'. In essence the prevailing wisdom within the social work team was that having had her first two children removed from her care, she was automatically unable to care for any other children. Her parenting capacity had been decided without fresh assessment, based upon prevailing attitudes that her children were not safe in her care. It is now three decades since I worked with this woman and sadly, I often find echoes of her story in that of other fathers and mothers that I meet.

More recently, I have met several women who were diagnosed with as autistic later in life, years after their children were removed from them. Perhaps with an earlier diagnosis their parenting might have been better understood and they might have received support, resulting in different professional decisions. Whilst I can't really know if this is true, I remain convinced that as practitioners we have a duty to undertake robust assessments and consider alternative explanations, which may at times challenge accepted opinions (hegemony) held by society, other professionals or our team, manager and colleagues. Taking this position can, at times, seem a lonely place because it is much easier to go with the crowd and agree with everyone else.

The Australian sociologist R.W. Connell used Gramscian theory in her work on gender, developing the concept of *hegemonic masculinity*. Connell theorised that masculinity is constructed through complex intersections of gender and class. This results in diverse and historically relative social codes which maintain and reinforce hierarchical gender positioning within society. Connell highlighted the way in which common idealised cultural representations of men – for example as physically strong, as breadwinners, or even as violent – enable them to maintain dominance over women (Connell, 1995, 2002).

It is difficult to know how much we acquiesce to cultural hegemonies in our social work practice. No one is immune to the norms their society has conditioned them to, or the culture of their organisation. A practitioner may strongly believe in challenging gender stereotypes, but somehow still find their practice dominated with traditional constructs of women as carers and nurturers, and thereby expect much more from mothers than fathers. Carey and Foster (2011) argue that deference to hegemony has increased as social work has become less structured, more uncertain and increasingly dependent upon unpredictable markets of social care. Whilst there are calls for social work to embrace diversity, there remains dissatisfaction with the hegemonic spread of Western models of social work (Brydon, 2012).

Modernism, postmodernism and post-traditionalism

Humans have always sought to understand the world we inhabit, and our comprehension and focus have shifted throughout history. Different systems classify these historical periods: for example, technical periods such as the Bronze Age, scientific periods such as the Age of Enlightenment, Marxist epochs based on class division and general time periods, such as ancient and modern.

Modernism

As a general classification, the *modern world* (and modernism) began with the Enlightenment and the attempt to construct societies based on scientific understandings of universal realities, reason and truths. The term *modernism* was first used in sociology by Georg Simmel (1858–1918) to describe social processes and forces brought about by the combination of social theories with the Enlightenment and industrialisation. Essentially, modernism was associated with progression towards a better human condition and social ordering (Garrett, 2018). While associated with progressive processes, modernism was fundamentally Eurocentric and Western in outlook and either by design, intent or accident, traditional ways and societies were replaced by modernist reordering of societies. Through modernism, traditional and cultural understandings were to be replaced by rationalist approaches. However, in practice this meant modernist imperatives to fashion social relations on concrete notions of scientific truth, reason and reality were used to promote and justify colonialism and imperialist actions resulting in the death and oppression of huge numbers of people (Garrett, 2018). Consider the experiences of Native Americans, or the European conquest in Africa and imperialism in India. Modernism is no longer perceived as wholly progressive because its foundation on conceptualisation of concrete (and universal) reality and truth is now recognised, at the very least, to be flawed.

Postmodernism

French-based philosophers Foucault, Derrida, Lyotard and Baudrillard challenged the grand narratives of modernism within what became known as *postmodernism*. Many contradictions are inherent within postmodernism – not least being that some of its celebrated adherents did not consider themselves postmodernists! Foucault never referred to himself a postmodernist, and Baudrillard maintained that he operated more or less within Marxism. Rather interestingly, there is no actual agreement about when the postmodern world began (Howe, 1994); there is even a debate about whether the modern world has actually ended (Garrett, 2018; Price and Simpson, 2007). As ever in philosophy, there are alternative opinions and theories, the existence of which challenges modernism's stance of singular truth and reality. In essence, postmodernism refutes that there can be a universally held and scientifically understood worldview or reality. The postmodernists studied post-industrial science, architecture, art, information technology, knowledge, communication, consumerism and globalisation, and were unable to find a transcendental truth or rule governing all situations. This led to doubts about the universality of modernist-held grand (big and all encompassing) narratives about truth and reality. Rather than discovering a collective truth or objective reality, they recognised a multitude of diverse discourses and multiple truths held by different groups (Healy, 2005). Concepts such as consumerism and globalisation are associated with the deconstructed postmodernist worldview, resulting in individualisation, identity and choice.

Postmodernism is concerned with language and discourse: a form of social interaction between people and within organisations (Van Dijk, 2011), and sociologically refers to how a particular subject is discussed and conceptualised (Tulle and Lynch, 2011). Michel Foucault (1926–84) highlighted how difference and diversity challenged modernism's notions of social conformity. He investigated groups whose lifestyles could be viewed as alternative or outside of mainstream society, for example prisoners and psychiatric patients. Foucault sought to show how socially constructed concepts such as sexuality, criminality and mental illness connected with the self and individuality. His examination of mental illness (Foucault, 2001) charted the way in which *madness* is disapprovingly categorised as an unacceptable state of being. Foucault reflected on how historical and cultural discursive practices set rules for organising and producing different forms of knowledge.

Jean-François Lyotard (1924–98) argued that 'language games' constitute the self, society and social relations in heterogeneous manners, sending out contradictory codes and messages (Lyotard, 1984/2005). Lyotard criticised the history of grand or meta-narratives which aimed to classify society within socially constructed homogeneous theories such as Christianity or class structure and promoted the notion of *petit narratives*, which were more personal and less universal. Swiss linguist Jacques Derrida (1930–2004) recognised that the words and language we use communicate a diversity of meanings and are understood in multiple ways. He highlighted normative and abnormal conceptual understandings, where people are viewed as one thing or another, either/or. In this way, personal social identity may be defined through an implied negative connotation. For example, someone may talk about their 'gay work colleague', but simply refer to their 'work colleague' when describing someone who is straight, because in our heteronormative society, heterosexuality is assumed (Derrida and Bass, 1995). Although the person may not even be conscious of it, their need to highlight one colleague's sexuality but not the other's validates and reinforces heterosexuality's normative dominance.

In relation to social work, Healy (2014) defines discourse as the knowledge of a specific group which helps to shape power relations, and professional knowledge is often theoretically driven. Therefore, discourses are essentially a form of communication that can privilege knowledge and power held by specific groups (Fairclough, 1992). If we think, for example, about a person visiting a psychiatrist. The person directly experiencing the mental health issue knows how it manifests and affects them, but invariably the psychiatrist controls the discourse about mental health. By communicating in an established language of symptomology and diagnostic labelling, and demonstrating familiarity and skill at navigating treatment pathways and services, the psychiatrist establishes their power in the form of expertise.

Postmodernism's influence upon social work is fairly recent (Healy, 2005), and most significantly felt in the field of critical social work (Fook, 2016), which we discuss later on in this chapter. Fook (2000) suggests postmodernist approaches to social work promote the deconstruction of professionalism in favour of context-specific partnerships between social worker and client. She further argues that social work practitioners deconstruct professional expertise to reconstruct practice in response to diverse situations. Postmodernism causes some difficulty as a social work theory: it positively stresses different locations of power, the importance of language, the diversity of groups and individuals and the plurality of perspective (Howe, 1994). However, the reduction of the authority of knowledge, along with the individualisation of practice, risks a negative move towards neoliberal and consumerist policy which individualises complex social problems. Corker and Shakespeare (2002) identify that postmodernism significantly overlaps theories of diversity such as feminism, queer studies, critical race studies and disability studies, whilst at the same time appearing to promote consumerism and individuality, thereby reinforcing notions of personal responsibilisation.

Post-traditionalism (new modernism?)

British sociologist Anthony Giddens (b. 1938), alongside others such as Ulrich Beck (1944–2015), has opposed the universality of postmodernism. Although he shares many of the postmodernists' views (i.e. the influence of consumerism and narratives), Giddens suggests modernity cannot end, as it is always a contemporary concept. It is the times we live in that change and so we are experiencing a *late modern* period in a *post-traditional* world. Giddens refutes sociological positivism, arguing that sociology is concerned with people and social interaction, and reflexivity is a given for sociologists as their research involves, at least to some extent, participation. His *structuration theory* (Giddens and Pierson, 1998) is concerned with human agency – our ability to act independently, to make free choices and influence our environment – and the influences of structure upon human action. Structuration draws upon hermeneutics, functionalism and structuralism. Whereas Durkheim (see Chapter 2) imagined structures as being almost physical in their existence, Giddens defines them as a more ethereal influence. The combination of social action/individual agency aligned with structural components of social institutions, such as knowledgeability and traditions, is related to structure but possessed by the individual. Whilst choice and reflexivity are very important factors in human actions, there are also unacknowledged conditions and unintended consequences of action. Structuration recognises that individual social actions are embedded within social structures. When social action is determined by a traditional outlook, individual agency is reduced because choice is already prescribed by traditions and customs. For example, a person's social activity may be a relationship that leads to marriage, where an unacknowledged condition may be patriarchy. These are subjective processes, not states of mind, and are sustained by the agent on an ongoing basis:

> It is entirely consistent with the status of structuration theory as an ontology of potentials that what may be for agents unintended consequences and unacknowledged conditions of action over a given historical period, may thereafter become discursively acknowledged by agents as ongoing outcomes of and conditions for their own social context. (Cohen, 1989, p. 55)

A post-traditional world allows for a range of options that encourage individual agency and choice through media exchanges. Individuals can appropriate knowledge which would not have been known or available to them without books, films and most strikingly, the internet. Therefore, modernity represents an increase in individual agency, choice and a democratisation of social structures. For Giddens (1992), people renegotiate intimacy as traditional approaches to relationships are eroded by advances in communication technology and the internet.

French sociologist Pierre Bourdieu (1930–2002) was primarily concerned with the dynamics of power in society. He explored the diverse and subtle ways in which power is transferred and social order is maintained within and across generations, as well as focusing on the production and reproduction of capital. Bourdieu extended notions of capital beyond traditional economic forms to include social, cultural and symbolic capital. Alongside social class, an individual's social space is defined by the relationships between the different forms of capital. The ways in which an individual operates within the different social world fields (such as politics, education, economy, etc.) create a complex set of social relations in which individuals engage daily.

Bourdieu theorised the family as a means of accumulating and transmitting social, cultural and symbolic forms of capital between generations (Bourdieu, 1986). For Bourdieu, the ways in which family is constructed represents both a fiction, and the most natural of social categories through which social relations, ties, bonds and affiliations are created:

> Their logical extension in the countless acts of reaffirmation and reinforcement that aim to produce, in a kind of continuous creation, the obliged affections and affective obligations of family feeling. (Bourdieu, 1996, p. 22)

The internal structure of the family unit is founded on social interactions that incorporate intimate paternal and maternal relations. These relations and the internal structuring of families reproduce cultural practices and *habitus* – ingrained ways by which individuals perceive the world – which in turn affect the individual. The ways in which habitus is constituted informs how individuals spontaneously respond to the social world. Family and tradition are important for Bourdieu and Giddens, the latter arguing that:

> Modernity always set itself against tradition, but in many areas of life, tradition persisted – particularly in everyday life. The reason was primarily the dominant position of the patriarchal family which remained undemocratized. That family form, together with the

norms of gender and sexuality associated with it, is now breaking down creating both opportunities and dilemmas in its wake. (Giddens and Pierson, 1998, p. 118)

For Giddens, the family has undergone democratisation with an emerging equality not only between genders but also intergenerationally between adults and children (Giddens, 1992). How people negotiate their intimate and personal (often familial) relationships is of fundamental importance, and therefore social work must take into account not only what people represent through traditionally ascribed roles and actions, but also their agency to negotiate and perform non-traditional roles.

Paulo Freire and critical consciousness

Paulo Freire (1921–97) was a Brazilian philosopher and educator most recognised for his seminal 1968 text, *Pedagogy of the Oppressed*. He was highly critical of traditional models of education, which he felt treated students as empty bank accounts into which teachers made deposits of knowledge: 'knowledge is a gift bestowed by those who consider themselves knowledgeable upon those whom they consider to know nothing' (Freire, 2006, p. 72). Freire thought this legitimised and perpetuated oppression, and dehumanised both teacher and student. To Freire, education cannot be a neutral act: it either disempowers people, or it liberates them. He argued that overcoming problems in society requires cooperation, unity, organisation and cultural synthesis. To achieve this, educators need to demonstrate humility, recognise that no one knows everything and equally no one is ignorant of everything, and have the courage to treat learners as co-creators of knowledge (Freire, 1998). Freire advocated that his ideas were adopted not just by educators, but also specifically by social workers (Freire and Moch, 1987). His work has significant influence on many key social work concepts such as empowerment, co-production, critical reflection, reflexivity and anti-oppressive practice.

The profession of social work mainly developed in Western contexts, premised on Western values and knowledge predominantly espoused by white, middle-class, heterosexual Christians. Unless we consciously recognise and explicitly challenge this, the superiority of Western discourses is assumed. This risks colonial practice which homogenises rather than celebrates the differences presented by an increasingly multicultural world (Cook, 2020). Critical consciousness (sometimes also referred to as conscientisation) is a key component of Freire's theoretical approach, which examines how knowledge is constructed within the context of culture, power and oppression. It requires that both parties in a relationship – student *and* educator, person using services *and* social worker – critically examine their social realities in order to become conscious of the oppressions they have experienced and the oppressions they have perpetrated. Once conscious of these oppressions, focus can shift to identifying and taking action against their root causes.

Radical social work

Radical social work emerged in response to social work's involvement in the welfare state delivery of public services and is generally accepted to have begun in the 1970s. It was initially influenced by Marxist analysis, and later incorporated feminist and anti-racist perspectives (Peas, 2009). In their seminal book, *Radical Social Work*, Bailey and Brake presented a series of essays critiquing social work education and practice: 'Radical social work, we feel, is essentially understanding the position of the oppressed in the context of the social and economic structure that they live in' (1980, p. 9). Bailey and Brake intended to make social workers consciously inspect their aims and methods in order to realign them more with the people than the state: 'Our aim is not, for example, to eliminate casework, but to eliminate casework that supports the ruling class hegemony' (1980, p. 9). Ferguson and Woodward (2009) suggest that proponents of radical social work had lasting impact by drawing attention to the ongoing nature of oppression based on social divisions due to class, gender, sexuality and so on.

Social work practice in the 1970s took place in the context of universal welfare support and freely accessible services. Viewed retrospectively, standard approaches of that time based on community development, prevention, emancipation and empowerment appear to be very aligned to Paulo Freire's philosophy. Radical social work was premised on social and political activism, which is difficult to sustain without compromise when working within state-led organisations. As the political agendas of the 1980s and 1990s moved towards managerialist and marketised models of social service delivery (see Chapter 3), radical social work dwindled and its practitioners became caricatured, bound up in the backlash against notions of political correctness and perceived to be as outdated as the fashions of the 1970s.

Social work has changed significantly since the birth of radicalism of the 1970s (Lee, 2014) and, in the early 21st century, exists under the shadow of austerity. Services are not universal, but rationed or even withdrawn; ideologies have significantly shifted from welfarism to individual responsibilisation (see Chapter 3). Deacon and MacDonald (2017) suggest that though often viewed as only a minor political movement, radical social work has continued to influence practice because its aims of identifying and challenging structural inequalities resonate with contemporary social policies and economic approaches: 'The challenge for social workers in the application of this theory [radical social work] is in the balance of collectivist action versus individual immediate need' (Deacon and MacDonald, 2017, p. 173). In her excellent book *Social Work for Lazy Radicals*, Jane Fenton (2019) asserts that radical social work is more relevant than ever, but feels that many students and practitioners believe that radical social work is not available to them because they do not view themselves as political activists. Fenton addresses this by aligning radical social work with all critical thinkers who oppose the neoliberal hegemony, some of whom may be political activists, some of whom may not.

Judith and Lloyd

Judith trained as a social worker in the 1980s, and has always proudly viewed her practice as radical. She sees her role as empowering and advocating for people who are experiencing inequality and is proud to have remained a frontline practitioner for over 35 years. Judith regularly takes part in political and environmental protests. She knows that some of her colleagues and management view her as a dinosaur left over from another time, but this doesn't faze her at all: she serves the public, not them. Judith has lived through huge changes in service design and delivery and is never afraid to challenge management and speak truth to power.

Recently, Lloyd joined the team as a newly qualified social worker, and Judith was really pleased to find an unexpected ally from an entirely different generation. Although radical social work was only discussed in an historical sense during Lloyd's training, teaching introduced him to ideas about structural inequality, oppression and marginalisation, and encouraged him to take a critical stance. Lloyd set up a social work blog in order to express some of his thoughts and by the time he qualified, he had a substantial following on social media. Lloyd's activism is online, rather than in person like Judith's, but they are equally passionate about challenging practices which reinforce rather than redress inequality.

Critical social work

Critical social work is generally accepted to have evolved from combining ideas and influences drawn from postmodernism, Marxism, critical theory and radical social work. Critical social work is used as an umbrella term to describe multiple perspectives which seek to address oppressive discourses and legitimise marginalised ones (Barak, 2016), such as feminist social work, anti-racist, anti-discriminatory and anti-oppressive practice (discussed below). Acknowledging Beck and Giddens' work on risk in society (see Chapter 7), Adams et al. (2009) suggest critical practice is a way for practitioners to process thinking and action through different and diverse perspectives in order to respond to risk and uncertainty. Fook (2016) highlights the critical tradition in social work as a helping profession, which emphasises the social context in people's lives. She aligns critical social work with postmodernism and advocates for critical analysis through reflection on practice situations in order to deconstruct dominant discourses and reconstruct emancipatory strategies and processes for change and support (see Chapter 8). Michael Unger (2004) proposes specific questions (which he refers to as *the two P's and three R's*) that social workers should carefully and honestly consider to achieve critical/postmodern practice:

Positioning

How are those being helped and those helping positioned in their communities?

What aspects of the community's life do both share?

What cultural, social, economic, political, ethnic, racial, or geographic characteristics do they have in common?

Where does the work of helping take place?

Power

Whose definition of the problem is heard the loudest?

Does the way a problem is defined place limits on the solutions being considered?

How do community members exercise power over their wellbeing?

Resource sharing

What resources do social services have available?

What resources do the communities with which social workers work have available?

What has the community asked for and what are outsiders willing to share?

How much money for services is under the direct control of community stakeholders?

Resistance

How can alliances be built between the community and social services workers?

What strategies can social workers use to involve government in community processes?

When is the system serving its own needs instead of those of the community?

Reflection

How can social workers as inside outsiders help community members reflect on the nature of their relationships with those with power?

How can professionals make their work transparent to the community?

What 'outside expert' knowledge is valued, or not valued, by a community?

What part of the system mandate does the community share?

Author's experience Cat

My first social work placement was with a charitable sector children's service. As it started, my off-site practice educator gave me a stack of sheets and said, 'fill one of these out every time that you work with a new kid, then bring them back to supervision'. Each sheet was split vertically down the middle: one half headed 'Me', the other with a space for me to write the child or young person's initials. The same questions were asked on both sides – I had to fill out the details of age, gender, ethnicity, economic status, level of education, level of autonomy, etc., for both myself and the child/young person.

In supervision, my practice educator asked me what I had learnt from the exercise. I replied that I was older than all of the children; I was the same gender and race as some, and different from others; I was economically independent, none of the children were; I had a higher level of education than all of the children; I was more autonomous than all of them. My practice educator asked me again what I had learnt from this exercise. I thought for a while and then said, 'it's about power/status, isn't it? My age, education etc. all give me power and status over these children.' My practice educator commended me and explained that effective social work needs to do more than recognise similarities and differences, it must identify what power relations are at play, and what can be done to redress the balance. He then showed me a sheet that he had completed, one side for him, one side for me, and we spent the rest of the session discussing the power imbalance in our relationship. At the end, my practice educator handed me more sheets. 'But I've got it, I understand!' I said. He replied, 'If you want to be any good, you'll do this exercise for the rest of your career.'

Exercise 4.2

Think about a person or family. Consider Unger's questions, or if you prefer, the exercise Cat has described above. What does this reveal about where the power lies? What can you do to shift the power from you to the person/family?

Feminist social work

Feminist social work is a critical perspective which recognises and challenges the way in which power is inequitably distributed in society on the basis of socially constructed notions of gender (see Chapter 2). Lena Dominelli (2002b) argues that key principles of feminism are directly relevant to social work, for example, recognising the diversity of women, considering women as capable decision-making agents, providing women with space for self-determination and looking for collective solutions. By taking a critical stance of gendered power relations, feminist social work opposes the privileging of any group over another.

Anti-racist practice

Anti-racist practice is a critical perspective which emerged in the 1980s to recognise and challenge the dominance of white-centricity by promoting the perspectives of different cultures, ethnicities and histories (Dominelli, 2008), and is most commonly associated with black perspectives. In social work education, anti-racist practice has largely been subsumed into more generalised notions around anti-discriminatory and anti-oppressive practice rather than being seen as a standalone issue (Butler et al., 2003). Some have also expressed concern that in practice, anti-racist approaches have been replaced and diluted by the less threatening notion of multiculturalism (Heron, 2004). The concern is that in identifying discrimination and/or oppression broadly and non-specifically, the racism experienced by specific ethnic groups is under-identified and intentionally or unintentionally minimised. Shocking, high profile injustices such as the killing of George Floyd raise extremely valid questions about institutional and societal values around race. Social work is not exempt from this. The Department for Education recognises that 'Non-white children appear to be slightly over-represented in the looked after children population, in particular children of mixed and black ethnicity' (2017, p. 5), and a systematic review undertaken by Barnett et al. (2019) identifies that detention under the Mental Health Act 1983 is significantly more likely for black, minority ethnic or migrant groups. These findings are extremely concerning and support our view that anti-racist practice needs to be a specific, rather than an implicit aim of social work education and practice.

Anti-discriminatory practice

Anti-discriminatory practice recognises that discrimination exists and should be challenged by acknowledging the diversity of people, and advocating for equality and social justice (Thompson, 2016). BASW's Code of Ethics (2014), in line with the IFSW, identifies challenging discrimination as a key social work value. Neil Thompson (1992/2016) developed the personal–cultural–social (PCS) model to help social work practitioners challenge discrimination by identifying:

P what prejudice(s) the **person** holds

C how the person's **culture** and community establish and normalise such beliefs

S how **structures** such as government, religion, media, etc. reinforce discrimination

Whilst anti-discriminatory practice recognises structural inequality and is associated with legislation to affect change (such as the Equalities Act 2010), the approach has been accused of not fully recognising how oppression is experienced. Dominelli (2002a) critiqued Thompson's PCS model for directing focus and energy to the perpetrator, rather than trying to understand the experience of inequality and oppression from the victim's point of view.

Anti-oppressive practice

Anti-oppressive practice is a critical social work approach which extends the ideas of anti-discriminatory practice by seeking to understand how structure and culture subjugate individuals on the basis of socially constructed concepts – for example, gender, race, disability and sexuality (Dominelli, 2002a). In this sense, it can be seen to incorporate the critical social work approaches discussed above, but as we highlighted in our discussion of anti-racist practice, this may have something of a diluting effect on specific issues. Sakamoto and Pitner (2005) caution against anti-oppressive practice imperatives resulting in people and their problems being defined *only* in terms of oppression. They also suggest that many social workers may feel so overwhelmed by the aim of eradicating structural oppression that they ultimately become apathetic.

Whilst the aims and ideas of critical social work are well established, there is much debate about the extent to which theory has translated into practice (Carey and Foster, 2011; Payne, 2014; Reisch and Andrews, 2001). Cocker and Hafford-Letchfield suggest that although the language of anti-discriminatory and anti-oppressive practice is embedded into descriptions of social work and its professional value base, 'whilst once they may have offered an alternative critique of individual and societal relationships, they have now become part of "status-quo" thinking, and have long since lost their political edge' (2014, p. 1). Neoliberalist ideologies have spawned managerialism and process-driven social work methods, which focus on efficiency and expediency. In such institutional cultures, space to critically reflect, appreciate unique experiences and situations, identify power relations and construct bespoke responses may not only be lacking, but derided as a wholly indulgent and unnecessary notion.

Conclusion

Critical and radical theories have had an enormous impact on how we think about and practise social work. Practising critically and/or radically requires that we aspire for critical consciousness to enable us to recognise the influence of cultural hegemony, power relations and normative assumptions which reinforce oppression at both macro and micro levels. In contemporary social work practice, scarce – if any – space is ring-fenced for meaningful critical reflection that can help us to understand not only the people we work with, but also ourselves. The emphasis is on protecting limited public funds by applying thresholds to reduce and prioritise the demand upon services, and where people do qualify for social work involvement, applying standardised processes in order to reach standardised outcomes. Critical and radical theories can help us to identify this construction of social workers as 'protectors of the public purse' as a hegemonic narrative. Critical and radical theories demonstrate that difference and diversity should be celebrated, plurality of perspectives embraced, and existing ideas and received wisdom continually challenged.

5 THEORIES OF HUMAN DEVELOPMENT

Introduction

Social workers need to be able to draw from a broad range of knowledge about how people develop socially, cognitively and behaviourally across the life course. In this chapter, we take a loosely chronological approach, starting by exploring key theories that consider how children develop from birth to adulthood, and moving on to theories of how we learn. We recognise that ageing is as much a social construct as it is a biological process, and that different roles and expectations of how people should behave at particular ages are based on normative cultural assumptions. Unfortunately, this contributes to discrimination in the form of ageism. The chapter concludes with theories of being older, and how people adapt and develop as they approach the end of their lives.

Psychosexual development – Sigmund Freud (1856–1939)

We introduced psychodynamic psychology in Chapter 2, noting that it was originated by Sigmund Freud. Freud believed that life centred on tension and pleasure: tension arising from a build-up of libido (sexual energy), and pleasure arising from its release. He proposed that children move through five stages of psychosexual development which help to establish their adult personality (Table 5.1).

Table 5.1 Freud's psychosexual stages of development

Stage & Age	Description
Oral **age 0–2**	The libido is centred around the mouth and gratification is achieved through feeding, sucking thumb/breast/bottle/dummy, babbling.
Anal **age 2–3**	The libido is centred around the anus, with gratification achieved through defecating/refusing to defecate. The child is introduced to societal expectations around toilet training.
Phallic **age 3–7**	The libido is centred around the genitals and masturbation becomes a source of gratification. The child becomes aware of anatomical differences between the sexes.
Latent **age 7–11**	The libido is dormant, and no psychosexual development takes place during the stage as children focus on developing social skills and acquiring knowledge.
Genital **11–adult**	The libido is centred around the genitals and gratification is achieved through sexual pleasure with others.

Whilst Freud's place in history is assured, his works have been the source of much reappraisal and criticism, not least by feminist scholars (Tong, 1989; Walby, 1997). Freud wrote during a very different time, which partially accounts for some of the inherent difficulties with his work, and from our side of history, his focus of sexual desire in children makes for very uncomfortable reading (Miller, 1990). Freud believed that children develop in a sexualised manner, using both repellent and attracting strategies in relation to their parents. He utilised the classical Grecian tale of Oedipus, who accidentally killed his father and raped his mother, to conceptualise this (Freud, 1890: 1954 print, 1949: 2011 print). In contemporary times, suggesting that children's relationships with their parents are based on subconscious sexualised attraction is extremely disturbing. Freud's disparaging attitude towards women and girls – whose behaviour he believed to be largely motivated by penis-envy – is equally unacceptable. Freud himself conceded that his Oedipal complex was rather more easily and acceptably adapted to male children than females. Carl Jung subsequently used another Greek myth to create a comparable conceptualisation of female children's development: the Electra complex. This theory (often mistakenly attributed to Freud) describes girls competing with their mothers for the affections of their fathers. Freud's work was also highly heteronormative: homosexuality and other sexual identities and preferences – including asexuality – were viewed as abnormal. Sexual gratification was something to be achieved only with a partner of the opposite sex, therefore masturbation beyond the phallic stage was also viewed problematically. Freud designated adolescence as a period of (hetero) sexual experimentation, which he considered successfully resolved through heterosexual marriage in the person's early twenties.

Psychosocial development – Erik Erikson (1902–94)

Erikson was heavily influenced by Freud's emphasis on the significance of childhood in explaining the adult self, and extended this through the concept of *generativity* – the desire to guide the next generation as a driving power in human organisation (Erikson, 1994). Erikson (1966) proposed an eight-stage model of psychosocial development across the life course (Table 5.2). Each stage presents a psychosocial crisis/task to be resolved, with successful resolution contributing to the development of a healthy personality, and conversely, inability to master the task resulting in difficulties and feelings of inadequacy (Erikson, 1963, 1970).

Table 5.2 Erikson's eight stages of psychosocial development

Age	Psychosocial Crisis/Task
Birth–18 months	**Trust versus Mistrust** Infants learn to trust adults who meet their basic survival needs and mistrust unresponsive caregivers.
18 months–3 years	**Autonomy versus Shame/ Doubt** Toddlers explore their world, learn that they can control their actions to get results and begin to develop preferences. They work to establish independence and complete tasks for themselves, which is why this is sometimes referred to as the 'me do it' stage. Children who are not enabled to develop autonomy may experience shame and self-doubt.
3–5 years	**Initiative versus Guilt** Children learn to plan and achieve goals while interacting with others. Children develop self-confidence and initiative if their caregivers allow them to explore within limits and support their choices. Children whose caregivers are over-controlling may develop feelings of guilt.
5–13 years	**Industry versus Inferiority** Children begin to compare their personal characteristics, family situation, social activities, academic achievement, etc. with their peers. If they perceive themselves to 'measure up', they develop a sense of pride and accomplishment, If they perceive themselves to 'fall short', they may develop feelings of inadequacy and inferiority.
13–21 years	**Identity versus Confusion** Adolescents begin to question who they are, what their purpose is, and experiment with different representations of identity in order to discover themselves. Adolescents who are successful at this stage have a strong sense of identity. Those who do not consciously search for identity, or are pressured to conform to others' expectations may develop a weak sense of self and experience role confusion.
21–39 years	**Intimacy versus Isolation** People who have successfully navigated the previous stages become ready to share their life with others. If some of the earlier stages have not been successfully resolved, the person may have trouble developing and maintaining successful relationships with others and experience feelings of loneliness and emotional isolation.

Age	Psychosocial Crisis/Task
40–65 years	**Generativity versus Stagnation** Generativity involves finding your life's purpose and contributing to the next generation, for example through childbirth, caregiving and/or meaningful work (paid or unpaid) which contributes positively to society. Those who do not master this may experience stagnation – a lack of connection with others and confusion about their role/purpose.
65 and over	**Integrity versus Despair** People begin to reflect on their lives. Those who feel satisfied and fulfilled by their accomplishments develop a sense of integrity. Those who do not master this stage may focus on what would have, should have, and could have been and feel a sense of bitterness and despair.

Cognitive development

Theories of cognitive development are most closely associated with the work of Swiss psychologist Jean Piaget, but the work of Soviet psychologist Lev Vygotsky, who died whilst still a young man in 1934, has posthumously been very influential.

Jean Piaget (1896–1980)

Piaget was concerned with explaining the acquisition of knowledge and development of intellect (Wadsworth, 2004). Through his observations of children, Piaget concluded that intellectual development is the result of both hereditary and environmental factors, as the child's constant interactions with the external world invent and reinvent knowledge. Piaget saw cognitive growth as an extension of biological growth, with intellectual development influencing emotional, social and behavioural aspects of child development.

Piaget devised the concept of *schemata* (the singular form is schema), intellectual structures that organise events as they are perceived, classifying them according to common characteristics to provide a reference point from which to deal with future situations. An initial schema, for a baby, is founded upon the desire to taste and eat and therefore a baby will suck objects almost indiscriminately (Piaget, 1953). As the child develops and grows, they are exposed to widening experiences and their schemata become more generalised, more differentiated, more mature, and ever more complex. Piaget used the term *assimilation* to describe the cognitive process by which a person or child integrates new perceptual, motor or conceptual matter into existing schemata or patterns of behaviour. With assimilation the schema evolves, therefore the baby still favours tasting objects, but learns not to put all objects into the mouth as a matter of course. Only when new stimuli cannot be assimilated into existing schemata are new ones developed; Piaget termed this *accommodation* (Piaget, 1955/1976). Piaget theorised that children use these twin processes of assimilation and accommodation as they progress through four, distinct cognitive stages which enhance their cognitive abilities (Piaget and Gruber, 1977) (Table 5.3).

Table 5.3 Piaget's stages of cognitive development

Stage & Age	Characteristics
Sensorometer **0–2 years**	Babies go through very rapid changes as they explore the world through their senses and motor activity. They begin to understand cause and effect and develop the ability to follow objects with their eyes. Initially, babies cannot distinguish between themselves and the environment and anything that they can't see does not exist. **The main goal of this stage is to learn *object permanence* – that objects continue to exist even when they can't be seen.**
Pre-operational **2–7 years**	Children develop better speech and communication, using syntax and grammar to express concepts. Memory and imagination are developing, and children can imagine the future and reflect on the past, but have difficulty distinguishing fantasy from reality (e.g. actors are the characters they play). Basic numerical abilities are developing. **The main goal of this stage is being able to attach meaning to objects with language.**
Concrete operational **7–11 years**	Concepts such as time, space and quantity begin to be understood and applied as children develop abilities of generalisation. **The main goal of this stage is to start developing *operational thought* – the ability to solve problems mentally.**
Formal operational **12 years onwards**	Strategy and planning become possible as children become able to organise information, understand abstract concepts, form and test hypotheses and reason scientifically. Piaget believed that once someone reaches the formal operational stage, they build upon knowledge, rather than changing how it is acquired or understood.

Piaget also strongly believed in the importance of play as a mechanism for children to explore, manipulate, experiment, question and search out answers for themselves (Piaget, 2001; Piaget and Inhelder, 2000). The implication of this is that adult caregivers and educators need to provide the children with the opportunity to grow naturally by encouraging new experiences, activities and venues for play (Wadsworth, 1978, 2004). Since Piaget's innovative studies, a body of work encouraging childhood development through play has emerged (Webster-Stratton, 2003).

Lev Vygotsky (1896–1934)

Although Piaget and Vygotsky were contemporaries, born in the same year, Vygotsky died at a young age, and remained relatively unheard of outside of the Soviet Union until his works were posthumously published in the West in the 1950s. Vygotsky was intrigued by Piaget's theory that children devise rules of behaviour and morality through play (Vygotsky, 1967). He concurred that children develop through stages, but attributed much more importance to the relationship between genetic nature and social environment. He viewed childhood play as a psychological tool, promoting maturation through the development of rules and abstract thinking. Whilst life is too immediate to allow young children to stop and formulate rules, play facilitates this very function, and allows rules learned through play to be transferred to real life. He gave the example of two sisters who play a game of being sisters: through this pretence they experimentally define their actual reality, formulating rules that are transferable to their real lives (Vygotsky and Luria, 1930).

At the time when Vygotsky was writing, people were generally viewed as either children or adults. Vygotsky asserted that adolescents were a distinct group because the teenage brain functions in a unique way: 'It is only when the child turns into an adolescent, that the final transition into the realm of thinking in concepts can occur' (Vygotsky, 1931a, no page). He studied structured learning approaches and believed that once something was learnt – such as riding a horse, or tying shoelaces – it cannot be unlearned. Vygotsky offered a more flexible conceptualisation of learning than Piaget. He termed the knowledge attained the *actual developmental level* (Vygotsky, 1978), and described the child developing learning at a level below this in the *zone of proximal development*:

> The zone of proximal development defines those functions that have not yet matured but are in the process of maturation, functions that will mature tomorrow but are currently in an embryonic state. (Vygotsky, 1978, p. 87)

The zone of proximal development is what the learner can learn with guidance (mentoring) (Figure 5.1).

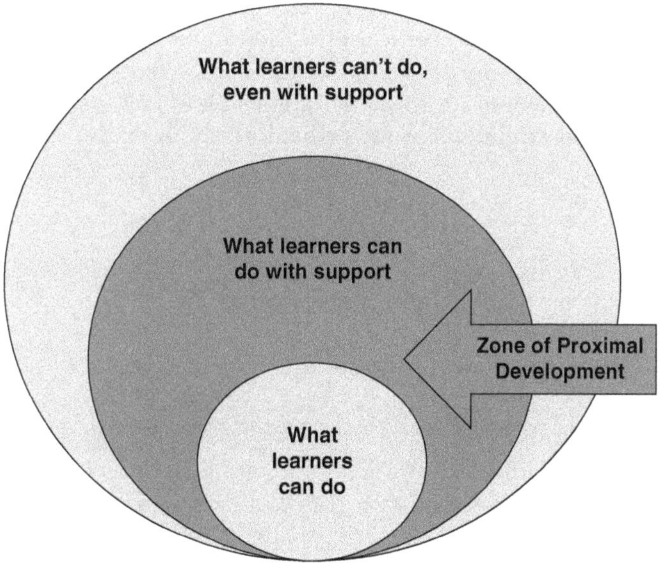

Figure 5.1 Vygotsky's zone of proximal development

Vygotsky's work on learning has had a lasting impact upon Western education. American psychologist Jerome Bruner (1915–2016) developed on Vygotsky's work to create the now commonly used pedagogical concept of *scaffolding*, where an adult or more advanced peer acts as a mentor, providing the child with structured and focused support to enable them to grow into the zone of proximal learning. This approach of scaffolding support around the learner empowers them to be active in their own learning through selection and discovery, rather than more traditional pedagogical approaches of mimicry and recollection (Bruner, 1978), so is consistent with some of Paulo Freire's radical views on learning (see Chapter 3).

Learning theory – Burrhus Skinner (1904–90)

Learning is a behaviour of development and we introduced the basic features of behavioural psychology in Chapter 2. Learning theory is most closely associated with the American behaviourist Burrhus Skinner, whose studies of rats and pigeons caused him to theorise that behaviour is historically contextualised so that when an action is rewarded, the subject will repeat it. This premise can be easily understood by thinking about how praise and reward are used to support an infant to progress from nappies to potty training, to using the toilet independently. Reinforcement of behaviours can be of a positive or negative nature, so undesirable behaviours are discouraged through negative consequence or punishment which signal to the child that they should not be repeated. Skinner explained, 'I look for antecedent events in the history of the individual to account for the origin of the behaviour' (Skinner et al., 1988, p. 245).

Skinner termed his theory *operant behaviourism* due to the behaviour inherently resulting from consequences to actions. Skinner saw behaviour as an evolving process because once a given activity has been chosen and the behaviour operationally reinforced, then the process of repetition takes on a mechanical aspect (Skinner et al., 1988). Effective parents utilise positive and negative reinforcement consistently to promote desirable behaviour and discourage undesirable behaviour. In less able families, however, patterns of reinforcement may be more idiosyncratic, troublesome and difficult for both the child and external observers to ascertain.

Author's experience Phil

As a practitioner, I often heard foster carers and other professionals describe a child's difficult behaviour having been learnt from their birth family. This 'learned behaviour' explanation is an enormous oversimplification which does not acknowledge the impact of cognitive processes. Certainly, many behaviours have very obvious links to events the child has experienced – for example, a child who has witnessed or been subject to violence may well behave violently. However, this does not explain why many children continue to present such behaviours once settled into nurturing, non-violent foster-care environments (Cairns, 2004), which by the same explanation should disincentivise the violence and reinforce positive alternative behaviours. Similarly, many children do not go on to repeat the violence they have experienced. As a practitioner I realised the simple explanations are easy but often limit our further exploration of what is really happening.

Social learning theory – Albert Bandura (b. 1925)

Social learning theory also recognises that behaviour is shaped in response to reward and discouragement, but it theoretically expands to include modelling behaviour as well as cognitively observed learning. In this way, the child's behaviour develops through socialisation and cognition, rather than assimilated schemata or operant conditioning. Influential Canadian American psychologist Albert Bandura has frequently sought to understand aggression. In the 1960s, he developed an experiment to consider patterns of aggression in young children by observing their reaction to a video of an adult attacking a bobo doll (a life-size inflatable figure, weighted at the bottom so that when pushed, it automatically returns to an upright position). The experiment incorporated three different endings to the video in which the adult was either rewarded, ignored or punished. Children were shown one of the three versions of the video, then left alone in a room containing a bobo doll whilst their behaviour was remotely observed without their knowledge. Bandura found that children who had watched the video where the adult was rewarded after attacking the doll behaved significantly more aggressively when left alone compared to the children who saw the aggression punished (Bandura, 1965). He proposed that human functioning was therefore responsive (at least partly) to external stimulus and behaviour was (at least partially) socially learnt. He viewed repertoires of aggressive behaviour as socially learnt through three principal sources: family, community and mass media (Bandura, 1978).

Bandura refuted the way in which Piaget's model implied that children are influenced exclusively by parents or teachers, arguing that multiple and conflicting influences of modelling and reinforcement occur in a child's life (Bandura, 1969). Bandura held that there are two components to behaviour: an internal, cognitive process through which it is justified, and an external, observable action. Although an action may appear impulsive, it is cognitively defended and justified by the individual's moral judgements. The *potential* for aggression and violence is therefore learnt through the child's observed experience; however, *engagement* in acts of aggression and violence follows on from an internalised moral justification of the act. Social learning theory, therefore, supports ideas that children learn behaviours through experiential observation, but also recognises that children acquire a sense of personal agency and employ cognitive processes to *select* which behaviours they enact and when. The perpetration of extreme and deplorable aggression has been justified many times historically on the grounds of personal principles and religious ideologies, supporting Bandura's theory that moral motivations are used to justify acts of violence cognitively rather than impulsively (Bandura, 1973, 1978).

The concept of *self-efficacy* is central to Bandura's social learning theory and the development of individual personality. Self-efficacy can be understood as a person's cognitive self-confidence in their ability to attempt/achieve purposeful goals and values (Bandura, 1977, 1994). Bandura theorised that self-efficacy is a major factor in determining personalised approaches to goals, tasks and challenges. The higher the person's sense of self-efficacy, the more likely they are to try something new; conversely, a lower sense of self-efficacy creates a poorer view of self-potential, making change seem much more insurmountable. Bandura has reflected on self-efficacy in childhood in different cultural contexts (Pastorelli et al., 2001) and he remains an influential figure in contemporary behavioural psychology.

Karen

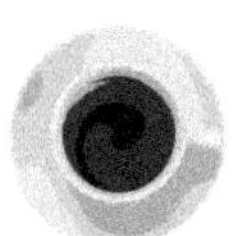

Over the course of her practice, Karen has worked with many people who have found change so frightening that they have chosen to stay in extremely difficult and dangerous situations instead. Karen has developed an exercise that she uses in this situation to help people explore and understand how they feel about change and introduce the concept of self-efficacy:

Imagine that you have lived your whole life on a remote island, completely cut off from the outside world. Life on the island is hard and lonely. You have to be resourceful and self-sufficient, particularly as you are not alone: a big scary monster also lives on the island. The monster is very dangerous and very unpredictable, and you have to be incredibly vigilant to always stay one step ahead of it. You have been fighting to survive for so long that every inch of the island is familiar to you – you know its terrain, its hiding places and how to use its resources.

One day, a boat washes up on the shore. You realise that your deepest wishes have come true and you can finally leave the island and escape the monster. Excited, you load the boat up with supplies and quickly set off. At first, it's plain sailing and it feels so amazing to be free. You have such a sense of relief and are full of hope and positivity about your future. But the journey is long and there is still no land in sight. After a while you begin to wonder where you are headed and if you have done the right thing. A storm breaks out and your little boat is being battered. You are scared, tired, wet and freezing cold; there is nowhere for you to shelter.

Do you keep going, or turn the boat around and head back to the familiarity of your island?

In Karen's exercise, the monster represents an existing threat (this could be a person, a situation or a behaviour) and the island represents their existing coping strategies. The boat represents change, which the person may engage with initially, but once an obstacle (the storm) appears, their self-efficacy will determine whether they feel able to 'ride out the storm' of change, or whether they revert to previous threats. Whilst the monster is terrifying, it is familiar, and the person knows that they have strategies for dealing with it. After explaining this, Karen encourages the person to think about what could increase and support their self-efficacy to make change more achievable and sustainable.

Exercise 5.1

Consider Karen's exercise.

What would you do? Why? What makes you more confident to implement change?

Ageing

Riley et al. (1972) proposed that society uses *age stratification* to hierarchically rank citizens into age groups. In Western societies, people are perceived to be most vulnerable at the polar ends of the life course, and therefore power and status is most commonly aligned with the time when we are neither very young, nor very old. Erikson aside, most of the theories that we have considered so far in this chapter have focused on childhood. Whilst our most rapid period of physical, cognitive and emotional development undoubtedly occurs in our early years, we continue to change and develop throughout the life course. The study of social, cultural, psychological, cognitive and biological aspects of human ageing is known as gerontology.

Age and ageing are socially constructed and relative, rather than fixed, concepts. Exactly *when* someone becomes old depends on culture and context – what seems old to someone in their teens seems young to someone in their eighties. Similarly, attitudes towards ageing are shaped by our experiences of interaction with role models, and the messages that we are given by the media, etc. (Swift and Steeden, 2020). Unfortunately, ageism – discriminatory behaviour premised on age – is extremely prevalent in society (see Chapter 15). Ageism affects all ages, just think about common stereotypes about snowflake millennials and the boomer generation. However, whilst youth is prized, the natural, biological process of getting older itself is very negatively perceived: although most people want to live longer, few people want to be old (Heslop and Meredith, 2019). We don't want the thinning hair, wrinkling skin, aching joints and deteriorating sight and hearing that change our bodies as we age. We think of ourselves as eternally young and are shocked to look in the mirror and see someone older than we were expecting, as if a *mask of ageing* has appeared on top of our true face (Featherstone and Hepworth, 1991). Dr Bernard Louis Strehler (1925–2001) studied ageing from a biological perspective. His classic work *Time, Cells, and Aging* (1962), proposed five criteria of biological aging:

Universal – it is experienced by all members of the human race.

Intrinsic – ageing is an innate part of the experience of being human.

Progressive – ageing is a continuous process.

Degenerative – not developmental.

Cumulative – multiple, ongoing aspects interact to produce the overall experience of ageing.

There are thousands of theories which seek to explain how and why we physically age, but ageing is much more than a biological process. To successfully respond to an increasingly ageing population, social work needs to make use of theories which seek to understand social and psychological aspects of ageing.

Author's experience Cat

I was teaching a seminar on older people and started by asking 'how do you feel about getting old?' I was not expecting many positive replies, and true to form, most people reported feeling pessimistic. However, I was really surprised by one student who forcefully declared that she would rather be dead than old. I knew her to be smart, caring and well intentioned. She would have vehemently challenged a peer who expressed racist, sexist or homophobic views, but was completely oblivious to the ageism her statement presented. I asked her to explain why she felt like this and she said she would hate to be frail and dependent, to lose her faculties through dementia or incontinence. I explained that I understood (and to an extent shared) these fears, but was interested in why they immediately came to mind when getting old was mentioned. As a group, everyone agreed that the first thing they had thought about when asked the question was declining physical and mental abilities.

For the next part of the seminar I asked each student to tell the group about a significant older person in their life. Students spoke warmly about relationships with parents, grandparents, neighbours and work colleagues who performed crucial roles in their lives as mentors, confidants, friends, role-models and supporters. These older people were variously described as wise, loving, inspirational, tough-talking, nurturing. I asked why the strengths and assets of these key people weren't the first things that came to mind when I asked about getting older. Most people felt that *their* older person wasn't a *typical* older person. The dominant negative discourse of ageing was so strong that it overshadowed deeply personal positive experiences.

Exercise 5.2

Think of representations of ageing and older people that you have seen recently in your day-to-day life – perhaps on TV, in the news or on social media.

Were they positive or negative?

How do they contribute to the perpetuation of ageism?

The social clock – Bernice Neugarten (1916–2001)

Neugarten was a pioneer in the field of ageing who was highly committed to challenging ageist public policy and working towards intergenerational equity. She was critical of staged models of development and argued for a more complex and diverse view of older people. Neugarten theorised that people are socialised into age-appropriate behaviour dictated by expected cultural norms. Rather than a biological clock controlling the ageing process, she proposed that people adjust their behaviour over their life course to meet the expectations of their culture's *social clock*. Age norms – for example the expected timescales for getting married and having children – vary from culture to culture, but whatever they are, people are judged by whether or not they are *on time*. People who conform to their culture's social clock gain acceptance, approval and status; people who do not conform are viewed with suspicion. Neugarten often used her own experience to illuminate her theory, explaining how she had been judged to be *late* according to the social clock because she reached academic milestones later than her peers after taking time out to raise her family.

Disengagement theory – Elaine Cumming and William Earle Henry

Cumming and Henry were functionalists (see Chapter 2) generally credited as creators of the first social science theory of ageing. They used data from a longitudinal study of hundreds of adults (the Kansas City Study of Adult Life) to develop disengagement theory and presented it in their 1961 book, *Growing Old*. They essentially proposed that as people get older, they naturally withdraw from society and society naturally withdraws from them. Cumming and Henry set out nine postulations (assumptions) of disengagement theory (Table 5.4).

Table 5.4 The nine postulations of disengagement theory

Postulation 1	People expect death, and their ability to engage with others deteriorates over time, resulting in the loss of ties to other individuals and society as a whole.
Postulation 2	Disengaging frees the person from the social norms that usually guide interaction. Non-conforming behaviour in residual social interactions causes further disengagement and the process becomes circular/self-perpetuating.
Postulation 3	Disengagement is different for men and women because they perform different roles in society.
Postulation 4	The desire to avoid the reputational damage of being seen to lose their skills and abilities motivates people to disengage. Younger adults are trained to develop the knowledge and skills needed to succeed those who disengage.
Postulation 5	Complete disengagement happens when both the person and society are ready for it. A disjunction occurs when one is ready but not the other.

(Continued)

Table 5.4 (Continued)

Postulation 6	People who have disengaged will experience personal and emotional difficulties unless they adopt new social roles.
Postulation 7	People become ready to disengage when awareness of the little time that they have left means they no longer wish to fulfil their usual social role. Society permits disengagement in order to provide employment for successive generations, to satisfy the social needs of a nuclear family (see Chapter 2) and because people die.
Postulation 8	Once disengaged, remaining relationships change.
Postulation 9	Disengagement theory occurs in all cultures and the form it takes is bound by the culture it occurs within.

Disengagement theory proved controversial almost immediately. It does not acknowledge the impact of class and reinforces gender stereotypes. Most troublingly, it presents older people as compliant tools of society, rather than individuals with agency. Although Cumming maintained her theoretical position, Henry went on to denounce disengagement theory in his later publications.

Activity theory – Robert Havighurst (1900–91)

Havighurst disliked and disagreed with disengagement theory, and developed activity theory in direct response. Activity theory – sometimes referred to as *the implicit theory of ageing*, *normal theory of ageing*, *lay theory of ageing* or *the busy ethic* – proposes that we can delay the ageing process and maintain or enhance our quality of life by staying physically active and socially connected. Activity theory concurs with disengagement theory that loss of role is an unavoidable part of ageing – children become independent and no longer need the same caregiving, occupation gives way to retirement. Where it differs, however, is in acknowledging the agency of the ageing individual to substitute former roles with other meaningful alternatives. Self-worth increases through this renewed sense of purpose and contribution to society, increasing happiness which may contribute to longevity (Havighurst, 1961). Critics of activity theory highlight that it does not consider how individual health and socioeconomic factors create inequalities which hinder older people from taking up new roles, and some people simply do not wish to do so.

Continuity theory – Robert Atchley (1939–2018)

Atchley first proposed continuity theory in 1971, and substantially developed it over his working life. Continuity theory proposes that our personalities are stable across the life course and influence the roles we assume and the satisfaction we attain. As we age, we persist with activities, behaviours, beliefs, preferences and relationships that characterised us in earlier stages of our lives. When we encounter physical, social and mental changes, we use adaptive strategies to link our pasts to our futures and create continuity. Internal continuity is maintained by forming personal links between new experiences and memories of previous ones. External continuity is maintained through interactions with familiar people and environments. Too little continuity makes life feel unpredictable and chaotic; too much continuity makes life feel stagnant and boring. Optimal continuity provides us with sufficient challenge to manage change without becoming overwhelmed (Atchley, 1989). Atchley's theory has been supported by subsequent research: for example, the World Health Organization (1997) found that people age most successfully when they carry positive health habits, lifestyles, preferences into later life. However, critics note that in drawing a distinction between *normal* and *pathological* ageing, this theory devalues people with chronic health conditions and neglects their experience.

Conclusion

The number of tables in this chapter will demonstrate to readers how frequently theorists tend to conceive of staged models of development! There can be a tendency to import these models into practice to rigidly use them as a checklist against which to measure children and adults' development. We strongly advocate against such an approach and caution you to remember how frequently the theorists we have explored in this chapter disagree with each other. There is no *right* way to develop and age because people, whether young or old, are individuals who each develop uniquely across their own life course. The theories that we have explored here can guide us to consider what is going on for each individual in their particular context, and to identify how biological, psychological and social factors influence behaviour.

6 THEORIES OF SYSTEMS AND RELATIONSHIPS

Introduction

Social work fundamentally focuses on people and their environments, the systems that they are part of and interact with (Connolly and Harms, 2012). This chapter considers theoretical perspectives of systems and relationships, and how the two form each other. We start by exploring systems theory and principles which apply to *all* systems, then introduce some of the key social systems theories which guide social work. Social work is a people-based profession where relationships are central to our practice. These relationships are multifaceted and reflect our work with people who experience difficulties, adversities and vulnerabilities. We need to understand our own relationships, those of the people we are working with and recognise that these are interlinked. The second part of this chapter, therefore, focuses on theories which help us to understand and explain why attachments are formed, how families operate, why social connections are essential and what happens when relationships are lost.

Theorising systems

A system is an entity made up of interdependent and interrelated components – think, for example, of the solar system, the digestive system, the education system. Systems theory is an interdisciplinary framework used to consider and describe both natural (organic, biological, chemical, etc.) and constructed (engineered, social, computerised, etc.) systems. In 1854, French physiologist Claude Bernard (1813–78) observed that when external factors (bacteria, alcohol, etc.) entered the bloodstream, the body had its own self-regulating mechanisms for maintaining optimal blood chemistry. He realised that other physiological processes behaved in the same way and concluded that in fact the whole body systematically self-regulates to restore and maintain equilibrium (optimum balance) in the face of external interference. Bernard described this as the *milieu interieur* (internal environment). Although Bernard is considered the founder of modern physiology, his theory didn't attract much interest until it was further developed by the American physiologist Walter Bradford Cannon (1871–1945). In his book *The Wisdom of the Body* (1932), Cannon reconceptualised the milieu interieur as *homeostasis,* proposing that all physiological systems resist change and seek constancy.

Homeostasis does not occur by chance, but as the result of organised internal regulation and self-government through processes known as *feedback loops* (Figure 6.1). A positive feedback loop reinforces the system to amplify and generate growth – for instance, a strong fruit crop due to favourable weather presents an increased food source and therefore animal breeding increases. A negative feedback loop self-corrects to stabilise and restrict growth – for instance, less fruit due to unfavourable weather results in food shortages and less breeding.

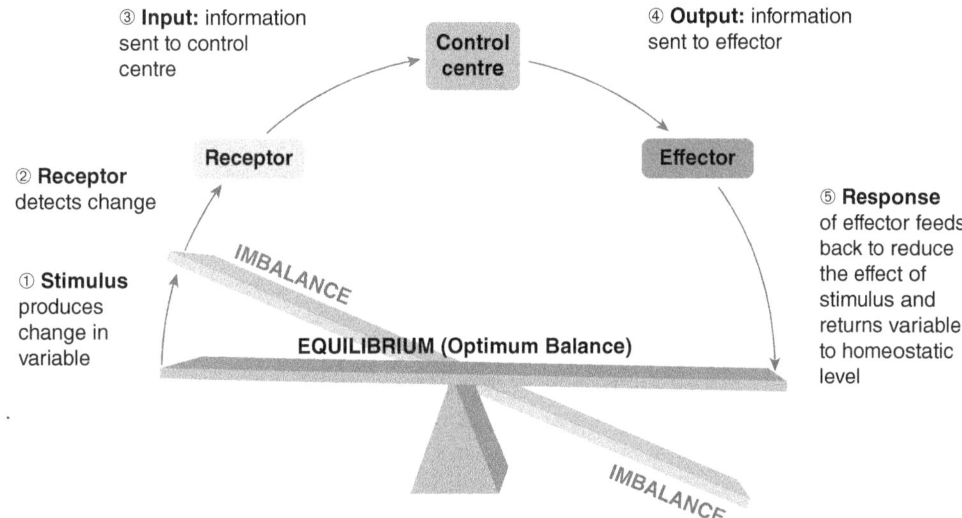

Figure 6.1 Homeostatic feedback loop

In 1922, Russian physician, philosopher, writer and revolutionary Alexander Bogdanov (1873–1928) published his philosophical thesis *Tectology: Universal Organisation Science.* He proposed that social, biological and physical sciences could be unified if they were considered as systems of relationships and efforts were made to identify the organisational principles underpinning them. Tectology was the forerunner to *general systems theory*, which was proposed by Austrian biologist Karl Ludwig von Bertalanffy (1901–72) in the 1940s. Bertalanffy sought to understand the underlying order of the universe through a new paradigm which focused not on separate domains of knowledge, but on interrelationships:

> there exist models, principles, and laws that apply to generalized systems or their subclasses, irrespective of their particular kind, the nature of their component elements, and the relations or 'forces' between them. It seems legitimate to ask for a theory, not of

systems of a more or less special kind, but of universal principles applying to systems in general. (Bertalanffy, 1968, p. 32)

Bertalanffy (1968) differentiated between open systems, which continuously interact with their environments, and closed systems, which are isolated from their environment (Figure 6.2).

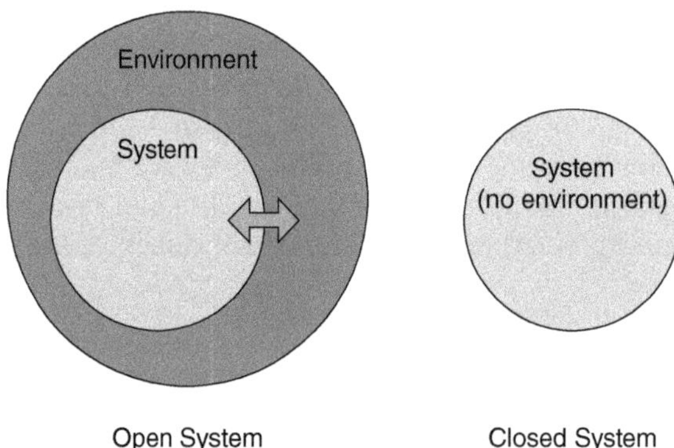

Figure 6.2 Open and closed systems

Connolly and Harms (2012) argue this knowledge of closed and open systems has helped social work understand risk and protective factors in families and with individuals. A family operating within an open system will be seen as more protective and less risky than one where members are closed off from their environment. General systems theory developed to see systems as plural, identifying boundaries between systems and their environments along with the interrelationship between subsystems (Turner and Baker, 2019).

Social systems theories

We have established that systems theory is a framework for understanding relationships and interconnections to a whole by trying to identify the internal and external rules that govern the system. When the systems being considered are social, rather than physiological, we generally refer to social systems theory.

Theory of social action – Talcott Parsons (1902–79)

The American sociologist Talcott Parsons developed his *theory of social action* in the 1950s and it is regarded to be the first generalisable theory of social systems. Talcott proposed that people take action by making subjective decisions about the goals that they wish to achieve and the means by which they will achieve them. Action is constrained by the actor's situational conditions (for example their genetic makeup, ecological factors) and governed by personal and cultural values, norms and expectations. Social systems survive through four *functional imperatives* which are referred to as the *AGIL paradigm* (Table 6.1).

Table 6.1 Talcott Parsons' AGIL paradigm

Functional Imperative	Description
Adaptation The system's capacity to interact with the environment	Securing sufficient resources from the environment and then distributing these throughout the system
Goal attainment The system's ability to set goals for the future	Establishing priorities and mobilising system resources for their attainment
Integration Coherent values and norms are agreed and established across the system	Coordinating and maintaining viable interrelationships among system units through common language, culture and laws
Latency (or pattern maintenance) Action taken by actors in the social system to manage tension and maintain the integration requirement (see above)	Assuming roles (based on gender, class, etc.) and establishing institutions (e.g. family, school), which mediate belief systems and values between generations

It is fair to say that Parsons' theory has been widely criticised, and it certainly has not dated well. Despite this, it undoubtedly remains influential – perhaps most significantly for its description of the *nuclear family* (see Chapter 2).

Systems theory – Niklas Luhmann (1927–66)

Functionalist social systems theory (see Chapter 2) conceptualised relationships between systems as linear and relatively simple, but this struggled to explain the apparent disorder, or entropy, in modern and postmodern society (Harvey and Reed, 1996). German sociologist Niklas Luhmann studied under Talcott Parsons, but dismissed his social systems theory and developed his own. Luhmann argued systems have the capacity for self-organisation (Luhmann, 1995), which allows for a more complex understanding of social interaction as well as difference with the environment. Luhmann held that the environment is (at least partly) a product of the system, rather than independent of it, so that as a system transforms, so too does the environment in which it operates (Luhmann, 1995). System and environment interact through communication: the system receives information about the environment and determines how to evolve in response. We can model this very literally by thinking about the current climate crisis (information about the environment) and the way society (and the various social subsystems which comprise it) is responding. Micro level responses to climate change may take the form of denial, personal behavioural change (e.g. recycling, adoption of a vegan diet), or collective action (e.g. school strikes, Extinction Rebellion). Macro level response to climate change may take the form of denial, government policy or international collaboration (the Paris Agreement, the United Nations Framework Convention on Climate Change).

Ecological systems theory – Urie Bronfenbrenner (1917–2005)

Russian-born American psychologist Urie Bronfenbrenner was a huge influence on thinking around childhood development, and we might just as easily have discussed his ecological systems theory in Chapter 5. In the USA, he is attributed with being the father of the *Head*

Start programme, which provides comprehensive early childhood support with education, health, and nutrition to low-income families (Cornell University, 2005). In the UK, his work is incorporated into the *Common Assessment Framework* (Calder and Hackett, 2003; Gill and Jack, 2007; see Chapter 8) – now referred to as the Assessment Framework – and influenced the *Sure Start* approach. Bronfenbrenner drew on the work of Vygotsky and Bertalanffy to develop his ecological systems theory (Figure 6.3), which provides a comprehensive framework of environmental influences on the developing child. He believed that the child's social and psychological development is strongly influenced by the nature of the dyadic mother–child relationship, and presupposed that within this, ideally both parties should undergo periods of growth (Bronfenbrenner, 1979). Bronfenbrenner conceptualised this relationship as embedded in and influenced by larger social systems of community, society, economics and politics, in a similar manner to a set of nested Russian dolls (Bronfenbrenner, 1977).

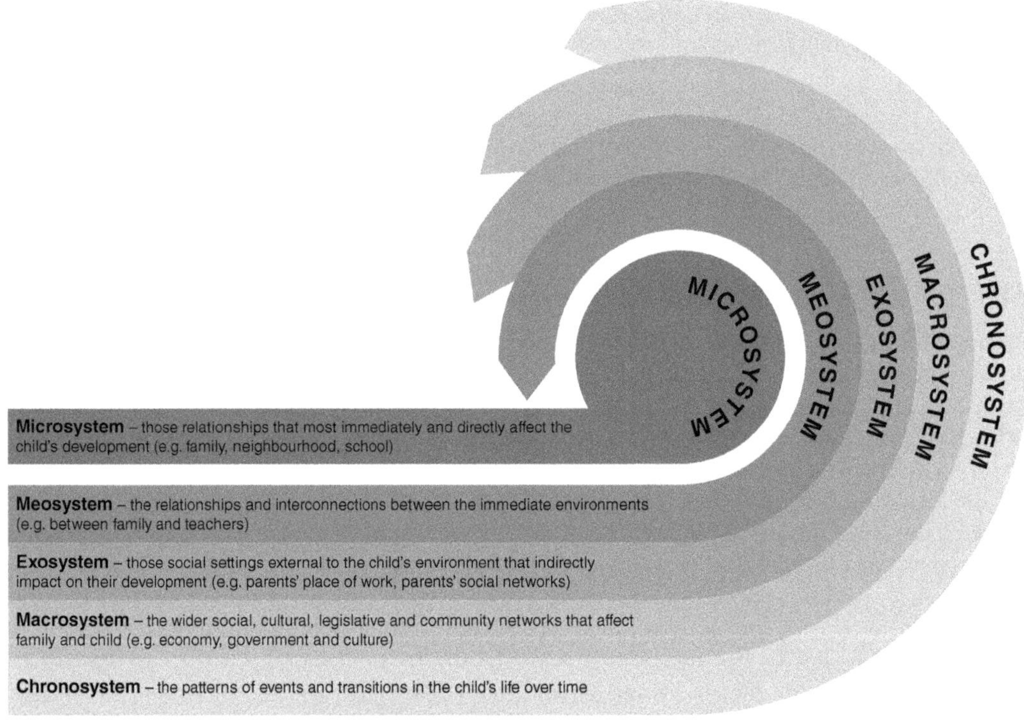

Figure 6.3 Bronfenbrenner's ecological systems theory

Over time, Bronfenbrenner refined and developed his original theory, adding in a fifth system, the chronosystem (the process of transitions, events and ageing). His focus on the mother–child dyad was based on gendered normative assumptions which quickly proved unrepresentative. Focus shifted to the parent/carer–child relationship, resulting in Bronfenbrenner's most famous quote:

> In order to develop, a child needs the enduring, irrational involvement of one or more adults in care and joint activity with the child ... Somebody has got to be crazy about that kid! (cited in Noddings, 2002, p. 25)

After Bronfenbrenner's death, Johnson and Puplampu (2008) suggested an update to his nested ecological system to reflect the increasing impact of technology on child development. They proposed the introduction of the *techno-subsystem* within the microsystem to represent how the child interacts with communication, information and recreational technology in their immediate environment.

Family systems theory – Murray Bowen (1913–90)

American Professor of Psychiatry Murray Bowen was a pioneer of family therapy. His family systems theory applied systems thinking to the complex interactions of the family, which he viewed as an intensely interdependent emotional unit (Bowen, 1990). Bowen believed that families profoundly affect their members as they, 'solicit each other's attention, approval, and support and react to each other's needs, expectations, and upsets' (cited in Kerr, 2000). As a result of this, he proposed that a change in one member of the family impacts on all other members. Bowen's family systems theory has eight, interlocking components which apply not just to families, but other groups, such as work and social organisations (Table 6.2).

Table 6.2 Bowen's family systems theory

Interlocking Component	Description
Triangles	A triangle is a three-person relationship system, the smallest stable relationship system and therefore the *molecule* of larger emotional systems. Couples therapy uses the therapist to complete the triangle, providing a neutral third party capable of relating to both sides of a conflict.
Differentiation of self	Families and social groups affect how people think, feel and act. People with a poorly differentiated self are heavily dependent on others for acceptance and approval, so can act as social chameleons, adjusting their behaviour to try and please others. Those who have a well-differentiated self recognise their dependence on others, but can cope with conflict, criticism and rejection without automatic capitulation.
Nuclear family emotional process	Four basic relationship patterns govern where problems develop in a family: 1 anxiety 2 marital conflict 3 dysfunction in one spouse 4 impairment of one or more children
Family projection process	Parents transmit their emotional problems to a child. Problems that most negatively affect the child are: • a heightened need for attention and approval • difficulty dealing with expectations • the tendency to blame (oneself or others) • feeling responsible for other's happiness • acting impulsively to relieve anxiety, rather than tolerating anxiety and acting thoughtfully

(Continued)

Table 6.2 (Continued)

Interlocking Component	Description
Multigenerational transmission process	Information is transmitted across generations through relationships and relationally and genetically transmitted information interacts to form the individual *self*.
Emotional cut off	Sometimes people attempt to manage unresolved emotional issues with family members by reducing or totally cutting off emotional contact. However, problems remain dormant, rather than resolved, and this may place other relationships under pressure.
Sibling position	People who grow up in the same sibling position have predictable common characteristics – for example, oldest children tend to be leaders, younger children followers and middle children exhibit characteristics of both their older and younger siblings.
Societal emotional process	Guided by the emotional system, people sometimes respond based on self-interest, whilst at other times they respond based on the interests of the group. Societal emotional functioning parallels this – over different periods of history, there have been tendencies for society to move in the direction of differentiation (regression) or togetherness (progression).

Complexity and chaos

The theories we have considered so far in this chapter are relatively accessible, and it is fairly easy to understand how they describe our experience. However, the systems that we encounter in practice are often chaotic and very difficult to understand. As systems theories have developed, they have progressively moved away from straightforward and linear explanations and our contemporary understanding is that social systems are certainly much more complex and chaotic than Parsons' functionalist perspective. Connolly and Harms suggest general systems theory has transformed into complex systems theory and observe:

> systems theories continue to be attractive to social workers, as undeniably social problems and environments have become increasingly complex and as such can easily be seen as 'complex systems'. (2012, p. 59)

Complexity and chaos theories originated in the natural sciences and computer technology, emerging in response to difficult to understand and apparently disorderly systems. The relationships and connections between components combine to form larger and less obvious relationships within larger and more complex systems, such as weather formations. These complex, often large, multifaceted systems are characterised by apparent unpredictability, non-linearity, interconnectivity and emergence.

We seek to understand situations by applying our existing frameworks of reference, and when they don't fit, we classify them as complex and chaotic (Heslop and Meredith, 2019). Predictable patterns do exist in complex social systems, but they are much harder to detect

Exercise 6.1

Let's think of a murmuration of starlings, where thousands of birds seem to fly as a single organism. Actually, each bird is responding only to the few birds immediately around it. As they all act responsively, the birds form a protective whole (a system!) which can quickly detect and avoid predators as they seek a place to roost for the night.

because they are non-linear (Harvey and Reed, 1996). Applying complexity theory to social systems, therefore, requires us to behave in a way which is counterintuitive. It has been argued that complexity theory's application to social work is helpful because it represents understanding of uncertainty, ambiguity and complexity, but is less helpful in identifying procedural ways to manage these very same situations (Fish and Hardy, 2015).

Intersectionality – Kimberlé Crenshaw (b. 1959)

Walby (2007, 2012) associates inequality with complexity and MacDermott (2014) argues complexity is concerned with the intersection of systems. Intersectionality emerged from critical feminist theory (see Chapter 2) and was inspired by Freire's practice of conscientisation (Krumer-Nevo and Komem, 2015; see Chapter 4). The term intersectionality was first used by Kimberlé Crenshaw (1989) in relation to black disabled women in North America. Traditionally, people have been assigned a singular or primary social inequality, such as sexuality or race. Intersectionality takes a far more complex approach, proposing that to understand the extent of disadvantage and marginalisation people experience, we need to appreciate how a plurality of social inequalities intersect to create new forms of oppression (Yuval-Davis, 2006).

Recognising intersectionality can help to overcome the tendency for competition between inequalities – for instance, race or disability – acknowledging instead that diverse inequalities encompass both. Mattsson (2014) suggests that because intersectionality focuses on the interplay and complexity between gender, sexuality, class and race, it is an excellent tool for critical reflection, and a mechanism through which to challenge oppression and inequality (see Chapter 4). Reflecting on the interprofessional context of health and social care in North America, Rubin et al. (2018) argue intersectionality is important to social work education and the training of future practitioners. They suggest a commitment to integrated interprofessional practice should embrace intersectionality of health care, social inclusion, justice and respect for people.

Systemic practice

Systemic practice is an umbrella term for social work approaches which draw from the key principles of theories that we have discussed so far in this chapter. Working in this way recognises that social systems are not static, they evolve over time, and are often hard to fathom. Jones (1996) suggests that the attraction of systemic practice is that it allows practitioners to consider wider societal factors and adhere to radical impulses, whilst preserving the intimacy of working with individuals and families. For example, an individualist approach might reductively pathologise a person as an addict, and directly or indirectly blame them for their own poor choice to abuse substances. Systemic practice would encourage a broader approach which considers the impact of context, connections and environment. In this way, an understanding may develop that the person is using substances as a coping mechanism to block out painful experiences from their childhood, when they were maltreated as a consequence of parental trauma, poverty and ill health.

Systemic social work practice often draws from elements of Bowen's systemic family therapy, which sees the family as a system of interconnected and interdependent individuals who form an emotional and physical unit (Kerr and Bowen, 1988). The therapist works with the family members together and supports them to consider what is happening in their system, and how they can navigate towards solutions. Both families and practitioners are often resistant to this approach. In support of systemic practice, Hills (2012) explains that social work's dominant method of working with family members individually, rather than collectively, is fundamentally flawed because it only facilitates change in one component of the family system.

Ahmed-Mohamed (2011) suggests the influence of practice perspectives based on general systems theory (Goldstein, 1973; Pincus and Minahan, 1973; Siporin, 1980) has ensured social workers continue to focus on systemic relationships between individuals and their environments through change agent systems, as well as the interactions between micro, meso and macro systems. Ahmed-Mohamed argues that social work is a normative discipline, which is created and recreated through ethical considerations (professional and societal), and therefore does not prioritise a contextual systemic intervention because this approach would value the service user's autonomy over professional, societal and ethical considerations.

Theorising relationships

Relationships occur within and between systems, and social workers need to draw from knowledge on how and why we relate to and interact with each other, and the consequences when we cannot. Our species is social; we have reached this point of existence by living together, cooperating with each other and organising ourselves to form a social mechanism. We need each other, and we seek relationships and connections from the moment that we are born.

Social capital

Social capital describes the importance of human connection. It is premised upon the idea that all social networks have value and that social groups function effectively through interpersonal relationships based upon trust, cooperation, reciprocity and shared identity, understanding, norms and values. American political scientist Robert Putnam offers a theory of social capital in his 1995 article 'Bowling Alone: America's Declining Social Capital', which he expands on in his book, *Bowling Alone: The Collapse and Revival of American Community* (2000). However, the concept of social capital has been around for a considerably longer period of time and Putnam himself acknowledges that the first recorded description of the term was in the 1916 writings of educational reformer L.J. Hanifan:

> The tangible substances [that] count for most in the daily lives of people: namely good will, fellowship, sympathy, and social intercourse among the individuals and families who make up a social unit ... The individual is helpless socially, if left to himself. If he comes into contact with his neighbor, and they with other neighbors, there will be an accumulation of social capital, which may immediately satisfy his social needs and which may bear a social potentiality sufficient to the substantial improvement of living conditions in the whole community. The community as a whole will benefit by the cooperation of all its parts, while the individual will find in his associations the advantages of the help, the sympathy, and the fellowship of his neighbors. (cited in Putnam, 2000, p. 19)

Social capital has gained currency to become a way to understand the dynamics of individual and community resources. Furstenberg and Kaplan (2007) acknowledge the measurement of social capital within families can be difficult, though they speculate that interpersonal family relationships and negotiating skills are important in defining family roles. Hawkins and Maurer (2012) feel that considering social capital during social work assessments can provide an analytical and theoretical basis for integrating different aspects of social networks, support and relationships, but conclude that the concept is sadly underused.

At the turn of the century, Putnam proposed that expansion of the educated middle classes, the spread of mass entertainment in industrialised society and political disengagement had increased individualism, and that as a result, 'By virtually every conceivable measure, social capital has eroded steadily and sometimes dramatically over the past two generations' (2000, p. 287). Johann Hari's internationally best-selling book, *Lost Connections: Why You're Depressed and How to Find Hope* (2018), presents a broad range of credible research evidence which supports the idea that rising rates of mental health difficulties are related to humans' declining social interactions.

Attachment theory – John Bowlby (1907–90) and Mary Ainsworth (1913–99)

Proponents of attachment theory are concerned with explaining human relationships by identifying common links and modes of behavioural classification. This theory has had an enormous impact on social work, particularly in relation to childcare. John Bowlby, the architect of attachment theory, was significantly influenced by the work of Freud (see Chapters 2 and 5). He developed attachment theory from studying maternal influence among 'delinquent' young males (essentially replacing the Freudian notion of libido with attachment behaviours). A second significant influence on Bowlby's work was Charles Darwin's theories of evolution and natural selection. Darwin studied the behaviour of iguanas in the Galapagos Islands. He picked the reptiles up and threw them onto the sand, hypothesising that when they landed, they would scurry to the sea to escape him (iguanas are excellent swimmers!).

Darwin was surprised to observe that instead the iguanas always made their way back to the same rocks from which he had first picked them up.

> Perhaps this singular piece of stupidity may be accounted for by the circumstance, that this reptile has no enemy whatever on shore, whereas at sea this reptile must often fall a prey to the numerous sharks. Hence probably urged by a fixed and hereditary instinct that the shore is its place of safety, whatever the emergency may be, it there takes refuge. (Darwin, 1839, p. 468)

Darwin concluded that the iguanas are evolutionarily predisposed to seek refuge on land and therefore will do so even when confronted by a new land-based threat. Bowlby saw attachment behaviour as a similar evolutionary response (with associated behavioural styles) in humans, the purpose of which is to ensure close, safe and affectionate bonds between caregiver and infant (Bowlby, 1997). The conceptualisation of attachment as an evolutionary response is highly significant – suggesting a biological aspect aligns it with the natural, as well as the social sciences. This association causes attachment theory to be perceived as more credible, which may in part account for the way in which it has come to dominate childcare social work.

Bowlby believed there to be four distinguishing characteristics of attachment:

Proximity maintenance – the desire to be near the people we are attached to.

Safe haven – returning to the attachment for comfort and safety when faced with fear or threat.

Secure base – the attachment figure acts as a base of security from which the child can explore the surrounding environment.

Separation distress – anxiety that occurs in the absence of the attachment figure.

Attachment behaviours, therefore, are an infant's predisposed survival strategies (such as crying or smiling) to elicit safe caregiving. Howe, in his guide for social work assessments, explains: 'put simply, attachment behaviour is activated whenever young children feel distressed and insecure and need to get into close proximity with their main caregiver' (1999, p. 13). The resulting response by the adult caregiver helps the child make sense of the world and promotes child development and the child's internal working model (or self-perception). Certainly, there can be little argument about the importance of adults in the care of children, but there is much debate about the almost universal generalisability of attachment styles.

Akram and Dianne

Akram has really struggled with lectures on theory at university. For example, Freud's theory of psychosexual development seems utterly bizarre and he has no idea why he needs to know about it, because there is no way that it is applicable in the present day.

Dianne, Akram's practice educator, does not disagree. She feels that social work is practical and hands on and whilst she considers many theories interesting, they are not always easy to stop and apply when working with people. Dianne does, however, value attachment theory and explains to Akram that 'it's about caring, bonding and the parenting relationship – it's practical and common sense'. She talks to Akram about situations in which this theory has guided her work with families, and Akram is really enthused to hear examples of *how* theory relates to practice. He does some more reading around attachment theory and is surprised to see that it was heavily influenced by ideas which can be traced back to Freud and Darwin. Akram feels like he has had a lightbulb moment – although he is pretty sure he is never going to use Freud's psychosexual development theory or Darwin's theory of evolution in social work practice, he can see how they connect to attachment theory which he will use frequently.

Attachment patterns

Mary Ainsworth developed the *Mother–Infant Strange Situation* test to assess the levels and patterns of attachment in children. This experiment involves observing an infant for 10 minutes immediately after their mother has left the room, and through it, she initially identified three attachment patterns: *secure*, *avoidant* and *ambivalent*. Main and Solomon, who were students of Ainsworth, worked on the *Adult Attachment Interview* (Main and Solomon, 1990) and identified a fourth attachment pattern – *disorganised* – which Ainsworth subsequently incorporated (Table 6.3).

Table 6.3 Attachment patterns

Attachment Pattern	Description
Secure attachment	Occurs when the carer is available, sensitive and responsive to the child.
Avoidant attachment	Occurs when the child perceives the caregiver to reject attention-seeking behaviour and therefore becomes more self-reliant.
Ambivalent attachment	Occurs when the child becomes uncertain how to seek caregiver's attention due to the caregiver responding sporadically, unpredictably and inconsistently.
Disorganised attachment	Occurs when the caregiver is frightening and rejecting, and the infant/child presents incoherent behaviour.

Attachment theory has become central to childcare social work practice, where understanding how an infant bonds/attaches – or does not – with an adult caregiver is a vital component of assessment. Attachment strategies continue across the whole course of a person's life, so our understanding of attachment theory is helpful for practice with adults as well as children. Our childhood attachment strategies influence our ability to regulate our emotions in relationships in adulthood. However, there is some debate amongst proponents of attachment theory – for instance, Mary Main (b. 1943) and Patricia Crittenden (b. 1945), both former students of Ainsworth, develop different perspectives. While tending to be categorised as an attachment pattern (see Table 6.3), Main viewed behaviour classified as disorganised attachment as usually occurring briefly during infancy and suggested wherever possible one of the other three patterns (secure, avoidant, ambivalent) should be identified alongside disorganised attachment (Reijman et al., 2018). Crittenden (2000) uses data codified from both the Strange Situation test and the Adult Attachment Interview (over two decades) to suggest a *dynamic-maturation model* where variables within behavioural patterns occur as a result of maturing, life changes and culture, whereby:

> The past is fixed, but its meaning is rewritten every time it is recalled. Maturation is the means, and mental integration is the process through which future functioning can be expanded to yield a nearly infinite range of human possibility. (Crittenden, 2000, p. 357)

Attachment theory is a dynamic field of study and the importance to social work is maybe at the expense of critical appraisal in an effort to utilise an approach (or methods) which essentially is concerned with analysis rather than a universally held conclusion to be applied with all families.

Theories of family relationships

What makes a family, a family? Much more than biology: we are biologically connected to distant relatives that we don't have any relationship with at all – we might not even know they exist! Conversely, people without any biological link to us become part of our families through fostering, adoption and intimate partnerships, whilst we frequently describe close friends as 'like family'. Collins et al. (2010) suggest that the purpose of a family is to maintain the wellbeing of its members by offering predictability, structure and safety so that they can mature and participate in society. In the 21st century, family relationships are diverse; below we briefly examine three theories of how families construct themselves and maintain their special relationship.

Family practice and display

Professor of Sociology David Morgan spent his career researching relationships and Manchester University's Morgan Centre for the Study of Relationships and Personal Life is named in his honour. Morgan (1996) argued that families are not concrete structures, rather they are created through fluid, everyday practices which take place in social contexts. Family participation is represented by activities within families where the emphasis is on the social actor recreating his or her world within the context of the family, and performing gender (West and Zimmerman, 1987) and family practices (Morgan, 1996) in everyday routines which overlap and intersect with other practices based on class, age, sexuality, ethnicity and culture.

British sociologist Janet Finch (2007) explored how families socially construct (see Chapter 2) themselves and define their roles through *display*. Finch proposed that within their everyday practices, families put on a show to 'convey to each other and to relevant audiences that certain of their actions constitute "doing family things"' (2007, p. 67). Drawing on both Finch and Morgan,

James and Curtis (2010) suggested that some families use displays of particular cultural understandings of family to affirm themselves, whilst others use normative, hegemonic displays of family to conform and smooth over internal challenges. They conclude that ideas of family take different forms, but all of these demonstrate a need to be understood as part of particular social and cultural worlds rather than as lone individuals. Within social work, these theories about the practice and display of family have been transferred to consider how foster (Rees et al., 2012) and adoptive (Jones and Hackett, 2011) families construct and maintain themselves.

Family scripts

John Byng-Hall was a pioneering British family therapist, and a close associate of John Bowlby (see attachment theory earlier in this chapter). He proposed that from early attachment experiences onwards, family members develop internal operating models which script how they behave and interact with one another (Byng-Hall, 1985). These *family scripts* help us to understand the roles and responsibilities of ourselves and others within our family – for example, what is expected of a father differs enormously from family to family, but your family script governs what is expected of a father within *your* family. Similarly, scripts govern how we learn to cope with difficulties within the family. Family scripts make family life predictable and safe by enabling us to develop routines which can be followed automatically to produce an expected result. Byng-Hall (1985) theorised that family scripts (and the routines, beliefs and values which emanate from them) are passed down through families, one parent's script blending with the others so that the child's script contains material from both. We replicate the scripts that we have learnt in our family of origin, often unconsciously, but sometimes in the full and explicit knowledge that we are acting like a particular relative or side of the family. We can deviate, but this takes effort and pushes us to an unfamiliar territory which may result in feelings of insecurity.

Families of choice

The idea of families of choice originated with American anthropologist Kath Weston, who noticed gay men and lesbian women were choosing networks of friends to provide the type of support and intimacy which would traditionally have been provided by biological families (Weston, 1991). She recognised that people were committing to chosen ties of intimacy, rather than those fixed and assigned by biological familial relationships (Ribbens et al., 2011). Anthony Giddens (see Chapters 4 and 7) argues that choice also transforms heterosexual relationships in modern post-traditional society. As media and information technology expose people to alternatives to traditional notions of family, tradition becomes less normative and alternative lifestyles become more widely available and accepted (Giddens, 1992; Giddens and Pierson, 1998). The development of families of choice within the LGBTQ+ community has resulted in some reflection on what the same-sex family represents, particularly as sexual orientation is now seen as much more fluid than it once was (Diamond, 2008). Individuals in same-sex couples produce new versions of masculinity and femininity as they perform gender within the families of choice discourse. The resulting perception of greater choice and openness in relationships, along with the aim to break away from heterosexually structured differences, has led to a feeling of openness to relationship possibilities within the non-heterosexual community (Weeks et al., 2007).

Theories of grief and loss

Grief and loss are most commonly associated with death and dying, but people can experience these emotions in response to other challenges such as the breakdown of a relationship, development of a serious health problem, redundancy or retirement from a fulfilling role. Losing a significant relationship impacts on how we relate to self, others and society. No one is helped by being told that grief is something that they can or should 'get over'; to consider grief as something that can be resolved undermines the importance of the lost relationship. However, theory can help us to consider the process of mourning and adaptation that follows loss. Most theorists identify phases, tasks or stages of grief. Each experience of loss is unique and the theories we present below are frameworks of understanding, but should never be interpreted as rules to follow or criteria against which to classify grief as 'normal' or 'abnormal'.

Attachment theory

We explored attachment theory in some detail earlier in this chapter. Bowlby ultimately presented his work across his *Attachment and Loss* trilogy (1969–80), the final volume of which, *Loss: Sadness and Depression*, was published in 1980. Bowlby suggested that grief is a normal, adaptive response to loss of an attachment figure. With his colleague Colin Murray Parkes, Bowlby (1970) proposed four stages of grief (Table 6.4).

Table 6.4 Bowlby and Parker's four stages of grief

Stage	Description
Shock and numbness	A self-defence mechanism which occurs in the immediate period. Shock and numbness protect the person from being completely overwhelmed by the emotional impact of their loss.
Yearning and searching	The person experiences a range of differing emotions (anxiety, anger, despair, confusion, sorrow, etc.) as they yearn for the return of their loved one and search for meaning in their loss.
Despair and disorganisation	The person begins to accept the reality of their loss and that their life is forever changed, causing them to experience despair or hopelessness.
Reorganisation and recovery	The person slowly begins to accept their 'new normal'. They do not stop grieving, but begin to become able to access positive memories about their relationship rather than focussing solely on the loss.

Kubler-Ross's five stages of loss

Swiss psychiatrist Elisabeth Kubler-Ross's (1969) model is the best-known theory of grief (Table 6.5), but it has become controversial, because it is very much misinterpreted and misapplied. The theory was actually devised whilst working with people diagnosed with terminal illness, to describe and explain how they adjusted to their coming deaths. It somehow struck a chord in popular culture, where the five stages have been generalised to apply to everything from bereavement to financial loss. Kubler-Ross later clarified that her five stages are not linear –

people may experience each stage multiple times – and passing through the five stages does not mean that the loss is necessarily resolved.

Table 6.5 Kubler-Ross's five stages of grief

Stage	Description
Denial	We react to loss by denying it and blocking the emotions associated with it, clinging to our old reality.
Anger	As we start to realise the reality of the situation, we become angry and frustrated that such an incomprehensible thing could have happened.
Bargaining	We feel guilty and review possibilities of what we could, should or would have done that might have resulted in a different outcome. Often people will express this as 'What if...?', 'If only...', 'I'd give anything...'.
Depression	We feel overwhelmed by our emotions, and begin to withdraw from the world.
Acceptance	We accept our new reality and learn how to live with it.

Worden's tasks of mourning

America psychologist J. William Worden (2009) proposes four tasks (Table 6.6) which must be accomplished in order to re-establish equilibrium following loss, but warns that grief is not a linear process and people experiencing it move back and forth from one task to another.

Table 6.6 Worden's four tasks of grief

Task	Description
Task 1 **To accept the reality of a loss**	Loss – particularly when sudden or unexpected – feels unreal. It may be accepted rationally, but not emotionally. Mourners go through rituals which help them to move closer to acceptance, for example, viewing the body, planning the funeral, scattering the ashes.
Task 2 **Process grief and pain**	Grief exists on a large spectrum and presents endless possibilities of emotion. People often try to delay or avoid experiencing these difficult emotions, perhaps through overworking or using alcohol or drugs. These complex feelings need to be expressed and worked through.
Task 3 **Adjust to the world without your loved one**	This task requires adjusting externally to the world, as well as internally to new emotional and spiritual needs. New roles and responsibilities are negotiated but this is not easy and takes time. This process slowly helps the person to understand the impact that the loss has created in their life.
Task 4 **To find a connection with the deceased while embarking on a new journey**	We need to maintain our connection to our loved ones, even as our own lives continue to change, to reaffirm that the relationship didn't end at death. Some value physical objects – perhaps wearing a piece of jewellery, or carrying a keepsake; many develop rituals, such as visiting the grave or sharing memories of the person at special occasions.

Continuing bonds

Klass, Silverman and Nickman (1996) propose that rather than detaching and disengaging from lost loved ones, we slowly find ways to redefine the relationship and maintain a continued bond. Just as our relationships with living people do not cease when we are not physically with them, so our relationships with people who have died endure. This theory has parallels with Worden's fourth task (2009), and may involve rituals and keepsakes, but extends the idea further, so that the deceased person is not just remembered, but still has influence in the ongoing relationship. An example of this is a person considering what their deceased loved one's view would have been when faced with a big decision, so as to make a choice of which they approve.

Relationship-based practice

Relationship-based practice is a social work approach/practice model concerned with how social workers can form meaningful, purposeful and mutually respectful relationships with people who use services. For most of us, this approach is embedded in our motivations to enter social work: we want to develop effective relationships and work together with people to improve their situations. Relationship-based social work may appear common sense to a humanistic-based profession, but technocratic and austere approaches have bureaucratised the delivery of social care services (see Chapter 3) to the extent that many social workers have relatively little time to spend with people. A survey of 600 social workers found that they spent an average of only 15% of their working week in face-to-face contact with people who use services (Burke, 2012) and the recent resurgence of interest in relationship-based practice responds to how disheartening many social workers, managers and services find such statistics. Relationship-based practice offers a person-centred and culturally diverse alternative and suggests that valuing the quality of the relationship a professional is able to develop with the person using services leads to improved outcomes (Dix et al., 2018; Ruch et al., 2010).

Conclusion

At its best and at its worst, human life is messy and complicated. This can feel so overwhelming that sometimes in the urge to simplify, reductionist approaches result in problems being viewed in isolation and individualised. When this happens, people who use services can feel that rather than being supported, they are being blamed for their own difficult situations. An understanding of theories of systems and relationships helps us to see the people we work with as inherently complex social entities influenced and defined by their connections and environments. The task for social work is to embrace this complexity, not resist it. Once we understand the key principles of systems, we can employ systemic and relationship-based approaches to take a broad, contextualised view of families, teams and communities. We can identify patterns of behaviour and realise that even when they are not helpful or desirable, they are serving some form of purpose. We can work together with individuals, families and groups to understand how to effect meaningful change within their systems.

7 THEORIES OF RISK AND VULNERABILITY

Introduction

This chapter considers theoretical knowledge underpinning two concepts core to contemporary social work: risk and vulnerability. We look first at key theoretical perspectives of risk, and consider safeguarding. Social work has a key role in protecting vulnerable people, and safeguarding children and adults has become a central component of practice. However, people are vulnerable to an abundance of risk factors which make their social experience difficult, and our practice needs to consider this both within and outside of safeguarding processes. Understanding risk involves identifying vulnerability, which is generally conceptualised as susceptibility to some form of threat. People are often seen to be vulnerable because they experience issues such as poverty, trauma, poor health and disability, but theories explored in this chapter support that view that vulnerability arises not from a condition, but from society's discriminatory response to difference.

Risk

Risk is commonly conceptualised as the possibility of something happening, or a strategic approach (think of the board game, Risk!). From a social constructionist perspective (see Chapter 2), risk is a contentious concept; it can have either positive or negative connotations depending on how it is located within particular historical and political contexts (Berger and Luckman, 1979; Hothersall and Mass-Lowit, 2010). For example, falling in love is a risk that most people take at least once in their lives, and even if the relationship ultimately ends, countless positives will have been gained from taking the risk. In modern society, negative dimensions of risk are frequently amplified whilst positive dimensions are muted. When risk is one-dimensionally characterised as negative, it follows that narratives focus on managing, avoiding and eliminating risk. This has become highly problematic for the social work profession, which takes a key role in responding to risks that present within the context of human lives and relationships.

Both German sociologist Ulrich Beck and British sociologist Anthony Giddens (whose work on post-traditionalism we explored in Chapter 4) theorised that modern society had become a *risk society*, preoccupied with ensuring future safety through the avoidance of risk. They suggested that because it was possible to assess and take preventative measures against risks produced by human actions in industry, society had become orientated towards the systematic reduction of risk in *all* areas of life. Hungarian-British sociologist Frank Furedi offers a complementary argument to Beck and Giddens' risk society: he argues that obsession with risk means that fear has acquired a commanding status in contemporary society, resulting in a *culture of fear.* Within this, focus endlessly shifts between uncalculated threats which may be posed by technology, foods, strangers, health, etc. Furedi (2018) is critical of this culture of fear as it restricts alternative viewpoints and drives to influence human behaviour through moral panics. He suggests that language has evolved to embrace the rhetoric of fear to the point where everyday conversations routinely centre on fear and panic.

Clearly, risk is a major influence on society, and a key driver of social work. Social work's relationship with risk manifests quite differently in contemporary social work compared to how it was approached in the past. In the 19th century the Charity Organisation Society (see Chapter 1) assessed needs and allocated resources based on their prediction of what would happen without them. Their assessment of need incorporated speculation of potential future outcomes – assessment of risk. Similarly, the restructuring of social services in the 1970s (see Chapter 1) advocated for universal services to meet needs. At both of these points in history, a century apart, needs were the primary driver of social work intervention and meeting needs was considered to preventively reduce risk of harm. Webb (2006) argues that an increasing dependence on process and rules (see managerialism, Chapter 3) has moved social work's focus from need to risk, prioritising safety above all else. Safety is seen to be the primary need and therefore intervention may only be offered if a threshold of risk has been met.

Karen and Judith

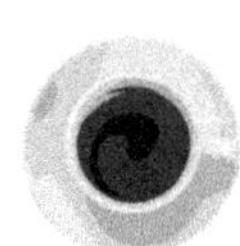

Judith and Karen are talking about risk. Judith is proud of her politics and how this has informed her practice. She tells Karen about a time in the early 1980s when she supported a politically engaged group of squatters who included young care leavers. Karen isn't sure whether or not she would have done this, but even if she wanted to, none of the managers she has ever had would have sanctioned it! Judith says she is sad that modern social work culture makes people focus more on protecting themselves from blame than helping the people that they work with to take positive risks. She says that people are far too ready to defer to managers when they should be challenging them. Karen is really fond of Judith and respects her a lot, but recognises that their situations are very different. As she has chosen to remain in frontline practice, Judith is only accountable for herself. Her years of experience enable her to push boundaries with management in a very knowledgeable way and often this works, but if she is proposing to take a risk that is considered too high, she will be overruled. Karen is a senior practitioner; as well as working with people who use services, she supervises other members of staff and therefore is partially accountable for the risks that they take. She needs to maintain her job and her registration – she cannot take the chance of being blamed when something goes wrong.

Exercise 7.1

Whose stance on risk do you associate with more, Judith's or Karen? Why?

Think of a risk that someone tried to stop you from taking. How did it feel? Did you follow their advice or not?

Risk assessment in social work

Risk and danger are not precursors for referrals to social work. A hang-gliding daredevil takes many risks but does not need a social work assessment. However, when a person who is perceived to have a need for care and support wants to go hang-gliding, professionals can get very uncomfortable! Notions of vulnerability and duty of care become bound up with fear of blame and repercussion. It is important that when people come within the scope of social work, we hold sight of the fact that risk taking is a core facet of human life and relationships and we cannot and should not seek to eliminate it. Social work practice has to approach risk with a nuance that recognises how sterile a totally safe life is and find ways of responding to risk reasonably, rather than excessively.

Smethurst (in Scragg and Mantell, 2011) asserts that good risk management processes are systematic, participatory, proportionate, least restrictive, clear, and are regularly monitored and reviewed. Kemshall (2013, cited in Maclean and Harrison, 2015) identifies three approaches to risk assessment:

- **Actuarial assessment** – developed from the insurance sector, actuarial assessment is based on scientific models of risk which draw upon statistical and quantitative analysis of data to calculate probability. This approach does not provide an individualised assessment or identify strengths, and is not a good predictor of serious and uncommon behaviours/ risks.
- **Unstructured clinical** – is based on the subjective knowledge, skills and experience of the assessor. While unstructured clinical approaches are individualised and contextual, they are very subject to bias.
- **Structured professional judgement** – this approach seeks to combine positive elements of actuarial (statistical calculations of risk) and unstructured clinical (individualised by skilled assessors) approaches. Kemshall explains that this approach is an important component of a practitioner's casework.

Safeguarding

Safeguarding dominates contemporary social work practice, reflecting legislation, policy and popular opinion which has been directed by tragedy. The unimaginably cruel abuse and deaths of children like Peter Connolly and Daniel Pelka rightly promote a reaction at every level of society. No one can comprehend how such events have happened and we all agree that we must do whatever we can to prevent similar occurrences. However, as distressing as these tragic events are, they are uncommon. Macdonald and Macdonald (2010) caution that in building social work around safeguarding models designed to minimise low-probability, high-cost outcomes such as homicide, uncertainty becomes mistaken for risk and possibility mistaken for probability. When social work is focused on avoiding low-frequency events, the allocation of scarce human and financial resources is skewed towards managing narrowly defined risks. Wider social needs go unmet and inevitably unmet needs develop into risk.

Various tools and methods have developed to support social work practice on risk and safeguarding, and facilitate risk assessments and action plans – for example, the statutory guidance *Working Together to Safeguard Children* (Department for Education, 2018), and the strengths-based practice framework *Signs of Safety* (Turnell, 2012; Turnell and Edwards, 1999). However, many feel that these tools promote *parent-blaming* by overlooking structural issues and instead make families responsible for circumstances outside their control. Baginsky et al. caution that practice frameworks are no substitute for theoretical knowledge:

> Further exploration of the theories that underpin the most frequently used frameworks and of social workers' understanding of how they relate to practice is needed. A framework is only a framework. It does not provide the necessary skills, tools and experience to work with children and families. That will come from understanding the theoretical underpinnings of the adopted framework. (2020, p. 13)

Whilst we in no way dispute the need to safeguard people of all ages from abuse, neglect and exploitation, we do worry that sometimes social work's role is narrowly conceptualised as responding *only* to these issues, and only when they are perceived to have reached a pre-designated level of risk. Abuse is enabled by inequality which gives power to one side and creates vulnerability on the other. In the remainder of this chapter we explore a range of notions and theories related to vulnerability, recognising how our society is premised on categorising people and affording or denying them status and opportunity.

Vulnerability

Many highlight the disabling consequences of labelling someone vulnerable (see, for example, Brown, 2011; Hollomotz, 2009; Hough, 2012). Conceptualising someone this way may infantilise them, promoting paternalistic practice which can compromise rights, autonomy and independence in order to prioritise safety. Others highlight a victim-blaming tendency to hold vulnerable people responsible for their own abuse (Roulstone and Mason-Bish, 2012;

Shakespeare, 2012). In 2008, whilst discussing criminal justice responses to disability hate crime, then Director of Public Prosecutions Kenneth Macdonald noted that:

> the label vulnerable was being applied ... [as] an innate, unchanging and unchangeable characteristic of disabled people. We are one step away from making the assumption that disabled people should expect to be attacked because of who they are. (cited in Crown Prosecution Service, 2010)

The implications of constructing vulnerability as an inherent characteristic of the disabled person, rather than the result of the perpetrator's disablist targeting, are discriminatory and extremely concerning. Roulstone and Mason-Bish (2012) suggest it is much more helpful to think of vulnerable situations, rather than vulnerable individuals. Innes and Innes' (2013) work on vulnerability to antisocial behaviour proposes three aspects of vulnerability which may coexist in a variety of ways (Figure 7.1).

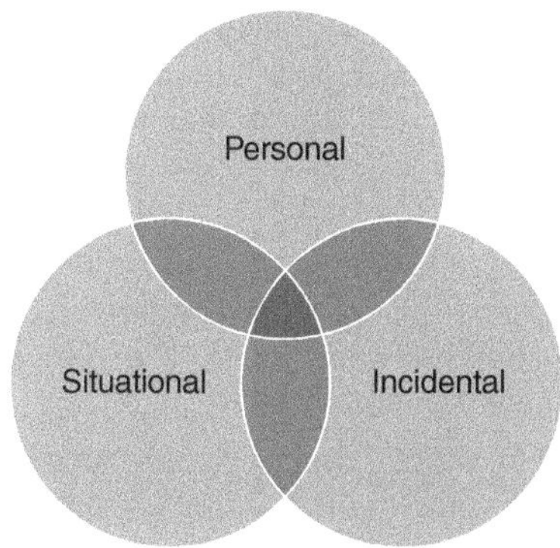

Personal vulnerability – resulting from an individual or group's characteristics, identity or status

Situational vulnerability – resulting from some aspect of the context, e.g. location, environment, intoxication, time of day

Incidental vulnerability – certain incidents promote vulnerability, including repeated occurrences and/or incidents perceived to be personally targeted, e.g. bullying

Figure 7.1 Personal, situational and incidental vulnerability (adapted from Innes and Innes, 2013)

Contextual safeguarding, developed by British social researcher Carlene Firmin, very much follows along these lines in work with children and young people. Context becomes increasingly important as children mature and become more independent, experiencing peer and community relationships where potential risks may include peer abuse, sexting, online exploitation and gang membership (Firmin, 2018). Contextual safeguarding nests the young person within their actual environment, recognising the impact of public and social influences *beyond* family for a more nuanced assessment of vulnerability and risk.

Vulnerability theory – Martha Fineman (b. 1943)

Martha Fineman is an American feminist legal theorist and political philosopher whose extensive work focuses on legal constructions of dependency and vulnerability. Her 2005 book, *The Autonomy Myth*, argues that Western culture is fixated with the idea that citizens are and should be autonomous, when the social reality is quite the opposite. She asserts that dependency is unavoidable in any society, as we are all interconnected and need care and support from other individuals and institutions at points throughout our lives. Fineman's *vulnerability theory* (2008, see Table 7.1) therefore holds that vulnerability should be understood to be universal and constant, inherent in the human condition, rather than defined groups. Through institutions of society, the state privileges segments of the population and disadvantages others, creating vulnerability. She therefore argues for increased state intervention rather than responsibilisation of the individual:

> A vulnerability approach argues that the state must be responsive to the realities of human vulnerability and its corollary, social dependency, as well as to situations reflecting inherent or necessary inequality, when it initially establishes or sets up mechanisms to monitor these relationships and institutions. (Fineman, 2017, p. 2)

Table 7.1 Core tenets of vulnerability theory (adapted from Fineman, 2008)

Rejection of responsibilisation (Fineman refers to rejection of the *liberal subject*, a term less readily applicable in the UK)	The level of autonomy people have is not determined by birth, but through a complex set of interactions with societal institutions. People are not equally able to determine the course of their lives and therefore cannot be responsibilised for the outcomes of all decisions.
Vulnerability is universal and constant	Challenging the discrimination and stigmatisation that arise from locating vulnerability in a particular group or condition. Recognising that at different times, in different situations and for different reasons we are *all* vulnerable and will need support.
Resilience is both built and destroyed by societal institutions	State (or state regulated) institutions are a core facet of every citizen's experience – families, hospitals, schools, councils, the inland revenue, the benefits agency, the criminal justice system, etc. Institutions build resilience and respond to vulnerability, but also create inequality in the way in which they allocate resources.
Equality should be Substantive, rather than Formal	In Formal Equality, laws and policy are applied to all persons equally, theoretically leaving each individual free to exercise their rights and choices. Substantive Equality recognises that people's situations are not all equal and advocates for laws which take into account discrimination, marginalisation and unequal distribution.
A more responsive state	The state is responsible for creating inequality that causes vulnerability because it legitimises and gives power to societal institutions. It must therefore take greater responsibility in identifying the ways in which institutions create inequality, and address this through law and policy.

Stigma

Stigma (plural stigmata) is a Greek word which originally denoted a mark that was cut or burned into someone to identify them as disgraced. In the modern day, it refers to the labelling of a person or group with a set of culturally determined, undesirable characteristics that mark them out as deviating from what is perceived to be the 'norm'. Stigma is a tool of oppression: it apportions shame to those stigmatised and privilege to those who are not. Founding father of sociology, Emile Durkheim (see Chapter 2), theorised about stigma as far back as the late 19th century, but it is most strongly associated with Erving Goffman.

Theory of social stigma – Erving Goffman (1922–82)

Goffman was an extremely influential Canadian sociologist who wrote many seminal texts and comprehensively theorised stigma in his 1963 publication, *Stigma: Notes on the Management of Spoiled Identity.* He observed:

> While a stranger is present before us, evidence can arise of his possessing an attribute that makes him different from others in the category of persons available for him to be, and of a less desirable kind – in the extreme, a person who is quite thoroughly bad, or dangerous, or weak. He is thus reduced in our minds from a whole and usual person to a tainted discounted one. Such an attribute is a stigma, especially when its discrediting effect is very extensive. (Goffman, 1963, p. 3)

Goffman proposed three types of stigma (Table 7.2).

Table 7.2 Three types of stigma (adapted from Goffman, 1963)

Type of Stigma	Description
Stigma of character traits	Negative judgements made about a person's individual character inferred from, for example, mental illness, imprisonment, addiction, unemployment, promiscuity, etc.
Physical stigma	Negative judgements made on the basis of physical differences in the body, for example, impairments of sight or hearing, body or limb shape, birth marks, etc.
Stigma of group identity	Negative judgements made on the basis of belonging to a particular race, nation, religion, etc.

Goffman's theory divides the individual's relation to a stigma into three categories:

- *the stigmatised*, who may experience discrimination, shaming and exclusion
- *the stigmatising* (Goffman originally referred to *the normal*, however this term reinforces stigmatisation and is no longer used), who increase their own status and self-esteem by depersonalising others into stereotypical caricatures; and
- *the wise,* who do not stigmatise others or bear the particular stigma (although they may be stigmatised through association)

Smith's (2012) study supported Goffman's three relationships to stigma, but made a further distinction by subdividing *the wise* into *active wise*, who challenge stigmatisation and the *passive wise*, who do not (see Figure 7.2).

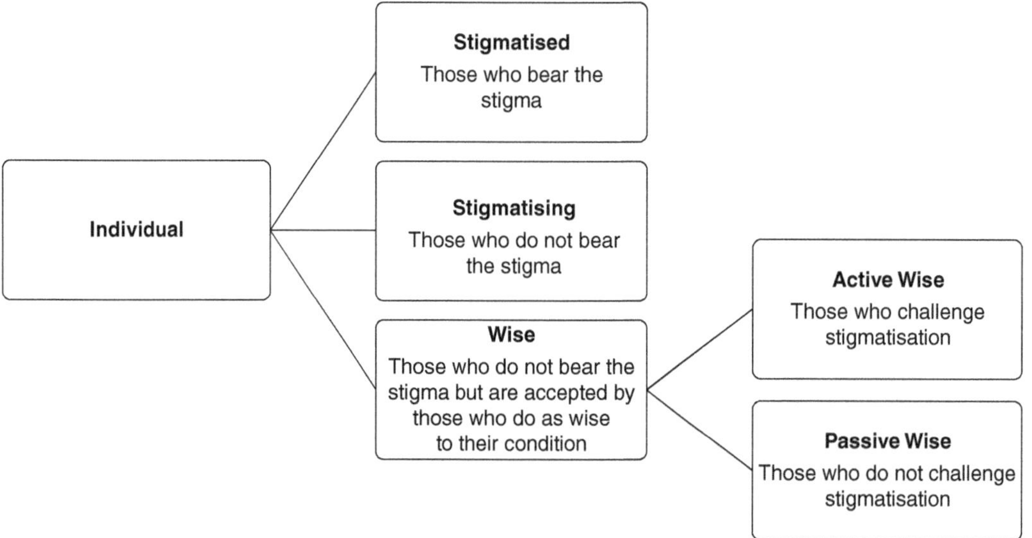

Figure 7.2 Relationship of the individual to stigma (adapted from Goffman, 1963 and Smith, 2012)

Goffman viewed stigma as constructed and relational, rather than fixed, as what is considered undesirable in one culture may be the norm in another, and views shift over time. Roles are not fixed either: as stigma arises from the relationship between an individual and the specific expectations of a particular social setting, a stigmatiser in one setting may be stigmatised in another. Some people, Goffman suggested, have stigmatising attributes which are not immediately apparent, and therefore they straddle two levels of social experience:

1 **Discreditable** – the stigma has not yet been revealed but may subsequently be, either intentionally by the person themself, or by factors beyond the person's control. Until this happens, the person may successfully conceal their stigmatising attribute for an indefinite period of time, which Goffman called *passing*.
2 **Discredited** – the stigma has now been revealed/ discovered and affects the behaviour of the person and those around them.

Jones et al. (1984) offered six levels of stigma which augment and correlate to Goffman's concepts of discreditable and discredited:

1 **Concealable** – the extent to which others can detect the stigma.
2 **Course of the mark** – how the stigma will increase, decrease, or disappear over time.
3 **Disruptiveness** – the extent to which the stigmatising characteristic and/or reactions to it disrupts social interactions.
4 **Aesthetics** – the extent to which the stigmatising characteristic elicits disgust in others.
5 **Origin** – how the stigmatising characteristic is perceived to have come into being – whether present at birth, accidental, or deliberate.
6 **Peril** – the danger or threat that others perceive (whether accurately or not) the stigmatising characteristic to pose to them.

Individuals will experience the six dimensions in differing combinations which determine the extent to which stigma impacts on their life – for example, a mental health issue may be concealable at times, whereas a physical impairment may not; however, a higher level of peril may be associated with mental health issues than with physical impairment.

Link and Phelan's components of stigma

Conceptualisations of stigma were criticised for having insufficient focus on the experience of being stigmatised and victim-blaming by locating the problem in the stigmatised person (Sayce, 1998), rather than the individuals and societies that stigmatise. American sociologists Bruce Link and Jo Phelan (2001) sought to respond to this by proposing that stigmatisation has four, coexisting components (Figure 7.3).

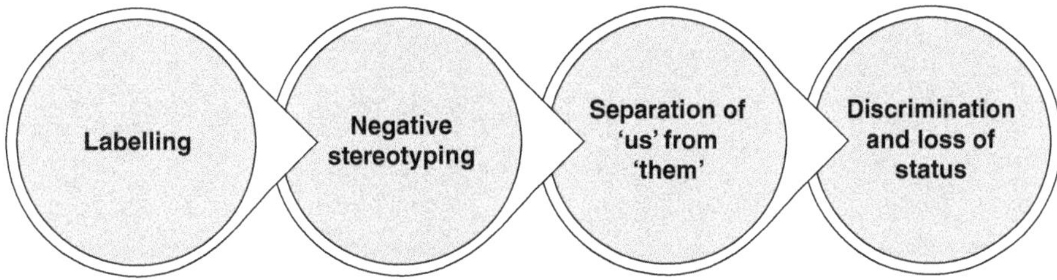

Figure 7.3 Link and Phelan's components of stigma

Labelling and negative stereotypes become embedded so pervasively that people are negatively perceived, not because of their individual behaviour or personal characteristics, but on the basis of prejudicial expectations of how *people like that* behave. A unique feature of Link and Phelan's model is their assertion that the underlying motivation for stigmatisation is always power – whether social, economic, or political.

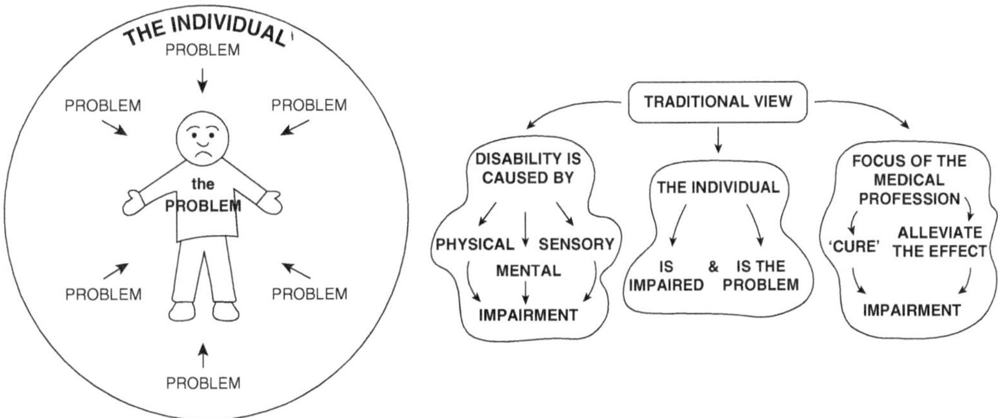

Figure 7.4 Medical model of disability

The social model of disability

In the UK, disabled activists Vic Finkelstein and Mike Oliver developed ideas originating from the Union of the Physically Impaired Against Segregation, and the Disability Alliance into the *social model of disability*. Unfortunately, society sets a normative expectation of cognitive, physical and mental function, and views anyone it perceives to deviate from this as disabled (Heslop and Meredith, 2019). In the deficit-focused medical model (Figure 7.4, see previous page), people are pathologised: the disability inhabits the person and problems arise from them.

The social model of disability (Figure 7.5) makes a distinction between the impairment a person has and the oppression they experience, defining disability as the product of the oppression, rather than the impairment (Shakespeare and Watson, 2002).

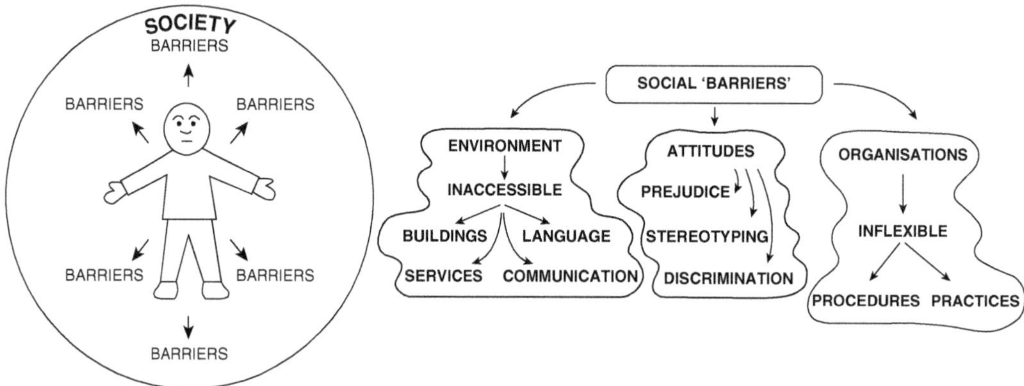

Figure 7.5 Social model of disability

The staircase of oppression and the empowerment track – Thesen, 2005

Janecke Thesen is a Norwegian medical doctor and researcher who has extensively explored the stigmatisation associated with medical diagnosis and the power relationships between medics and patients. Her work draws from Norwegian philosopher Hans Skjervheim's (1926–99) classic text, *Objectivism and the Study of Man* (1959), which recognises how one person can reduce another to an object of study, rather than a person to be engaged with. Skjervheim's concept of objectification is sometimes referred to as othering, dehumanising or pathologising. Janecke Thesen designed the staircase of oppression and the empowerment track as simple, visual models which can be used to consider how power is used with vulnerable and/or stigmatised groups. Whilst designed for medics, her staircase models are equally highly applicable to social work practice.

Social work takes place with people who are experiencing problems, but it is critical that we retain our humanity and see the person, as well as the problems. The staircase of oppression (see Figure 7.6) is built upon a foundation of objectifying, from which negative use of power insidiously creeps, step-by-step, to an end result of professional oppression. When we objectify, rather than seeking to ascertain the person's actual experience, we begin to stereotype; stereotyping promotes prejudicial views that promote discriminatory behaviour, ultimately resulting in our oppression of the person that we are tasked with supporting.

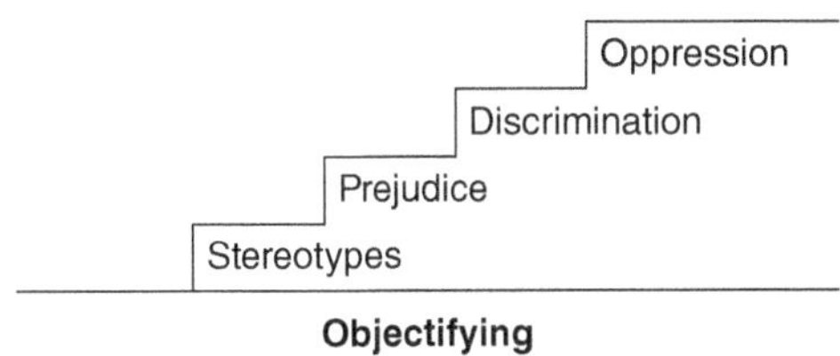

Figure 7.6 The staircase of oppression

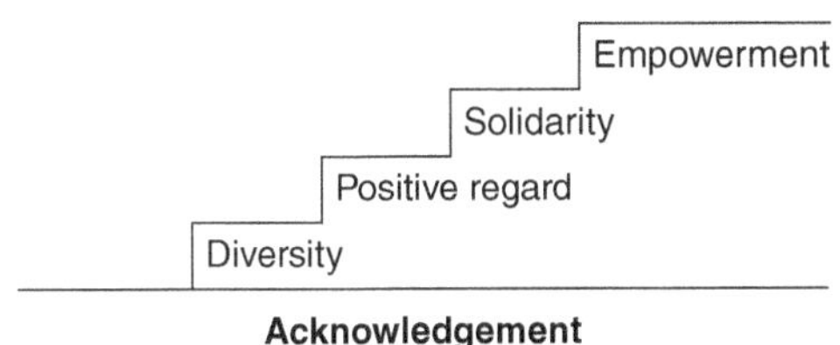

Figure 7.7 The empowerment track

The empowerment track (see Figure 7.7) offers an alternative staircase founded upon acknowledgement of the other person's unique experience. By recognising human diversity and treating the other person with unconditional positive regard (see Carl Rogers, Chapter 2), solidarity develops between person and professional, enabling empowerment.

Social role valorisation – Wolf Wolfensberger (1934–2011)

Social role valorisation (SRV) began as a concept termed normalisation, a human rights-based response to the segregation of people with learning disabilities. The concept is believed to have originated with Niels Erik Bank-Mikkelsen, who led work on Denmark's highly progressive 1959 Mental Retardation Act (we recognise that presenting an historically accurate account involves using some terms which are problematic in the modern day), which sought to secure people with learning disabilities the right to the same community-based existence as everyone else. Director of the Swedish Association for the Mentally Retarded, Bengt Nirje, continued work on the principle of normalisation and wrote about how institutionalisation denied people with learning disabilities access to the *normal rhythms of life* – getting out of bed on a morning and getting dressed at a time and in a manner that suits the individual person, rather than for the smooth running of the establishment; going to a place of occupation, and to other places for social and leisure activities, rather than everything happening within the institution; days which are different, rather than monotonous, and weekends which are distinct from weekdays. It is depressing to note that 50 years after Nirje first wrote about normal rhythms of life, the shift patterns of support staff still dictate what activities many people with learning disabilities can participate in (please check out www.StayUpLate.org and support the campaign). Nirje subscribed to a social model of disability, recognising that people with learning disabilities were disabled by:

- the factual impairment
- other people's responses to impairment
- the awareness of being different (Nirje, 1992)

German American psychologist Wolf Wolfensberger became enthused by Nirje's work and in 1972 published the seminal text *The Principle of Normalization in Human Services.* Central to this text was the idea that the biggest obstacle people with learning disabilities face is society's (conscious and unconscious) attitude towards them. Once people are seen as being different in ways that are negatively valued, they are relegated to lower social status and experience socially sanctioned rejection, segregation and lack of opportunity. For example, there is a largely unquestioned acceptance that children with learning disabilities will attend 'special' schools; in acting out society's belief that segregation is better, the education system renders the belief to be natural. Proponents of normalisation argued that segregation must end and people with learning disabilities – even those whose behaviour is viewed to present concerns and challenges – should be supported to live in ordinary houses, have ordinary relationships and engage in ordinary activities of daily living at ordinary times of the day and week in concordance with the normal rhythms of life (Jones et al., 2016).

The term normalisation proved difficult: it was often mistakenly assumed to categorise people with learning disabilities as 'abnormal' and needing to conform to the 'normality' of people who do not have learning disabilities. This unhelpful confusion ultimately led to the adoption of the alternative term *social role valorisation* (SRV) in 1983. SRV developed to the extent that it became distinct from normalisation and a social theory in its own right. SRV is built upon the premise that the good things any society has to offer are more easily accessible to those who have valued social roles and much harder to come by for those who have devalued or marginally valued roles (Osburn, 2006). Wolfensberger defined SRV as the use of culturally valued means to enable, establish, enhance, maintain and defend valued social roles for all people (1983, 1998, 2000). Its application, therefore, is relevant not only to people with learning disabilities, but to any group vulnerable to devaluation within society, including and not limited to: people with mental health issues, older people, people from different ethnic backgrounds, people experiencing poverty or homelessness, and people with addictions. Devalued people, groups and classes are far more likely than other members of society to be treated badly, and may be subjected to systematic patterns of such negative experiences where they are:

- perceived as 'deviant', due to their negatively valued differentness
- rejected by community, society, family and services
- cast into negative social roles such as 'subhuman', and 'burden on society'
- put and kept at a social or physical distance
- represented with negative imagery and language
- the object of abuse, violence, and even death

SRV recognises that people and groups are devalued and suffer these negative experiences not just through the actions of individuals, but by the actions of society as a whole. Action to enhance the value and status afforded to devalued people, groups and classes is therefore required at every level, as described in Table 7.3.

Table 7.3 Social role valorisation action implications (adapted from Thomas, 1999 and Osburn, 2006)

Level of Action	Action Primarily to Enhance Social Images	Action Primarily to Enhance Personal Competencies
Individual person	Supporting physical and social conditions that are likely to enhance positive perceptions of the indvidual.	Supporting physical and social conditions that are likely to enhance their competencies.
Primary social systems e.g. the person's family	Supporting physical and social conditions in the primary social system that are likely to enhance positive perceptions of the individual within and via this system.	Supporting physical and social conditions of a person's primary social system that are likely to enhance their competencies.
Intermediate and secondary systems e.g. neighbourhood, community, services	Supporting physical and social conditions in secondary social systems that are likely to enhance positive perceptions of the individual and others like them within and via those systems.	Supporting physical and social conditions in secondary social systems that are likely to enhance the competencies of people in them.
Entire society of an individual, group, or class of people	Supporting physical and social conditions throughout society that are likely to enhance positive perceptions of different individuals, groups and classes of people.	Supporting physical and social conditions throughout society that are likely to enhance the competencies of different individuals, groups and classes of people.

Theory of dementia care (personhood) – Thomas Kitwood (1937–98)

English social psychologist Tom Kitwood researched, wrote and taught extensively on dementia. Kitwood is generally credited as originating the now commonly used term *person-centred care* in 1988, building on principles of humanist psychology and particularly Carl Rogers' core condition of unconditional positive regard (see Chapter 2). Kitwood developed a theory of dementia care which focused on the individual's *personhood*, 'a standing or status that is bestowed upon one human being, by others, in the context of relationship and social being' (1997, p.8). Personhood is therefore enhanced through positive regard, creating wellbeing, and diminished without it, leading to 'illbeing'. Kitwood recognised that all humans have psychological need for five elements which contribute to the expression of love: Comfort – the feeling of trust that comes from others; Attachment – security and finding familiarity in unusual places; Inclusion – being involved in the lives of others; Occupation – being involved in the processes of normal life; Identity – what distinguishes a person from others and makes them unique. Kitwood theorised that these needs are heightened for people with dementia because they are usually more vulnerable and less able to take action to ensure they are met. This is compounded by the relative invisibility of people with dementia in society, which contributes to them being devalued and depersonalised.

Kitwood believed that care practices with people experiencing dementia routinely undermined their personhood and left them in a state of illbeing. As dementia progresses, the dominance of the medical model increasingly draws focus to the disease, prioritising medical and physical needs and diminishing personhood by failing to recognise or meet psychological elements. Kitwood described behaviours that undermine a person's wellbeing as *malignant social psychology*. The solution he proposed was person-centred care, where caregivers recognise personhood through *positive person work* in order to enhance wellbeing (1993, 1997; see Table 7.4).

Table 7.4 Examples of malignant social psychology and positive person work (adapted from Kitwood, 1997 and Mitchell and Agnelli, 2015)

Examples of Malignant Social Psychology	Examples of Positive Person Work
Disempowerment – preventing the person from using the abilities they still have	**Facilitation** – enabling the person to do what otherwise they would be unable to do
Infantilisation – treating the person like a child	**Negotiation** – consulting the person wherever possible about their preferences in care and their daily lives
Stigmatisation – treating the person as an outcast	**Celebration** – celebrating the person's achievements and joining in with their celebrations irrespective of the reason
Outpacing – providing information/choices too quickly without accommodating the person's communication needs	**Holding** – providing a safe psychological space or environment to enable people to truly express themselves
Invalidation – not acknowledging the reality of the person	**Validation** – accepting the reality of the other person, even if it is as a result of hallucinations or misperceptions
Banishment – excluding/segregating the person (physically or emotionally)	**Giving** – accepting whatever kindness the person with dementia gives
Objectification – treating the person as an object, rather than a fellow human	**Recognition** – acknowledging the person's unique thoughts, feelings and preferences
Ignoring – behaving as if the person is not present	**Collaboration** – carrying out tasks in partnership with the person

Poverty

In Chapter 3 we considered how neoliberal economic policy has reduced the welfare state and reinforced notions of individual responsibilisation; a policy of managerialism has led to social work becoming increasingly proceduralised and standardised; and a policy of austerity has increased demand for social care services whilst simultaneously reducing social care budgets. When trying to work within the constraints of an overstretched service, it is sadly all too easy to see the problem as the people creating the demand, rather than explicitly recognising how structural decisions have made them vulnerable. BASW's Anti-Poverty Practice Guide for Social Work (2019a) cautions that 'there is a temptation, one that social workers are not immune from, to place the blame for people's poverty completely or almost completely on their own personal choices and characters'.

Government policy (see discussion of *Troubled Families* in Chapter 3) has associated people who live in poverty with cultures of worklessness, even suggesting that this is transgenerationally transmitted, resulting in families who have never worked. Although research directly contradicts such claims (e.g. Shildrick, 2018; Shildrick et al., 2010, 2012; Valentine and Harris, 2014), other means lend them credence – for example the high scrutiny that benefits claimants are placed under and stereotypical characterisation through poverty porn programming (BASW, 2019a). Employment is not necessarily a route out of poverty, the Joseph Rowntree Foundation's annual report *UK Poverty 2019/20* highlighted that:

- Around 14 million people are in poverty in the UK – more than one in five of the population.
- Of these, 8 million are working-age adults, 4 million children and 2 million pensioners.
- Around 56% of people in poverty are in a working family. Seven in 10 children in poverty are in a working family.
- Of the 13 million people with disabilities in the UK, 31% live in poverty (around 4 million people), compared to 20% of the non-disabled population (Joseph Rowntree Foundation, 2020).

Poverty is multidimensional in nature – for example, a lack of financial resources impacts on every aspect of the human experience, denying opportunity by limiting the ability to participate socially, culturally and relationally. In 2016, International Movement ATD (All Together in Dignity) Fourth World joined with Oxford University to launch an international participatory research project which aimed to identify the experience of poverty across six very different countries – Bangladesh, Bolivia, France, Tanzania, the United Kingdom and the United States. The findings (Bray et al., 2019) demonstrate that whilst people's daily lives vary greatly across the different territories, they share common experiences of poverty, many of which are not commonly recognised in policy and research. The findings were used to develop the model presented in Figure 7.8. The inner circle represents the individual's *core experience* of poverty, the decagons represent the often-overlooked *relational dimensions* of poverty, and the hexagons represent the *privations* of poverty – the lack of resources upon which poverty policy narratives most frequently focus. All dimensions are closely interdependent and typically experienced concurrently. The triangles represent the *modifying factors* which Bray et al. (2019) found could either intensify or mitigate poverty.

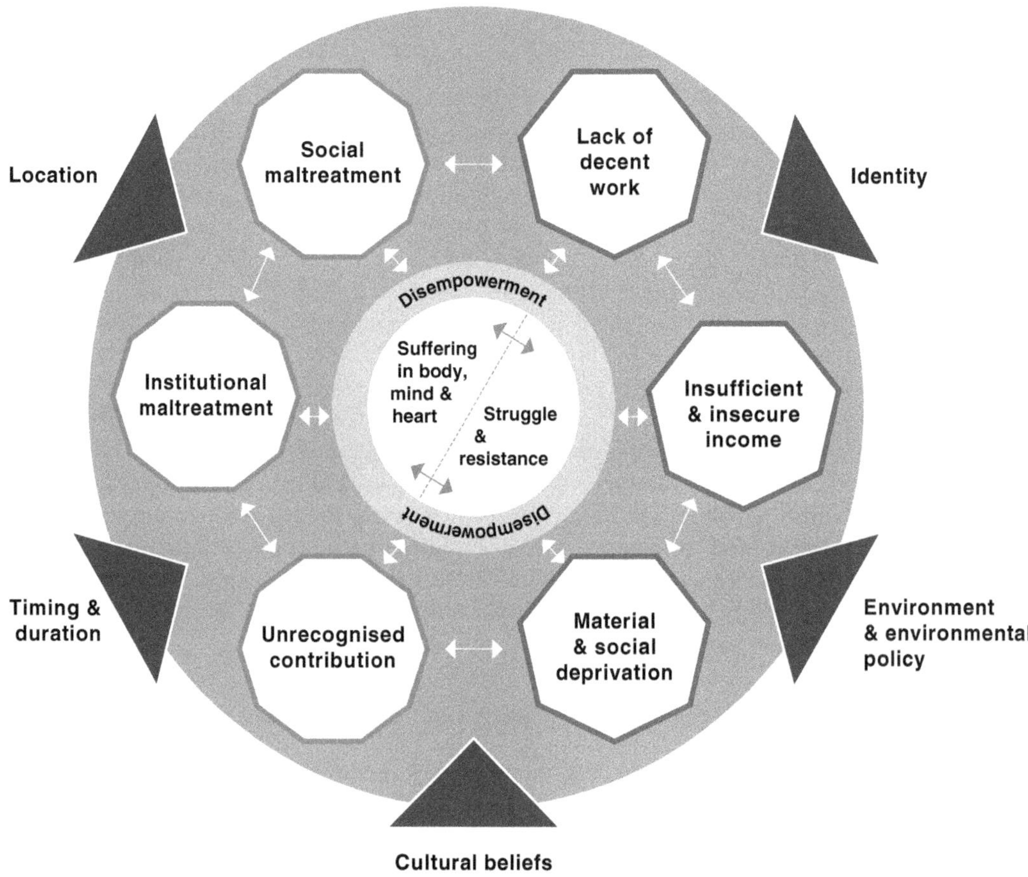

Figure 7.8 The Dimensions of Poverty (Bray et al., 2019)

Health is very often a social issue. Public Health England's *Health Profile for England* (2017) demonstrates that those living in the most deprived areas have the lowest average life expectancy and spend nearly 20 fewer years in good health than those who live in the least deprived areas. Although deprived areas are found in all regions of England, there is a considerably higher concentration in the north and therefore a north–south health divide persists. Back in 2008, the Labour government commissioned Professor of Public Health Michael Marmot to review what could be done to reduce health inequality across the UK. His subsequent report, the *Marmot Review* (Fair Society Healthy Lives, 2010), held that health inequalities are not inevitable and could be significantly reduced through a policy approach of proportionate universalism in order to:

- give every child the best start in life
- enable all children, young people and adults to maximise their capabilities and have control of their lives
- create fair employment and good work for all

- ensure a healthy standard of living for all
- create and develop healthy and sustainable places and communities
- strengthen the role and impact of ill health prevention

But in the same year that the Marmot Review was published, the Coalition government came into power and introduced its policy of austerity which was in direct opposition to Marmot's recommendations. A decade later, *Health Equity in England – The Marmot Review 10 Years On*, makes for grim reading:

> Austerity has taken its toll … From rising child poverty and the closure of children's centres, to declines in education funding, an increase in precarious work and zero hours contracts, to a housing affordability crisis and a rise in homelessness, to people with insufficient money to lead a healthy life and resorting to foodbanks in large numbers, to ignored communities with poor conditions and little reason for hope. And these outcomes, on the whole, are even worse for minority ethnic population groups and people with disabilities. (Marmot et al., 2020, p. 5)

Bibby, Grace and Abbs (2020) examine how the coronavirus (COVID-19) pandemic has brought health inequalities into sharp focus. Those who face the greatest deprivation are at highest risk of exposure to COVID-19 and also suffer the most social and economic consequences of measures to control the spread of the virus. The disproportionately high death rate amongst Black, Asian and minority ethnic communities exposes the structural disadvantage and discrimination they have long faced.

Martin and Akram

Bobbi is 6 and her school has reported concerns about her low attendance and scruffy appearance. Teachers have started bringing food in for her because sometimes she visibly shakes with hunger. They have tried talking to her parents, but her mum doesn't seem interested and they wonder if she drinks as she often looks unsteady. Dad isn't about much. Martin asks Akram to accompany him on an initial home visit and asks him what he thinks that they will find. Akram says that Bobbi is clearly being neglected, and as Bobbi's mum hasn't wanted to engage with the school, she will probably be quite hostile towards him and Martin. When they get to the house, Akram is shocked at how cold and bare it is. Bobbi's mum, Kendra, explains that the family has sold a lot of furniture in order to cover rent and bills. Kendra has multiple sclerosis, and Martin and Akram observe how she trembles and keeps shifting her position because she is in pain. Kendra's disability benefit was withdrawn when she was found to be fit for work, but she has not been able to get a job – employers don't want to risk taking on someone with her diagnosis. Bobbi's dad works as a delivery driver on a zero-hour contract basis. He works as many hours as he can, but after meeting the costs of fuel and maintaining his van, earns very little. The family uses a local foodbank, but sometimes things don't stretch as far as they need to and if they have nothing to sell, they go hungry. Kendra breaks down in tears and tells Martin and Akram that she feels desperate and was so ashamed when the school spoke to her that she just made her excuses and fled.

Exercise 7.2

What assumptions were made and by whom in advance of this visit?

How are the key dimensions of poverty (Figure 7.8) apparent in Bobbi's family situation?

Link and Phelan's theory of fundamental causes, 1995

American sociomedical researchers Jo Phelan and Bruce Link observed that despite public health initiatives such as screening and vaccination, people with lower socioeconomic status (SES) continued to have poorer health outcomes. Their research led them to propose social conditions as fundamental causes of disease. Link and Phelan's theory (1995) suggests that individuals with lower SES lack resources (or access to resources) which individuals with higher SES use to secure good health outcomes, hence disparities in health persist regardless of beneficial intervening mechanisms (see Table 7.5). For example, despite the introduction of smear tests for all women aged between 25 and 64, women of lower socioeconomic status have a higher risk of cervical cancer than those of higher socioeconomic status (Shack et al., 2008).

Table 7.5 How socioeconomic status affects resources which impact upon health outcomes (adapted from Link and Phelan's theory of fundamental causes, 1995)

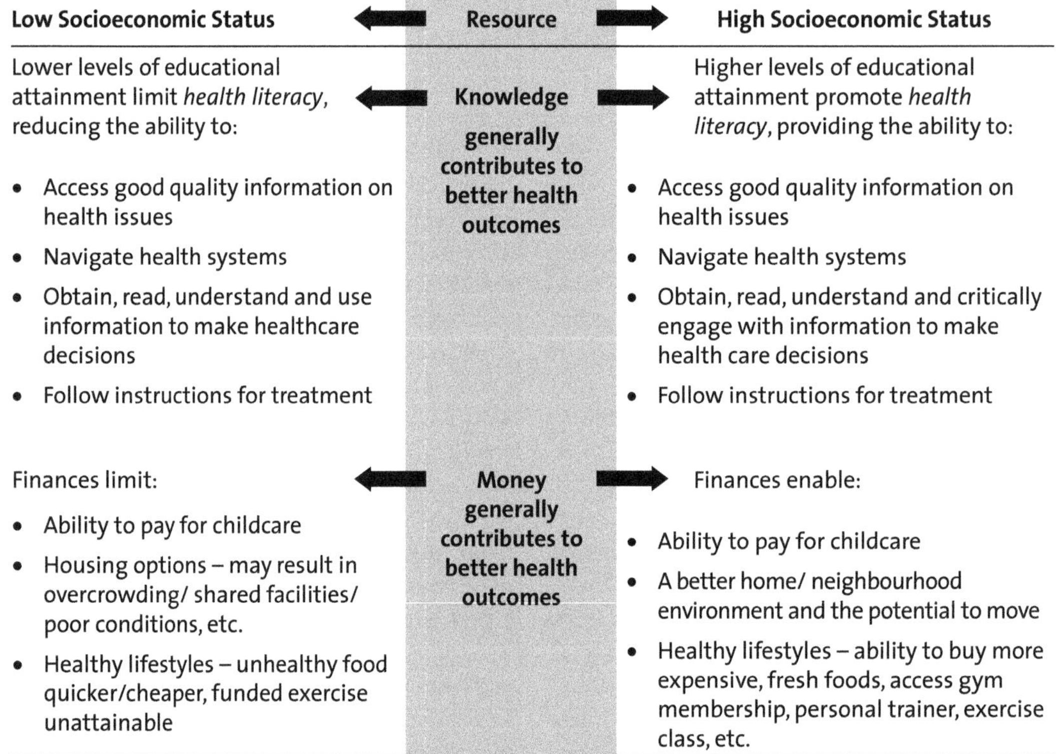

Low Socioeconomic Status ⟵	**Resource**	⟶ **High Socioeconomic Status**
Lower levels of educational attainment limit *health literacy*, reducing the ability to: • Access good quality information on health issues • Navigate health systems • Obtain, read, understand and use information to make healthcare decisions • Follow instructions for treatment	**Knowledge** **generally contributes to better health outcomes**	Higher levels of educational attainment promote *health literacy*, providing the ability to: • Access good quality information on health issues • Navigate health systems • Obtain, read, understand and critically engage with information to make health care decisions • Follow instructions for treatment
Finances limit: • Ability to pay for childcare • Housing options – may result in overcrowding/ shared facilities/ poor conditions, etc. • Healthy lifestyles – unhealthy food quicker/cheaper, funded exercise unattainable	**Money generally contributes to better health outcomes**	Finances enable: • Ability to pay for childcare • A better home/ neighbourhood environment and the potential to move • Healthy lifestyles – ability to buy more expensive, fresh foods, access gym membership, personal trainer, exercise class, etc.

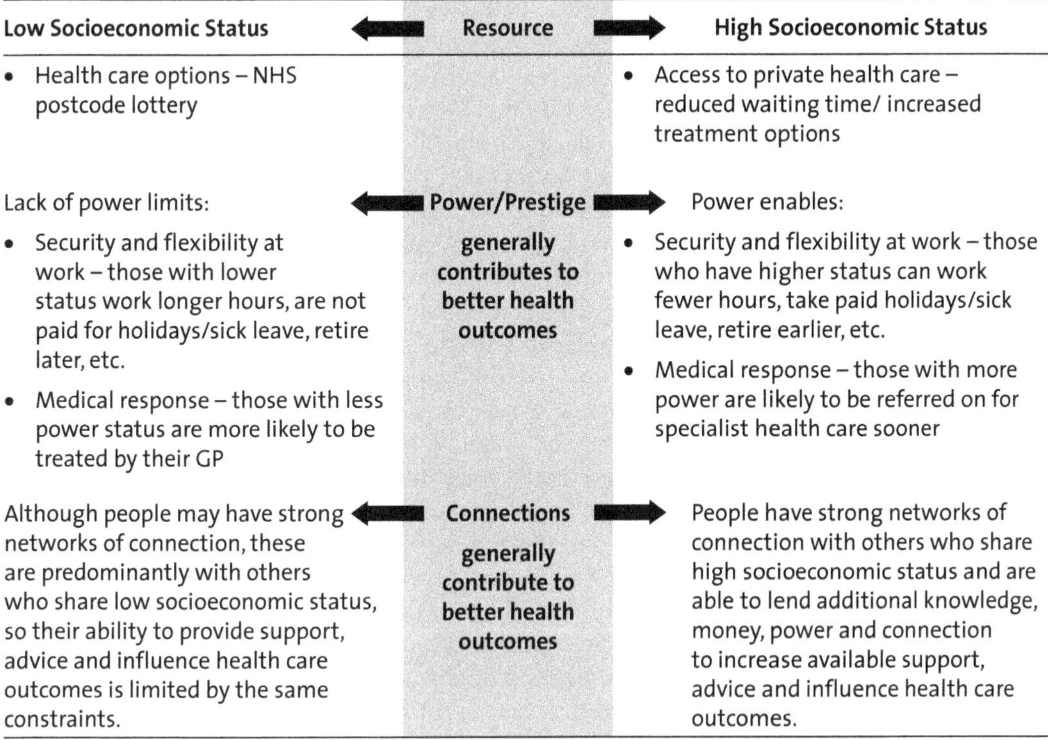

Low Socioeconomic Status	Resource	High Socioeconomic Status
• Health care options – NHS postcode lottery		• Access to private health care – reduced waiting time/ increased treatment options
Lack of power limits: • Security and flexibility at work – those with lower status work longer hours, are not paid for holidays/sick leave, retire later, etc. • Medical response – those with less power status are more likely to be treated by their GP	**Power/Prestige** **generally contributes to better health outcomes**	Power enables: • Security and flexibility at work – those who have higher status can work fewer hours, take paid holidays/sick leave, retire earlier, etc. • Medical response – those with more power are likely to be referred on for specialist health care sooner
Although people may have strong networks of connection, these are predominantly with others who share low socioeconomic status, so their ability to provide support, advice and influence health care outcomes is limited by the same constraints.	**Connections** **generally contribute to better health outcomes**	People have strong networks of connection with others who share high socioeconomic status and are able to lend additional knowledge, money, power and connection to increase available support, advice and influence health care outcomes.

The theory of fundamental causes has been applied broadly to recognise how socioeconomic status disadvantages other outcomes (see, for example, Khan et al., 2017 on mental health; Barkan and Rocque, 2018 on criminality), and in social work it presents an extremely helpful method for identifying the barriers poverty has created and considering how these can be addressed.

Trauma

Farrell (2008) recognises that references to psychological trauma appear as far back as the Greco-Roman wars of 1500 BC. The realisation that difficult events have impact is not new, and yet often social work practice takes a focus on what is happening now, without properly grounding this in what has gone before. American psychiatrist and trauma theorist Judith Herman defines trauma as something which

> overwhelm[s] the ordinary human adaptations to life... Unlike commonplace misfortunes, traumatic events generally involve threats to life or bodily integrity, or a close personal encounter with violence and death. (Herman, 1992, p. 33)

Trauma damages sense of self, leaving people feeling out of control and unsure of how to maintain their safety in evolving relationships and connections (Howell, 2005). The symptoms of trauma may be clinically diagnosable as post-traumatic stress disorder (PTSD), but can manifest in numerous other ways. There is strong evidence linking trauma to mental distress in the form of self-harm (Brodsky et al., 1995), and diagnoses such as borderline (emotionally unstable) personality disorder (Van der Kolk et al., 1991), depression (Maercker et al., 2004) and psychosis (Varese et al., 2012). This casts significant doubt on biological models which attribute mental illness to genetic vulnerability and chemical imbalances.

Transgenerational, or intergenerational trauma is a psychological theory which suggests that trauma is transferred between generations. Notions of transgenerational transmission are well established – we have already looked at Bourdieu's conceptualisation of the family as a means of accumulating and transmitting capital between generations (Chapter 4), and Erikson's theory of generativity (Chapter 5). The idea that trauma could be passed vicariously from one generation to another first developed with the recognition that a disproportionate number of children of Holocaust survivors were seeking help with mental health issues. Selma Fraiberg (1918–81) was an American social worker and child psychoanalyst, whose classic text, *Ghosts in the Nursery* (1975), built upon Freudian (see Chapter 2) notions of repressed and subconscious memories. She theorised that like ghosts, repressed negative experiences live on in the subconscious and haunt parents' behaviours with their own infants, impairing their ability to empathise with their children and understand their feelings. In turn, their children repress these experiences and the pattern repeats until someone breaks the cycle. American psychiatrist Daniel Schechter (b. 1962) realised that many mothers who were requesting psychiatric assessment of their children's behavioural difficulties had themselves experienced childhood maltreatment and been given psychiatric diagnoses such as PTSD, major depression, dissociation and personality disorder (Schecter et al., 2005). He observed that despite their best intentions, many of these traumatised mothers struggled to 'read' or tolerate their child's distress, and the child would start to replicate the mother's behaviour in order to maintain the attachment (see Chapter 6).

Adverse childhood experiences (ACEs)

The *CDC-Kaiser Permanente Adverse Childhood Experiences (ACE) Study* is one of the largest investigations of how childhood experience links to health and wellbeing issues later in life. Between 1995 and 1997, over 17,000 patients receiving physical health examinations completed confidential surveys regarding their childhood experiences, and their current health status and behaviours: 64% reported at least one type of childhood maltreatment or household dysfunction, and nearly 13% reported four or more (Felitti et al., 1998). The study demonstrates a correlation between rates of ACEs and over 40 negative health or behavioural outcomes in later life, including obesity, diabetes, depression, suicide attempts, sexually transmitted diseases, heart disease, cancer, stroke, broken bones, smoking, alcoholism, drug use, academic achievement and domestic violence (Centers for Disease Control [CDC], 2019). The ACE study theorises that trauma causes neurological disruption resulting in social, emotional and cognitive impairments which significantly impact on the person's life course (see Figure 7.9).

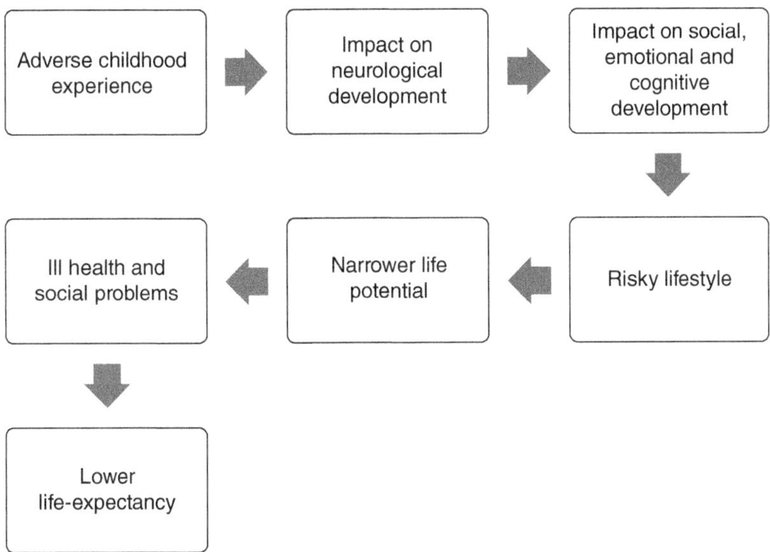

Figure 7.9 Impact of adverse childhood experience across the life course (adapted from CDC, 2019)

The ACEs movement has grown significantly in America, and begun to influence policy and practice in the UK. The *Welsh Adverse Childhood Experiences (ACE) Study* (Public Health Wales NHS, 2015) has been undertaken and *Delivering for Today, Investing for Tomorrow: The Government's Programme for Scotland 2018–2019* (Scottish Government, 2018) committed £1.35 million to an *ACE Aware* trauma training programme. But the ACEs movement is controversial. Macvarish and Lee (2019) analysed social policy specialists' views and found that they expressed widespread doubt about ACEs scientific reliability and validity, and significant concern about the way in which the approach negatively constructs parents and individualises complex social issues. The original study defined adversity as physical, sexual and emotional abuse; neglect; domestic violence; parental substance abuse; mental illness; suicide or separation. This narrow stance does not accommodate other adverse experiences which may contribute to long-term outcomes, such as poverty, hunger, homelessness, illness or bereavement. Walsh (2018) questions the language of ACEs, which implies that:

> adversity of any kind is bad or traumatic. While abuse and neglect should always be considered fundamentally wrong, traumatic and preventable, the same cannot always be said for adversity. Everyone will experience adversity at some point and there is often strength and hope to be found in it. Our responses to adversity can nurture resilience and loving relationships while also defining our identities.

The ACEs movement may make people feel defined by early negative experiences which condemn them to an inevitably lower standard of health and attainment, regardless of the fact that many people who experience childhood trauma go on to do well. Walsh (2018) suggests that whilst difficult childhood experiences must not be ignored, inverting the discourse to a positive, affirmative stance of 'hopeful childhoods' would promote a much more optimistic message of empathy, love, compassion and social justice. Trauma-informed social work can represent a powerful, non-pathologising challenge to unhelpful, stigmatising and dehumanising approaches. From a social model, we can look beyond categorisation and seek to understand how the trauma carried from difficult past experiences manifests in unhelpful behaviour in the present, and work with people to develop strategies for moving forward with hope.

Conclusion

This chapter has considered a range of theories which offer understanding of different ways in which people within our society may become vulnerable to risk. There are many, many more theories relevant to this discourse, but we have tried to look across a range of needs around which services are usually organised (physical and mental health needs, disability, learning disability, dementia, etc.), and beyond to socioeconomic factors that cause vulnerability. The theories that we have explored can help us to understand how certain individuals, groups and classes of society become vulnerable to the actions of others at individual and societal levels. This knowledge facilitates a more nuanced perspective of risk that moves beyond locating problems solely in individuals. Social work should safeguard people in the broadest, not the narrowest sense of the word, by recognising how inequality and discrimination create vulnerability and risk and taking action to support empowerment.

PART II

PRACTICE: USING THEORY IN OUR WORK WITH PEOPLE

8 APPLYING THEORY IN PRACTICE

Introduction

Everyone who studies social work at qualifying or post-qualifying level will be familiar with the requirement to relate theory to practice. For some this is straightforward, but many find it confusing. Hopefully, you will have had the benefit of academic teaching that demonstrates how theory relates to practice, and practice education where you are supervised and supported to apply theory in practice. Unfortunately, we know that not everyone experiences this and that, sometimes, links between theory and practice are only made in order to satisfy the requirements of the assignment. When the focus is on how to satisfy the requirements, rather than how to think critically, procedural practice is established, and the likelihood is that this will continue. Newly qualified social workers feel enormous pressure to demonstrate that they can *get on with the job* and that can often mean expedience triumphs over theoretically informed practice. In this chapter we consider the mechanisms you can harness to make applying theory a meaningful aspect of your everyday practice.

Praxis

Praxis is a Greek word associated with the ancient philosopher Aristotle, who proposed that humans perform three basic functions:

- *Theoria,* which can be translated as *thinking*, and is the origin of the word *theory*.
- *Poiesis*, which can be translated as *making*, and is the origin of the word *poetry*.
- *Praxis*, which can be translated as *doing*, and is the origin of the word *practice*.

Praxis describes how theory is enacted, embodied or realised, and is the basis of the ubiquitously used social work term *practice*. Praxis is the translation of thoughts to action, the process by which our theories, formal and informal, become our practice (Teater, 2014. Bernstein (1983) describes praxis as the interplay between ends and means, thoughts and actions: we decide upon the action to be taken in a particular situation through deliberation, using theoretical knowledge to both contemplate what we need to achieve, and construct and refine ways in which we might achieve it.

It's important to recognise that we incorporate theory in our practice in all kinds of ways: purist applications are very rare in social work. We select and weave together elements of different theories to create understandings and responses to individual situations, and this eclectic approach is a key strength of the social work profession (Heslop and Meredith, 2019). But it is also important not to overclaim the use of theory. Are you applying systems theory, or simply recognising that systems, social and cultural factors have impact? Are you assessing a child's attachment pattern, or simply describing a parent and child interacting? It is extremely beneficial to use theory to inform our understanding of a situation, but overstating our expertise is dishonest and unhelpful.

Practice experience Phil

Very soon after qualifying as a social worker, I attended training delivered by an experienced barrister. He explained how he relished social workers citing theory in the witness box because it enabled him to instil doubt on their evidence during cross-examination. He described how he would invite the witness to explain their expertise in this or that theory, quickly establishing the limits of their knowledge with pre-prepared obscure questions which they could not possibly answer. Sometimes he would go so far as to ask the social worker for their views on the work of a particular leading expert, only to reveal that he had made the author up to demonstrate the witness's lack of credibility. In high pressure situations, people can feel tempted to overstate their expertise in order to appear professionally competent. I learnt that it's best to stick to defensible facts when providing evidence to the courts. Although I was committed to using theory to inform my practice, I recognised that different arenas require different approaches and was always circumspect of making claims that I knew more than I actually did.

Critical reflection

Ferguson identifies that in social work, the 'need for professionals to use reflection to learn about and develop their practice is now a universally stated goal' (2018, p. 415). This view is evidenced by the *Professional Capabilities Framework for Social Workers in England* (BASW, 2018a), which includes Critical Reflection and Analysis as its 6th domain. The human need to review actions and learn from experiences in order to develop is obvious, and theoretical concepts of reflection can be traced back to the ancient philosophers. In contemporary times, American educational theorist David Kolb's (b. 1939) work on experiential learning has directly influenced reflective practice. Kolb proposed that individuals learn differently, with some preferring abstract conceptualisation by reading books whilst others prefer active experimentation through participating in an activity. Kolb identified that whilst individuals may have a preferred learning style, everyone is helped to learn through an ongoing process which combines four stages:

- **Concrete experience** – a classroom or real-life situation.
- **Reflective observation** – reviewing the concrete experience to identify its significant elements.
- **Abstract conceptualisation** – using knowledge (theory) to analyse and understand what has happened (theorising).
- **Active experimentation** – making plans and trying out what has been learnt.

Criticality involves interrogating and evaluating information, rather than taking it at face value, therefore when we critically reflect, we focus on identifying and understanding complex or overlooked issues and perspectives. This links very much to Paulo Freire's approach of *critical consciousness* (see Chapter 4), where a person takes active steps to become conscious of previously hidden truths about self and others. Smith stresses the importance of higher education equipping students to critically reflect, because 'Explicitly teaching critical reflection is a logical step towards students being able to recognise and negotiate complex ethical and professional issues' (2011, p. 211). The terms *reflective* and *reflexive* are often conflated and applied interchangeably, however they are distinct. In a postmodern sense, reflexivity involves the practitioner examining their own, unique *positionality* within social systems (Foucault, 1982; Giddens, 1976), for example identifying how core, personal beliefs about the identities of mother or father influence their behaviour towards people who are undertaking those roles. Archer (2003, 2007) considers reflexivity to be the practitioner's sense making process, which is constructed through their relationship with the environment and their internal and external conversations. Cook (2020) explains, 'the professional role requires a critical consciousness – consulting the "self" to facilitate reflective practice and reflexivity. Reflexivity can help us explore the value placed on knowledge and how it is acquired and applied.'

Donald Schön's hugely influential book *The Reflective Practitioner* (1983) is not a social work-specific text, but its impact on the profession is undeniable. Schön explored how professionals improvise responses to meet the challenges of their work, describing how theory and practice are integrated through cycles of experience and lessons learned. Professionals constantly review and evaluate these improvised responses to refine their practice through processes of 'reflection in action' (during practice) and 'reflection on action' (after practice) to think about and link their practice to knowledge (Schön, 1983). Maclean and Harrison (2015) recognise *reflection in action* as the real-time, internal conversation social workers have with themselves as they negotiate situations and take action, but they suggest that this approach is limited in terms of criticality because its short-term nature relies on the practitioner's perspective alone. They believe that the retrospective nature of *reflection on action* allows for much more careful consideration (whether alone or with others) of key events and perspectives. Though it may not pay sufficient attention to aspects of practice which are considered small or routine, it will nevertheless provide valuable learning (Maclean and Harrison, 2015).

Ferguson (2018) is more circumspect about reflection in action, identifying that it is not always possible or desirable. His research following child protection social workers identified that although they sometimes thought critically about what they were doing, often the demands of their interactions were so great that opportunities for reflection were limited. On other occasions, practitioners actively avoided reflection in order to protect themselves from sensory and emotional impact and make their work 'bearable and doable' (Ferguson, 2018, p. 424). Ash (2013) describes similar findings with social workers safeguarding adults. She uses the metaphor of a 'cognitive mask' to explain how practitioners in her study protected themselves from the full force of the distressing situations they encountered. Whilst the mask made their work bearable, she found that it obscured their vision of the wider social, political and cultural context of their work, preventing them from meaningful critical reflection. Ash's metaphor is all the more powerful now that literal mask-wearing has become a common feature of daily life, and we can readily understand how much it alters our experience.

Nobel Prize winning economist Daniel Kahneman (2011) offers another way of considering our thought processes. He identifies two interrelated dimensions to thinking: *fast thinking*, a highly efficient way of using past experience to narrow focus down to a few important details, and *slow thinking,* which incorporates much more information and examines it critically (Figure 8.1). This has obvious similarities with Schön's states of reflection in action and reflection on action. Kahneman (2011) states that fast thinking is our default mode – more than 95% of our thoughts are believed to be unconscious and automatic. However, when we encounter new situations or are under stress, fast thinking is problematic. Fast thinking shuts down our curiosity in order to narrow down our focus and enable us to make fast decisions. The problem is the brain is instinctively prioritising fast decision-making over accurate decision-making. We need to be able to identify when to disrupt our natural instinct and switch to critically reflective slow thinking.

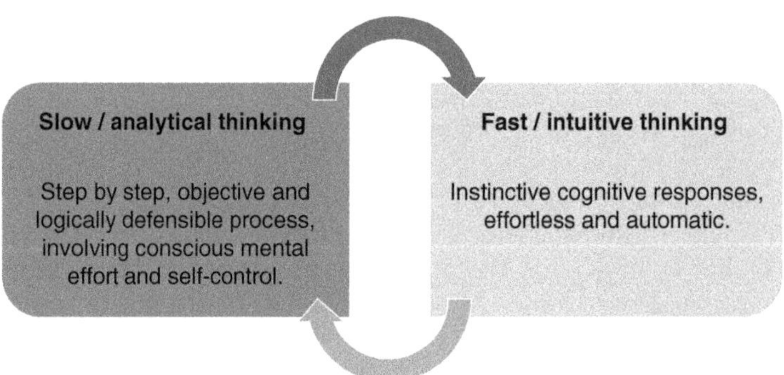

Figure 8.1 Slow thinking/fast thinking

Critical reflection is a complex, multidimensional process where lots of factors are at play. Having reviewed the literature relating to critical reflection, Smith (2011) identified that it largely relates to four interrelated domains (see figure 8.2) through which existing theory is applied as part of sense making, and theorising utilised to develop possible new explanations. Fook's (2002) critical reflection to reflective practice model offers a four-stage process through which practitioners can develop their own practice theory (Figure 8.3).

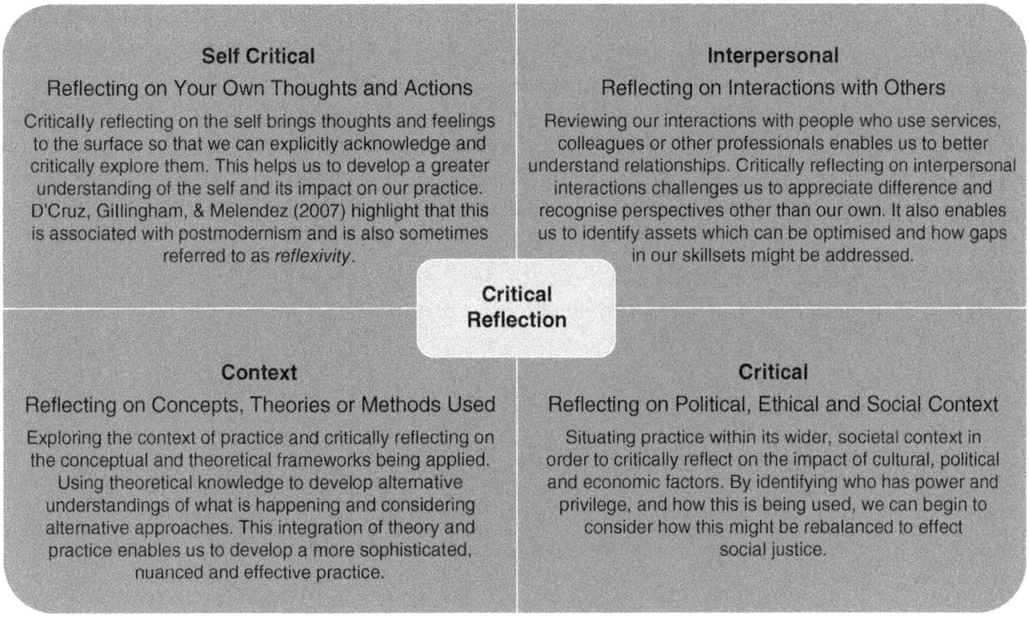

Self Critical
Reflecting on Your Own Thoughts and Actions
Critically reflecting on the self brings thoughts and feelings to the surface so that we can explicitly acknowledge and critically explore them. This helps us to develop a greater understanding of the self and its impact on our practice. D'Cruz, Gillingham, & Melendez (2007) highlight that this is associated with postmodernism and is also sometimes referred to as reflexivity.
Interpersonal
Reflecting on Interactions with Others
Reviewing our interactions with people who use services, colleagues or other professionals enables us to better understand relationships. Critically reflecting on interpersonal interactions challenges us to appreciate difference and recognise perspectives other than our own. It also enables us to identify assets which can be optimised and how gaps in our skillsets might be addressed.
Critical Reflection
Context
Reflecting on Concepts, Theories or Methods Used
Exploring the context of practice and critically reflecting on the conceptual and theoretical frameworks being applied. Using theoretical knowledge to develop alternative understandings of what is happening and considering alternative approaches. This integration of theory and practice enables us to develop a more sophisticated, nuanced and effective practice.
Critical
Reflecting on Political, Ethical and Social Context
Situating practice within its wider, societal context in order to critically reflect on the impact of cultural, political and economic factors. By identifying who has power and privilege, and how this is being used, we can begin to consider how this might be rebalanced to effect social justice.

Figure 8.2 The four domains of critical reflection (adapted from Smith, 2011)

Identifying a critical incident from practice (the existing narrative is told)
Analysing this within a theoretical context
Reflecting and deconstructing dominant discourses (the existing narrative is deconstructed)
Reconstructing emancipatory strategies and processes for change (a new narrative is constructed)

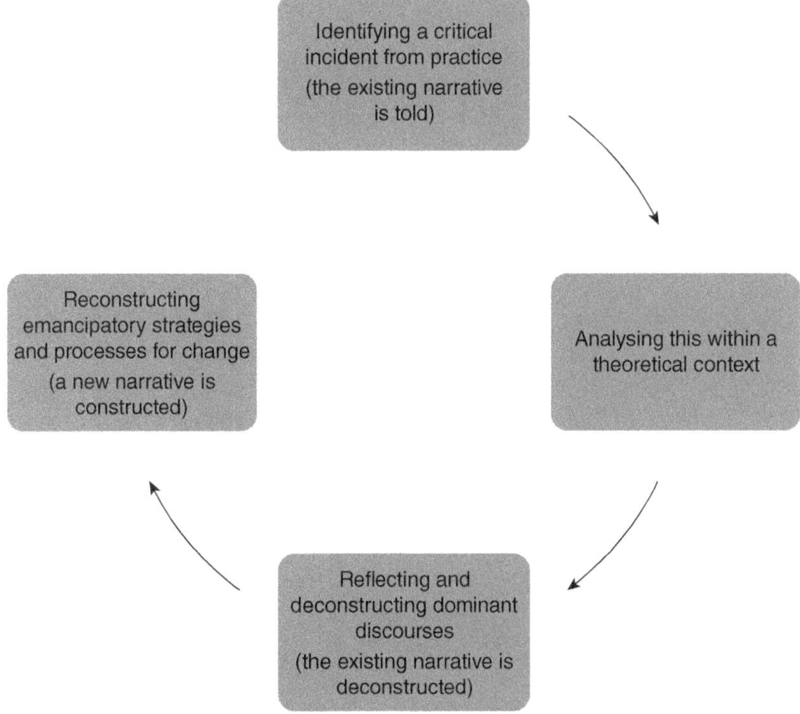

Figure 8.3 Fook's model of critical reflection to reflective practice (2002)

Critical reflection is often incorporated into formal supervision, which we discuss later in this chapter. Many people find writing a helpful tool for reflective practice. The process of organising and articulating thoughts into the written form allows us to apply theory, develop new insights and illuminate previously unnoticed 'gaps' in our understanding. Reflective writing often takes the form of a journal which may be shared in supervision to inform and enhance a critically reflective dialogue. Smith cautions students against proceduralising this opportunity by '[completing] a reflective diary as a perfunctory account of their actions, rather than recognising its potential to improve their thinking or learning' (2011, p. 215). An increasing number of social work practitioners share their critically reflective writings through social media blogs which enable them to establish conversations across the wider social work community.

Lloyd

As a student on placement, Lloyd found keeping a reflective journal to be an extremely helpful tool for using theory to think through practice situations. When working with someone experiencing mental distress, Lloyd began to think about his own, similar experience. He realised for the first time that although he had never thought of himself that way, he had been a mental health service user. Lloyd thought and thought about this and couldn't make sense of this duality of identity, so he decided to write about it. He explored how in one context he had felt powerless and desperate for help from services, and now he was the professional exercising the power of the service to support someone with similar issues. He drew from postmodernism to critically explore how language and context create identities which are allocated status, affording or denying a person power. Lloyd shared his writing in a closed social media group of people on his course, and asked for others' thoughts on it. Lloyd really enjoyed the discussions that ensued, and decided to set up his own blog where he could critically explore issues and share his ideas. Before long, he developed a strong following and regularly engaged in social media discussions with other social work students, service users and professionals across the world. Lloyd realised that his social media interactions became acts of critical reflection as other people's views further developed, challenged and changed his understandings.

Exercise 8.1

There are hundreds of excellent social work blogs – subscribe to one and consider how theory manifests in the blogger's writing. Better still, start your own!

Theoretical and conceptual frameworks

We have thoroughly explored and defined theory throughout this book, so let's briefly turn our attention to concepts before we consider frameworks. Concepts are ideas conceived in the mind, which act as the foundation for mental representations that we can communicate to others. We use the word concept in a lot of ways – blockbuster films are often referred to as 'high-concept'; advertisements may describe a new toothpaste as a 'revolutionary concept', or the latest vehicle as a 'concept car'. In relation to theory, concept is most commonly used to convey essential features of abstract ideas, principles or plans, for example, 'the concept of social justice', 'the organisation has held onto its original concept of providing free advice to anyone in need'.

A framework is a supporting structure which holds something up or contains it – we commonly associate it with buildings, pictures and computer systems. In these examples, a strong framework will provide a great foundation for the object it is supporting, whilst a weak, damaged or incomplete framework will be unstable and might result in serious problems. Theoretical and conceptual frameworks work in exactly the same way, providing structure and stability (or not, as the case may be!) to research and practice. The terms are often used interchangeably, but they are different:

- **A theoretical framework** is the theory – or combination of theories – that underpins your thinking and approach to developing an understanding. It comprises existing theory (or theories) which have been proposed, tested and validated by others.
- **A conceptual framework** is a 'logical structure of connected concepts that help provide a picture or visual display of how ideas relate to one another within the theoretical framework' (Grant and Osanloo, 2014, p. 17).

Social work is guided by legislation and policy which is peppered with concepts which have particular meanings within the social care context – for example, care, support, autonomy, capacity, wellbeing, eligibility, threshold, parenting, vulnerability, service, participation, assessment. These words form our professional language or discourse (see Chapter 4), and are used so frequently that it is easy to forget they are actually a means for quickly and readily conveying enormously complex, theoretical ideas.

Dianne

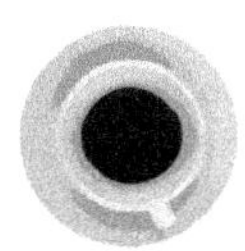

Dianne is working with Jenny, who has experienced long-standing domestic abuse. The local authority has statutory duties towards Jenny under Article 3 of the Human Rights Act 1998, which states, 'No one shall be subjected to torture or to inhuman or degrading treatment or punishment', and under Section 9 of the Care Act 2014, which requires that her care and support needs are assessed, and possibly Section 42, which requires that safeguarding enquiries are made in particular circumstances.

(Continued)

The local authority has incorporated this legislation into its policy and procedures, which form the basis of Dianne's conceptual framework. She is *safeguarding* Jenny from *coercion* and *abuse*, by *assessing* the *risks* to Jenny and identifying Jenny's *needs*. She will *empower* Jenny by providing information, options and *support*. Dianne's tendency to operate with the concepts alone is reductive and makes her a somewhat procedural practitioner. These concepts sit within a complex framework of well-established theories such as *systems theory*, *feminism*, theories of *vulnerability*, *risk, power and control*. Greater understanding of these theories and recognition of how they relate to Jenny could elevate Dianne's practice and create a more individualised response which may be more genuinely empowering and therefore more effective.

Exercise 8.2

Think about the concept of safeguarding. How do you understand it? If you had to explain it to someone who was totally unfamiliar with it, what would you say? What other concepts would your explanation incorporate? Which theories relate to these concepts?

Theorising and hypothesising

Simply put, theorising is the means by which we recognise and develop explanations, whether by applying theories which already exist, or developing new theoretical understandings. We theorise *all of the time*, whether we are conscious of it or not, so in a sense, becoming a more theoretical practitioner is as simple as recognising what you already do! In social work, we theorise at many levels:

- **About the nature of the world** – for instance, why people are disadvantaged, the role of the state, notions of risk, how we conceptualise deserving and undeserving, etc.
- **About the nature of social work** – for instance, what is our role and what are its limits? What is social work practice? What is social work research? When, why and how should we intervene?
- **About the nature of situations faced by communities and individuals that we are involved with** – for instance, how can we best engage with them? How have they been affected by their environment and relationships? How can behaviours be explained?

A theory is a well-established explanation which has been tested in some way and found to produce consistent outcomes, therefore it can be generalised to multiple situations. A *hypothesis* is much more tentative: it is a suggested or possible explanation which has not yet been tested. Hypotheses are sometimes referred to as working theories. They are proposed explanations formed from initial evidence which acts as a starting point for further investigation. In social work, hypothesising provides a formalised mechanism for practitioners to test decision-making processes and early stage assessment opinions through evidence and analysis. It is all too easy to make a snap decision about what is going on in a situation based upon assumption. Singular explanations create singular solutions which lack nuance and personalisation. The process of hypothesising allows for multiple explanations to be explored, so that practitioners can hold concurrent opinions about what is going on, gradually eliminating possibilities to arrive at a defensible conclusion.

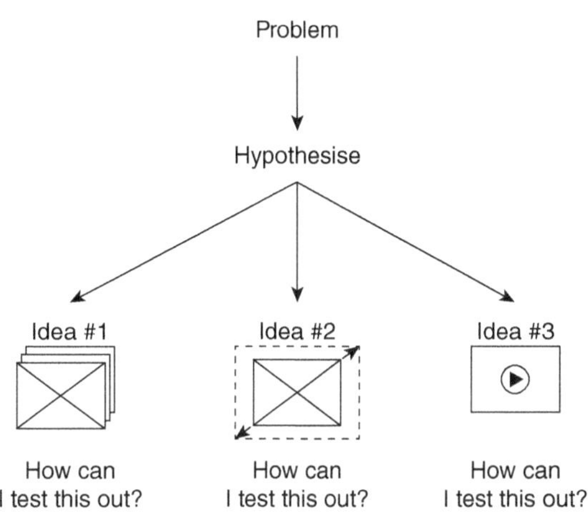

Figure 8.4 Model of hypothesising

Akram and Karen

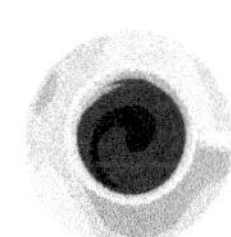

Akram is managing the duty desk with Karen overseeing his work. He opens a referral from a School Safeguarding Lead about a 15-year-old girl, Clara, who is not previously known to services. The referral states that over the past few months, teachers have noticed a marked change in Clara's behaviour which seems to have coincided with her mother marrying a much younger man, Jeff. The standard of Clara's work has dropped, and she has been uncharacteristically rude to teachers, swearing and on a handful of occasions, walking out of school. Clara's mother is apologetic but not particularly concerned when the school contacted her about this. Clara talks a lot about Jeff and today, one of her friends disclosed to a teacher that Clara had told her that she and Jeff are in love and he is waiting until she is 16 to leave her mother and run off with her.

Akram is extremely alarmed and tells Karen that he has received a referral about a man grooming and sexually abusing a 15-year-old girl. Karen reads the referral, then tells Akram that he needs to take a step back and not jump to conclusions. She asks him to take 10 minutes and develop three different hypotheses for what might be going on, think about how they could be tested out, and then come back and discuss them with her.

Exercise 8.3

What could be the negative consequences of running with Akram's first instinct?

From the information you have, develop three other hypotheses to offer possible explanations for what is happening.

How could you test these hypotheses to rule them in or out?

Supervision

Supervision in social work takes many forms, but loosely speaking, is space to reflect and be guided and mentored by others in marrying values, knowledge and skills. The Munro Review of Child Protection (2011) described supervision as the

> core mechanism for helping social workers critically reflect on the understanding they are forming of the family, of considering their emotional response and whether this is adversely affecting their reasoning, and for making decisions about how best to help. (Munro, 2011, para. 4.10)

Munro's stance that good quality supervision is integral to good quality practice was shared by the Social Work Reform Board (2012), who recognised supervision's central role in best supporting children, adults and families involved with social services. BASW (2011) propose that 'good quality supervision should improve social worker's capacity, confidence, competence and morale, leading to a better service for those who need social work.' (BASW, 2011, p. 5). However, the same policy highlights that increasing emphasis on managerial approaches to supervision 'has led to the reduction in the reflective aspects of supervision, loss of professional autonomy in decision making and a poorer service for service users' (BASW, 2011, p. 5).

Harris (1998) identifies how new managerialism (see Chapter 3) shifted perceptions of supervision: in the 1970s and early 1980s it was seen primarily as a supportive and developmental tool for the practitioner, but from the late 1980s onwards, it has increasingly followed an administrative model, becoming a mechanism for performance management and managerial/agency control. This is evidenced by Donnellan and Jack's research with Newly Qualified Social Workers (NQSWs) and their managers (2008). Whilst NQSWs reported wanting supervision to provide the opportunity to discuss cases in depth, and develop reflective practice skills, the researchers found that supervision tended to focus much more on what agencies needed NQSWs to know and do, than it did on supporting NQSWs to develop their individual professional identities. Contemporary social work supervision combines multiple purposes (Baginsky et al., 2010; Beddoe, 2010), which gives conflicting and confusing messages to practitioners. For example, in a supervision where the casework comes first on the agenda and performance second, a social worker may be advised to spend more time assessing a person to get a clearer understanding of their situation, then later be warned that their recording is not up to date and must be prioritised over direct work. It seems that the multiple purposes which supervision is used to meet can mean that it starts to mirror the often reactive nature of practice, becoming a place for meeting organisational demands, rather than a supportive space to pause, think and apply theoretical knowledge (Noble and Irwin, 2009).

There is also evidence that the nature, frequency and quality of social work supervision is inconsistent (BASW, 2011; Manthorpe et al., 2015; Noble and Irwin, 2009). Manthorpe et al. (2015) explored how NQSWs, managers and directors viewed and experienced supervision. They found that many line managers spoke of maintaining an open-door policy for *informal* supervision. Whilst it is important to have opportunities to critically reflect with managers and colleagues, informal supervision is by definition not ring-fenced time, and its on-the-hoof nature makes it subject to interruptions and time constraints. Informal supervision is more likely to be directive or advisory than explorative and theoretical.

So, what should good supervision look like? Unsurprisingly, research highlights that the nature of the relationship between supervisor and supervisee is critical (Carpenter et al., 2012). Carpenter et al. (2012) identify that social work supervision is of good quality when it explores worker effectiveness, pays attention to task assistance, and provides social and emotional support. The often highly emotionally charged nature of social work makes it important that supervision provides opportunities for reflection (Carpenter et al., 2012), and support which is 'rigorously reflective, analytical, and critical, taking fully into account the feelings and sensory experiences that may have been split off in action and not thought about' (Ferguson, 2018, p. 427).

Manthorpe et al. (2015, p. 59) asked NQSWs, 'What do formal supervision meetings with your line manager usually cover?' Fewer than a quarter of those in their first year of practice reported that supervision helped them to apply theoretical approaches or explanations to their work, and by the second year after qualifying, this fell to less than one in 10. One manager noted:

> I can almost still say what are my major influences theory-wise, which I think is especially important in front-line social work because it is so reactive, and we lose reflection, we lose the theoretical underpinning, we lose sight of a lot of what happens, and we're just reacting daily due to the resources issue and everything else. But I think it's our job as front-line managers to try and bring some of that back in with supervision. And it's surprising actually, the lack of that. (Manthorpe et al., 2015, p. 59)

This view suggests that consideration of theory as a key component of supervision is dependent on how much the supervisor values theory. Research supports our strong belief that supervision should be critically reflective and theoretically informed, because the benefits of this extend much further than the individual situation being discussed. Williams and Rutter (2015) propose that critical dialogues and questioning in supervision develop learning and knowledge and increase efficacy. On an individual level, critical questioning encourages reflexivity by drawing out assumptions, underlying thoughts, personal givens and accepted truths. Skilled, critical questioning from an experienced and supportive supervisor enables the practitioner to relate theory to their practice and move beyond description to a more meaningful analysis. Collectively, dialogue and critical questioning become continuous conversations which can help to create a whole workplace culture of learning (Williams and Rutter, 2015). Ferguson (2018) suggests that good experiences of supervision can provide a blueprint for practitioners to develop their own 'internal supervisor' to help them to navigate difficult practice situations and tolerate anxiety in order to allow 'vital insights about the service user and helping process to arise' (2018, p. 425).

Exercise 8.4

Does theory feature in your supervision? How? If theory doesn't feature on your supervision agenda in a regular or meaningful way, ask for it to be included as a standing item.

Using the mechanisms we have introduced in this chapter you could:

- identify a particular theory which you want to explore in relation to a piece of practice and read up on it before supervision
- start a critically reflective journal to use in supervision
- theorise about a piece of practice in supervision, developing different hypotheses to test out
- work with your supervisor to identify the conceptual and theoretical frameworks you have been working under/will be working under.
- use Smith's four domains (Figure 8.2) to guide your critical reflection on a piece of practice
- use Fook's critical reflection to reflective practice model (Figure 8.3) to develop your own theory of practice.

Author's experience Cat

As a social work student on my final placement, I was pretty shocked when one of the social workers I was introduced to told me that she looked forward to having students in the team because she learned so much about theory. I expected I would be learning about theory from the practising social workers, not the other way round! Over the course of the placement I came to see what she actually meant. The team – like all social work teams – was extremely busy, and outside of supervision, there was precious-little space for reflective discussion and theorising. My presence changed that dynamic because I asked questions which made the social workers explain their behaviour, assessments and decision-making and in the process of articulating this, it ceased to be instinctive and unconscious. Others in the office would chip in, expanding the discussion with alternative views and insights, and they seemed to thoroughly enjoy the opportunity to learn from each other and theorise together. I didn't know the word praxis at that time, but that is exactly what was happening. I was delighted to be included in these discussions and to be the stimulus for them, although a little sad to think that the practitioners saw them as indulgent unless they were for the benefit of a student.

Many years later, I was given a newly created post where I was responsible for the supervision of staff in a large, multidisciplinary mental health team. I set up a supervision group at which anyone in the team could present practice situations that they were struggling with. The multidisciplinary mix of the group provided new theoretical perspectives, which often led to new insights on how to move forward and invigorated previously deflated staff. Many children's social work teams now utilise systemic models of practice which incorporate group supervision as a fundamental element of their approach. Opportunities to share and think about our practice with others is enormously valuable as it challenges us to articulate our thoughts, theorise together and recognise aspects that we may have missed.

Conclusion

If social work was a process that could be learned and then followed, professional social workers simply would not exist: anyone can follow a process. Social work is a highly skilled role, because the situations that we work in are complex and the consequences of our decisions are very serious, so it is vital that our practice is robust and fit for purpose. Theoretical knowledge is not a luxury, only to be used in academic assignments or an indication that a practitioner has too much time on their hands. It must not be the first thing that is sacrificed when we are pushed for time and the stakes are high – in fact, this is exactly when we need to make time to critically reflect and use theory to consider what is happening, what we are doing and why. We hope that this chapter has helped you to consider how to incorporate theory into your everyday practice.

9 CHILDREN AND THEIR FAMILIES

Practice context

Internationally, the civil, political, economic, social and cultural rights of children are established through a human rights treaty – the United Nations Convention on the Rights of the Child (UNCRC, 1989). This represents an enormously significant commitment to the world's youngest citizens, and as UNICEF describes, is premised upon the profound idea that children

> are not just objects who belong to their parents and for whom decisions are made, or adults in training. Rather, they are human beings and individuals with their own rights... childhood is separate from adulthood, and lasts until 18; it is a special, protected time, in which children must be allowed to grow, learn, play, develop and flourish with dignity. (UNICEF, 1989)

The UNCRC is the most widely ratified human rights treaty in history, and the UK has been signed up to it since 1991. Nations that ratify the UNCRC are bound to it by international law, and required to periodically report on the status of children's rights in their country. The four countries of the United Kingdom (England, Wales, Scotland and Northern Ireland) each have their own national legislative process regarding childcare; whilst these legislative processes are all slightly different, they each relate to the UNCRC. Article 18 of UNCRC obliges states to allow parents to exercise their parental responsibilities. Parental responsibility (PR) is defined in Section 3(1) of the Children Act 1989 as being: 'all the rights, duties, powers, responsibilities and authority which by law a parent of a child has in relation to the child and his property'. The term attempts to focus on the parent's *duties towards*, rather than their *rights over* their child. PR provides legal authority to make important decisions in relation to a child, such as:

- choosing, registering or changing a child's name
- deciding where a child lives

- deciding the religion a child should be brought up in
- deciding about education and where a child goes to school
- consenting to a child's operation or medical treatment
- appointing a guardian for a child in the event of the death of a parent

Where PR is shared, important decisions must be made jointly. Children may be regarded to be 'looked after' by the local authority due to many situations, for example, safeguarding concerns, issues relating to parental capacity, parental unavailability, however, even in cases where a child is made subject to a care order, the local authority shares parental responsibility with the parent(s) and must include them in its decision-making. A living parent with PR does not lose it unless the child is legally adopted.

In England and Wales, children's welfare is addressed primarily under the framework of the Children Act 1989 (in Scotland the Children (Scotland) Act, 1995 and in Northern Ireland the Children (Northern Ireland) Order, 1995) and parents are assumed to care appropriately for children unless assessed otherwise. All organisations involved with children are responsible for their welfare and for safeguarding them from harm (Children and Families Act 2014), and legislation places a duty on local authorities, NHS Clinical Commissioning Groups and the police to work in local partnerships to support children's needs in their area (Children and Social Work Act 2017). However, the local authority has overall lead responsibility, and childcare social workers have a statutory mandate to respond to child welfare concerns, make reasonable checks (with for instance family, health, education and police), safeguard the welfare of children in need (Section 17, CA89), and undertake child protection enquiries (Section 47, CA89) to ensure children are safe and cared for appropriately. *Working Together to Safeguard Children* (Department for Education, 2018) provides detailed statutory guidance on the appropriate actions professionals should take where

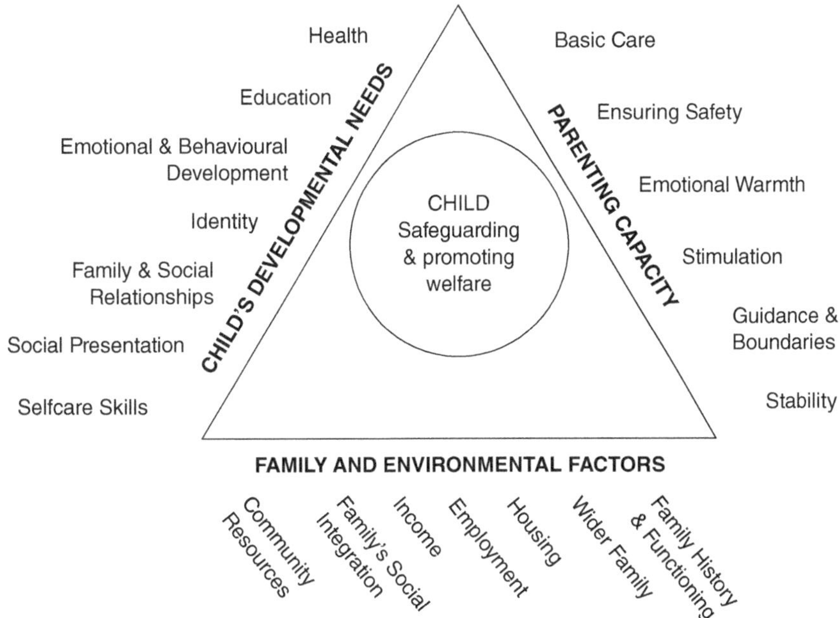

Figure 9.1 Framework for Assessment (Department for Education, 2018, p. 27)

there are safeguarding concerns. It includes the Framework for Assessment (see Figure 9.1), which is based on the ecological systems theory (see Chapter 6), and a series of flow charts outlining actions to be taken by professionals at different stages (see Figure 9.2, for example).

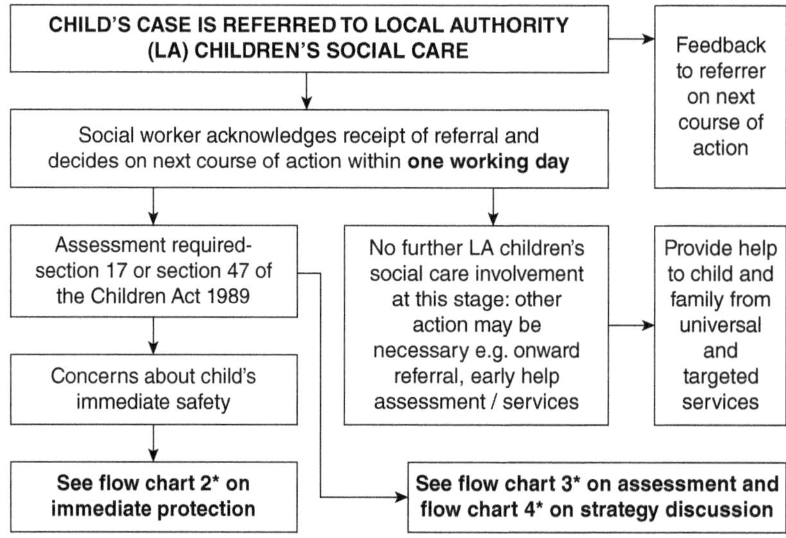

Figure 9.2 Action taken when a child is referred to local authority children's social care services (Department for Education, 2018, p. 32 [* to see flow charts 2, 3 and 4 see Department for Education, 2018])

The English safeguarding model is therefore a combination of a techno-rational approach involving prescribed procedure, and professional assessment dependent on the social worker's decision-making (Helm, 2011). A study by Vibeke and Turney (2017) compared professional judgement forming in England, which they argue is bureaucratised through process, with Norway, which is less dependent on process and relies more on practitioner autonomy in decision-making. They concluded that neither approach is problem-free. Where professional judgement guides decision-making, there is little requirement to clarify how decisions are made; conversely, constraining professional judgements to a procedural model may undermine practitioner' confidence and critical thinking (see Chapter 8).

Trish's Safeguarding Assessment

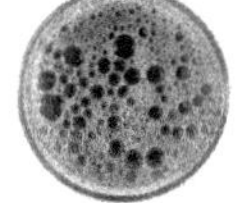

You can read more about these theories and concepts in the following chapters:

- Responsibilisation; Proceduralism – Chapter 3
- Systemic approaches; Family relationships; Attachment (insecure, disorganised) – Chapter 6
- Social learning theory – Chapter 5
- Risk; Victim-blaming; Safeguarding – Chapter 7
- Critical thinking; Supervision; Hypothesising – Chapter 8

Trish is covering the office duty desk, and a referral is handed over from the out of hours Emergency Duty Team (EDT). In the early hours of the morning, police alerted the EDT that an 8-year-old boy, Noah, had fallen down the stairs of the family home during a domestic assault on his mother by her partner. Noah and his mother were taken to hospital; the partner was arrested and taken into police custody. Trish checks the local authority records and finds that Noah spent some time living with foster carers when he was 3, whilst his mother served a short prison sentence. More recently, school contacted Children's Services to highlight concerns about Noah's aggressive behaviour with other children. This was not deemed to be a **safeguarding** issue, and resulted in a referral to an educational psychologist. Although Trish very much believes in **responsibilisation** and that parental responsibility is sacrosanct unless there are **safeguarding** concerns, she feels this was a missed opportunity to assess Noah's home situation and act sooner to protect Noah.

Trish contacts the hospital and learns that Noah is recovering and will be ready for discharge later on today. Unfortunately, his mother is much more seriously injured and has not regained consciousness. A decision about where Noah is going to be cared for upon discharge needs to be made quickly, and Trish consults her manager, Ali. Ali agrees for Trish to acknowledge receipt of the referral with the police and to make further checks before considering undertaking a Section 47 Enquiry (Children Act 1989). He will not yet be drawn on whether or not Noah needs to be accommodated by the local authority – he encourages Trish to **think systemically**, consider **family relationships** and identify any possible persons connected to Noah who can care for him. He also suggests, as a precaution, she contact the local authority placement officer to advise about the situation and agrees that he will liaise with his manager about potential funding of an emergency foster placement for Noah.

The police advise Trish they are seriously concerned about Noah's wellbeing and are considering arresting his mother for pushing him down the stairs. They want Trish to go to the hospital with them so that they can speak to Noah, but Trish is concerned about doing this without parental consent. From the records held by the local authority, Trish is unable to identify any family support available to Noah. She speaks to Noah's school, his educational psychologist and the school nursing service, none of whom know of any family other than Noah's mum. A more worrying picture begins to emerge as the professionals Trish speaks to express multiple concerns about Noah's aggressive behaviour, his inability to make **relationships** and form friendships, and his self-esteem. It seems that he has frequently presented at school with minor, unexplained injuries. Trish weighs up this information as she receives it, mentally assessing the historical **risks** indicated, and analysing how they may relate to Noah's current situation and inform what she needs to do to keep him safe. She thinks Noah may have been witnessing or suffering domestic abuse for some time, which would account for his injuries and behaviour at school. His aggression may be **socially learnt** through witnessing domestic violence. Trish considers that Noah may experience **insecure attachments** because of his relationship with his mum – maybe she prioritises her partner over him? Trish recognises this is a **hypothesis** but feels it is certainly worth considering because it can help explain his behaviour towards other children, which could be categorised as **disorganised**.

The hospital calls again, asking about the discharge arrangements for Noah. Trish goes back to Ali, emphasising the police concerns and the evidence she has collated from Noah's records and from speaking to education and health. She explains her **hypothesis** and strongly advocates for a Section 47 Enquiry and application for an Emergency Protection Order (EPO) to enable the local authority to provide immediate short-term protection and make alternative care arrangements for Noah. Ali is sceptical about Trish's **hypothesis** – whilst he acknowledges that it seems plausible, he reminds her that she has not yet spoken to Noah or his mum, who surely represent the most vital sources of information here. He stresses that the urgency of the current situation should not mean that assumptions are made about Noah's life or his mum's parenting, and encourages Trish to think critically to avoid falling into **victim-blaming** someone who has suffered a very serious assault.

Ali's **supervision** helps Trish to pause and recognise how overwhelmed she has felt by the immediacy of this situation and pressure from the hospital and police. Ali helps her to differentiate between long- and short-term considerations. In the short-term, the pressing need is to safely place Noah somewhere whilst his mother is in hospital. Ali agrees that as Trish can't speak with Noah's mum, and is not aware of anyone else with PR, an EPO seems appropriate. It will give the local authority the legal authority to look after Noah when he leaves hospital. EPOs last for eight days, with a possible extension of up to a further seven days, to a maximum of 15 days. Ali agrees to speak to the legal team, emphasising his hope that during the time frame of an EPO, Noah's mum will regain consciousness and be able to take part in decision-making. Ali instigates a Section 47 Enquiry and directs Trish to arrange a Strategy Discussion. However, he cautions Trish to retain a curious stance within this **procedural response**, remaining open to alternative perspectives and developing and exploring **multiple hypotheses** in order to understand Noah and his mum's situation.

Reflective exercise 9.1

Imagine yourself in Trish's position. Firstly, how do you feel about Noah's situation and how might you react to your feelings? ? Secondly, consider two theories which Trish could use to understand Noah's mum's situation.

Martin and Akram's Looked After Child Review

You can read more about these theories and concepts in the following chapters:

- Child development – Chapter 5
- Attachment – Chapter 6
- Trauma; Medical/Social models (pathologising); Labelling – Chapter 7
- Learning disability – Chapter 14

As part of Akram's induction with the team, he is given the chance to attend a Looked After Child Review with Martin. Children looked after by local authorities should receive regular reviews (at least every six months) and this one is for a young woman, Nadia, who is 16 and living in foster care. There isn't long until the review at the foster carers' home, and Akram can't ask Martin about Nadia as he is at a meeting off-site and intends to meet him there. Akram wants to be prepared, so he decides to quickly read what he can from Nadia's electronic records. He learns that as a young child, Nadia fled a war zone with her family. For a time, they lived in a refugee camp where conditions were very difficult and privacy and safety extremely hard to maintain. During this time, both Nadia and her mother were sexually assaulted.

The family eventually managed to relocate to England, and Nadia began attending primary school. Shortly afterwards, the school made a referral to Children's Services, noting that physically Nadia presented as much older than her actual age of 10, but developmentally she presented much younger. She was diagnosed as being globally developmentally delayed with possible **learning disability** and moved to a special educational needs school. At the new school, staff became concerned about Nadia's withdrawn behaviour, neglected appearance and poor personal hygiene. Akram notes that a Section 47 Enquiry was undertaken by Martin, and this established that the whole family had been severely **traumatised** by their experience as refugees and that Nadia was experiencing neglect, and emotional abuse. Eventually, the ongoing complexity of the family situation led to Nadia being accommodated by the local authority. She moved to her current foster placement four years ago when she was 12. Akram had not expected any of this and feels extremely emotional after reading about Nadia's history. He can't imagine how difficult it must have been for the family to go through so much in order to try and reach safety, only to achieve this and then be torn apart by the impact of trauma. He stops reading Nadia's records and heads off to get the bus and meet Martin.

Akram meets Martin outside the carers' home and they are welcomed inside. It is immediately obvious how much Nadia and the carers like Martin, and that they have been looking forward to seeing him – Nadia has made a cake. Akram is surprised to find that Nadia is a typical 16-year-old; she seems happy, confident and relaxed, and speaks clearly with a local accent. The review is very positive, Nadia is making excellent progress at school and she is considering her sixth form options. She would like to attend university and the carers have said they will look after her until she finishes university, at which point they intend to retire from fostering. Martin gives Akram a lift home. He explains what an impact Nadia had on his practice, and how much he has learned through working with her. When Nadia first came to the attention of Children's Services, she had been through so much and spoke very little English. Adoption of a **medical model** meant that rather than considering how **trauma** had impacted on her development, her presentation was pathologised. Nadia lost what few relationships she had developed in England when she was sent to a different school. A short while later, Martin's assessment was instrumental in the decision that Nadia could no longer live with her parents, and although he knew that this was in her best interests, he was acutely aware that Nadia was left with no established relationships. Over the next few months as Nadia moved from short-term placement to short-term placement, Martin was an important point of consistency for her, and inevitably became an **attachment** figure. When Martin eventually managed to organise Nadia's current placement with long-term foster carers, she blossomed in her new, stable and loving environment and felt a sense of belonging with the family. She quickly caught up on developmental milestones and was transferred into mainstream school.

Reflective exercise 9.2

Why do you think Nadia benefited from Martin's long-term support? Do you see any problems with him remaining involved? What would you do?

Karen's parenting assessment

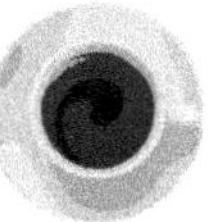

You can read more about these theories and concepts in the following chapters:

- Anti-oppressive practice – Chapter 4
- Grief and loss: Systems theory; Relationships – Chapter 6
- (Intergenerational) trauma – Chapter 7

Karen has been working with a little girl, Ella, aged 2, and her mother, Tanya. Karen knows that Tanya has a long history of difficult involvement with local authority social workers. As a child, Tanya experienced a great deal of adversity stemming largely from her parents' addiction to opiates. Tanya experienced neglect and missed a great deal of school. Eventually she was placed in residential care, and around this time she started to cut herself. Tanya's lifestyle is typically described as chaotic: she self-harms, is intermittently alcohol-dependent and has had several abusive relationships. Tanya's two older children have been removed from her care – one has been adopted and one lives in residential care. Tanya was eventually given a diagnosis of emotionally unstable personality disorder. Labelling someone as personally disordered is controversial, but Tanya found it enormously helpful to have an explanation for her situation. She attended a dialectical behaviour therapy (DBT) group and this helped her to develop coping strategies and abstain from self-harm and alcohol. Tanya formed a new relationship and became pregnant with Ella. With a great deal of support and careful monitoring from Children's Services, Tanya initially managed well, and Ella appeared to be thriving in her care. Unfortunately, Tanya's partner unexpectedly died, and her **grief** led her back to destructive coping strategies and significantly impacted her ability to care for Ella. Ella has been living with her paternal grandmother, but this arrangement is short-term.

Karen likes Tanya and really feels for her. She recognises through an **anti-oppressive** stance that Tanya's current situation is very much related to her own experiences of childhood maltreatment and oppression. Karen's knowledge of **systems theory** informs her understanding of how people's relationships and environments affect them. She uses a genogram (a **systemic** tool) to identify patterns of **intergenerational trauma** over three generations of Tanya's family. Karen has tried really hard to engage Tanya, but she has refused to cooperate with the assessment, won't attend parenting classes and has been quite aggressive with the psychologist. Unfortunately, Karen's assessment, supported by psychology reports, concludes that Tanya cannot safely parent Ella and the child's future wellbeing should be supported through adoption. In her court report, Karen includes the genogram and an ecomap to highlight the **systems of**

relationships and support available to Tanya and Ella. Whilst providing evidence at court, Karen is careful not to overclaim her expertise – she reflects on Tanya's childhood experiences and mentions **intergenerational trauma**, but keeps within the scope of her parenting assessment. The court agrees with the local authority Care Plan and the plan for adoption. Karen knows that this outcome perpetuates Tanya's negative view of social workers, and that the removal of another child will inflict further **grief, loss** and psychological **trauma**. Karen hopes that placing Ella with adoption carers will give her a positive experience of stable family life and break the cycle of intergenerational trauma, but she is experienced and realistic to know that adoption brings its own problems. Social workers cannot predict the future, and only time will tell whether Ella's adoption is successful and even if it is, what emotional and psychological impact it has had on her.

Reflective exercise 9.3

How do you think Tanya will react to Ella's adoption? Now consider two different theoretical perspectives which contextualise Tanya's experiences.

10 FOSTER AND KINSHIP CARE

Practice context

In the UK, foster care is a state-regulated activity where children unable to reside with their birth family are 'looked after' by approved foster families (Department for Education, 2011a, 2011b). A child enters the looked after system either through a voluntary agreement between a person with parental responsibility and a local authority under Section 20 of the Children Act 1989, or when a court order places a child in the care of the local authority (for example a care order under Section 31 of the Children Act 1989).

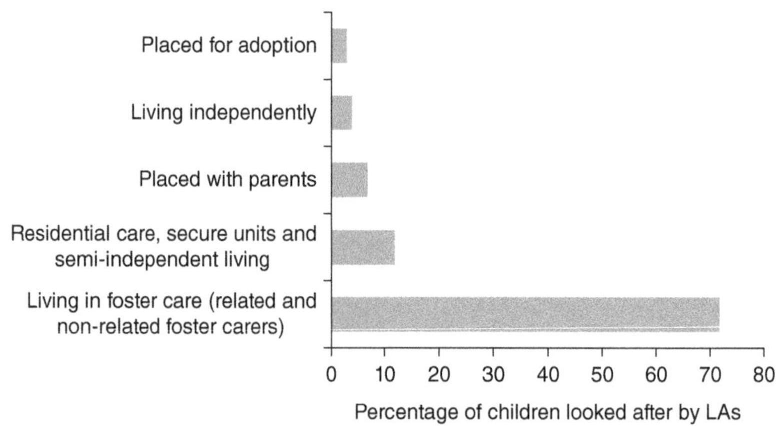

Figure 10.1 Placement types and their frequency (Department for Education, 2019)

Table 10.1 Types of UK foster care placement

Type of Fostering	Description
Emergency fostering	Placement for a child which is made during an emergency, often with little notice, and intended to last only a few days or weeks. Information on the child and family may be limited.
Short-term fostering	Planned placements to meet a short-term need, or to bridge until a long-term permanent option is identified. Sadly, it is not uncommon for children to remain in short-term placements for years in lieu of an approved permanent placement.
Long-term fostering	Such placements are intended to provide children with stability and a place to live and be cared for until adulthood.
Kinship care or family and friends fostering	Related foster carers are formally approved and supported, though local arrangements for this are variable. Kinship care, when formally arranged, is also known as family and friends fostering, related foster carers and connected person.
Fostering for adoption	The Children and Families Act 2014 placed a new duty on local authorities. Where a looked after child may be adopted, the local authority should consider placing the child with foster carers who are also approved as prospective adopters.
Remand fostering	Specialist foster carers who provide a placement for children and young people who are on remand and awaiting sentencing.
Short break fostering	Packages of care support which may include overnight stays for the child with a foster carer. The child does not become a 'looked after' child unless this extends beyond 14 consecutive nights or 38 nights during a year.

More specifically:

> A child is looked after by a local authority if s/he is in their care by reason of a care order or is being provided with accommodation under section 20 of the 1989 Act for more than 24 hours with the agreement of the parents, or the child if s/he is aged 16 or over (section 22(1) and (2) of the 1989 Act). (Department for Education, 2015, p. 16)

There are over 75,420 children and young people in the care of English local authorities and of these, 55,200 are placed in foster care (CoramBAAF, 2018). Figure 10.1 breaks down placement types by frequency and Table 10.1 describes the different kinds of foster care.

The majority of looked after children in foster care live with carers to whom they have no biological link. The Fostering Regulations (Department for Education, 2011a) relate to foster carers approved by local authorities as well as those approved through authorised fostering agencies (third sector and independent agencies). Approximately a third of all children living in foster care are placed with independent foster care providers (Foyle, 2015). Foster carers are required to undertake an assessment which is presented to a fostering panel, though the final decision on approval is made by the fostering agency decision-maker. The 'CoramBAAF Form F assessment' is the most commonly used format to assess prospective foster carers (Chapman, 2019). Foster carers are supported by a *supervising social worker* (sometimes known as a *link worker* or *fostering officer*), defined by the National Minimum Standards for Foster Care (Department for Education, 2011b) as distinct from the child's social worker. Research indicates foster carers feel austerity has had a negative impact, with many reporting the allowances they receive have been cut and that they experience reduced access to social workers and other services (Cann and Lawson, 2016).

Approximately 18% of looked after children are fostered by family members or friends, arrangements usually referred to as *kinship care* (CoramBAAF, 2018). Kinship care has increased over the last decade (Wijedasa, 2015) and is seen as a cost-effective option when compared to residential or stranger-based foster care (Azizet et al., 2012). Most kinship arrangements are made informally within families without any social work involvement, and can relate to part-time and short-term as well as long-term and full-time care. In some situations, kinship carers are approved as foster carers – for example, when they are caring for children looked after by a local authority, during court order applications or when kinship carers seek additional support.

Judith – young person missing from placement

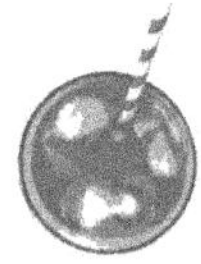

You can read more about these theories and concepts in the following chapters:

- Radical perspectives – Chapter 4
- Erikson's psychosocial stages of development (Identity versus Confusion) – Chapter 5
- Safeguarding; Risk; Culture of fear – Chapter 7

Judith is working with foster carers who look after Magda, who is 16 years old. Last night Magda went missing from her foster placement. Government statistics show that during 2018, incidents of children and young people being missing or away from placement were reported for 11% of looked after children. The statistics report that when children/young people go missing they tend to do so multiple times with an average of 6.2 missing incidents per child who went missing (Department for Education, 2019). Judith contacts the foster carers for an update and fortunately, Magda was safely returned by the police during the night. The foster carers are very uncomfortable with the situation and ask to meet with all involved professionals and the police to agree protocols to control Magda's behaviour in order to **safeguard** her.

Judith is concerned about Magda's welfare as she regularly goes missing. She is also aware that the foster carers impose a very strict curfew, and her knowledge of **Erikson's psychosocial stages of development** informs her that Magda is at the stage of ***Identity versus Confusion***, testing boundaries as she moves through adolescence towards adulthood. Judith is very conscious that it is important for Magda to explore her **identity** and wonders whether or not the foster carers are able to proportionately respond to her need to seek independence and autonomy. She knows that the carers are really committed to Magda, but her knowledge of **risk** and **cultures of fear** helps her to contextualise how frightened they are that they will be held accountable if she comes to any harm. Judith has been in this situation many times before and it always makes her feel conflicted. Her **radical perspective** is that the state should not seek to control its citizens – young people have the right to make choices about how they socialise. She firmly believes that young people should be supported to form their **identity**, which includes learning from making mistakes. It is important that Magda is not held to a higher standard than any other young person of her age would be, just because she is in foster care. However, Judith is also experienced and realistic enough to be aware that Magda may be placing herself at **risk** when her whereabouts are unknown, or there may be unrecognised reasons why she is going missing that need to be identified and considered.

Judith recognises that it is critical that Magda does not feel that she is being excluded from discussions and planning about her, or that decisions will be made on the basis of the carers' perspectives without the balance of hers. Judith wants Magda to know that her increasing maturity is being recognised and respected, even if people disagree with some of her behaviours. She sets up a planning meeting to include the foster carers, professionals and Magda. Judith feels that this approach can facilitate an open dialogue and frank exchange of views. It reconciles her **radical** values that young people should have autonomy and choice with the need to identify and manage the **risks** that Magda's behaviour may present.

Reflective exercise 10.1

Consider how age and gender may influence the ways practitioners work with young people. Identify an alternative theoretical perspective Judith could have adopted when working with Magda.

Akram's kinship care support

You can read more about these theories and concepts in the following chapters:

- Theory and social work (informal and formal theories) – Chapter 1
- Responsibilisation – Chapter 3
- Social learning – Chapter 5
- Systems theories; Attachments; Secure base model – Chapter 6
- Risk; Safeguarding – Chapter 7

Akram has been asked by his practice educator, Dianne, to work with some kinship carers whose usual supervising social worker has just left post. Dianne tells him that they are a lovely couple in their mid-sixties who look after their two granddaughters aged 5 and 7. Akram remembers a lecture at university about how **responsibilisation** and reduced state involvement prioritises support within families and that legally, social workers should consider kinship care, in accordance with the Children Act 1989, when parents are unable to look after birth-children.

Akram doesn't see any problems with this; he fully believes that families are best able to support their members. He believes that as state resources are so limited, social work has to focus on the area of greatest need – responding to **risks** and **safeguarding** issues. Akram is unsure about working with these grandparents, as he feels that this is a family situation and there is no role for social work, but he arranges a home visit.

Ahead of the visit, Akram thinks about theories he has been taught at university which might be relevant to this family's situation – perhaps **systems theory**, **attachments** and **social learning** apply here? But Akram is not yet really sure how these theories fit in practice or how he would use them. He feels apprehensive and worried the carers will only see him as a student when he wants to be seen as a professional. He doesn't want to come across as naive or false by pretending to use theory that he doesn't understand. He decides he will undertake the visit first, and think about theory later.

Akram observes that the home is very pleasant and clean. The children interact with their grandparents in a confident, relaxed and loving way. They are clearly entertained and well stimulated by a range of appropriate toys and books. Akram is reminded of his own childhood relationship with his grandparents and is slightly irritated that Dianne has involved him in a situation where there are no **risks** to address. He chats with the grandparents, explaining that he will be working with them for the next five months in place of their regular supervising social worker. The grandparents share how worried they are about their daughter (the children's mother), who has serious mental health issues. Akram encourages them to focus on strengths and highlights that the children are obviously happy and thriving. He congratulates them for providing the best possible circumstances for their grandchildren in their mother's absence. He leaves on an extremely positive note, feeling that his strengths-based approach has helped the grandparents to see how well they are doing.

The grandparents discuss Akram after he leaves. They both agree that he was nice, but superficial. Their supervising social worker had always been very supportive. She would listen to their concerns and empathise, then tailor subsequent sessions to give them more knowledge and understanding of how to manage their new role. For example, she had explained the **secure base model of attachments** (Schofield and Beek, 2014) which they had found very useful. The grandparents feel a bit ashamed that they are finding things really difficult at the minute. Although they dearly love their daughter and grandchildren, what was originally a short-term arrangement has now become permanent, and they are struggling. Gautier and Wellard (2014) highlight how grandparenting carers report finding it more challenging bringing up a grandchild than their own children; many experience reduced income due to giving up a job, increased risk of ill health and complex family relationships. The grandparents feel disappointed that Akram diverted them from exploring their concerns, and are worried that his positive attitude will make it difficult for them to be honest about how much caring for their grandchildren full-time is affecting their health.

Reflective exercise 10.2

Reflect on Akram's visit and how the grandparents feel. Consider how informal and formal theorising has influenced Akram's perspective. What can Akram do to turn this situation round? What theory might help him to better understand the grandparents' situation and what they need from him?

Martin's foster carer assessment

You can read more about these theories and concepts in the following chapters:

- Social learning theory – Chapter 5
- Relationships; Systems theories; Systemic practice; Family displays; Family scripts; Attachment; Secure base model – Chapter 6
- Trauma – Chapter 7

Martin enjoys assessing potential foster carers because the process is concerned with **relationships** and social networks around the **family**, and enables him to use **systems theories** and systemic **practice**. He enjoys working creatively and visually, using **systemic** tools such as genograms and ecomaps during foster care assessments. Ecomaps can help to identify an individual's environmental and social networks, while genograms focus on **family relationships** (see McGoldrick et al., 2008). It has been argued by Chapman (2019) that the assessment of prospective foster carers has two connecting aspects: firstly, an evaluation of what a candidate can offer, their suitability along with their strengths and weaknesses; and secondly, to assess and develop that candidate's ability to change or grow with fostering.

Martin is approximately midway through the assessment home visiting stage. During the last visit they used a genogram to reflect on family relationships. This interested Martin a lot because he felt he was beginning to understand the family dynamics. Martin had arranged this visit to coincide with the couple's two children (13 and 15) returning home from school so he could observe the family's interactions. He was aware that he was observing a **family display** and **family scripts**.The children had obviously been told to be on their best behaviour and were almost unnaturally polite! They feigned interest in everything that he and their parents said, but he occasionally caught them looking bored or rolling their eyes at each other. Martin was tickled by this, they were typical teenagers and there was nothing wrong with their behaviour, but the fact that they were prepared to make a special effort for him evidenced a family that respected each other and worked well together. Martin felt he had observed very positive relationships and so far, they seem a suitable family to foster.

During his next visit, Martin plans to consider how the couple might manage some of the stresses that foster caring can bring. He plans to discuss the types of **trauma** that foster children might have experienced, the ongoing psychological and emotional impact of this, and the difficult behaviours that it can sometimes cause. Martin will explain the basic premise of **attachment theory** and in particular the **secure base model** (Schofield and Beek, 2014). Martin recognises fostering is about keeping children safe but also feels it is about providing children with a home life where a child can bond and attach with foster family members and feel a sense of belonging.

Reflective exercise 10.3

Identify three aspects of family life you think are important to understand when assessing potential foster carers.

How would you explain **attachment theory** to the foster carers if you were Martin?

11 OFFENDERS

Practice context

Social work has a long-established history of supporting people who are or have been involved with the criminal justice system. Sometimes offending behaviour is the specific focus, but more often our primary purpose is responding to care and support needs, and offending behaviour is an element considered within this. Crime and the criminal justice system are always under close public and political scrutiny. There are multiple perspectives on the causes of criminal behaviour, the extent to which individuals are accountable, and the role that socioeconomic and political factors play. Pinkney et al. (2018) argue that although youth offending is not a new phenomenon, it is increasingly linked to factors such as poverty, domestic abuse, trauma, fear, lack of opportunities, school exclusion, lack of community resources and hostile government policies. High profile cases have also demonstrated how law enforcement and public services can get things wrong. The children and vulnerable young women sexually exploited by the Rochdale child sex abuse ring were initially problematised and criminalised, rather than their abusers.

Traditionally, probation workers were social work qualified, but since the 1990s, probation's training and operation have increasingly moved towards criminological models (Raynor and Vanstone, 2016). However, social work and probation services continue to work in frequent partnership through Multi-Agency Public Protection Arrangements (MAPPA), Multi-Agency Risk Assessment Conferences (MARAC), Youth Offending Teams (YOTs) and Liaison and Diversion Services. Multi-agency Youth Offending Teams (YOTs) were established in 2000 by the Crime and Disorder Act 1998 and are coordinated by local authorities, overseen by the Youth Justice Board. The Ministry of Justice's Standards for Children in the Youth Justice System (2019) directs practitioners to uphold rights, encourage children and young people's wider social inclusion and work to minimise their involvement in the criminal justice system through prevention, diversion and 'minimal' intervention, building on strengths to develop 'pro-social identity for sustainable desistance from crime' (p. 6)

Social workers in YOTs undertake childcare assessments, pre-sentence reports, work in prisons – including Secure Children's Homes, Secure Welfare Centres and Youth Offending Institutes, and attend court to identify and recommend sentencing options to magistrates and judges. They supervise and support young people aged between 10 and 18 years who have committed offences and have received a Youth Caution, Youth Conditional Caution or an order from the court, or who are considered 'at risk' of offending. When a child/young person receives a criminal justice court order (such as a Youth Rehabilitation Order), YOT case managers work under the Youth Justice Board's *AssetPlus* assessment framework (see Figure 11.1), coordinating interventions to meet the order's requirements. The case manager will regularly review any significant change and take action with regard to compliance, enforcement, or early revocation of the order.

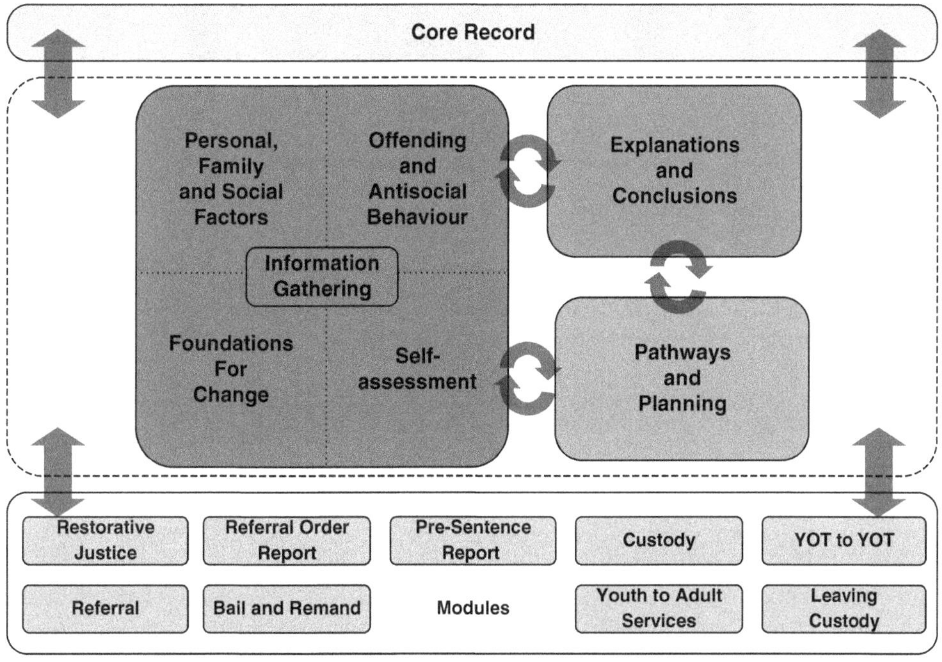

Figure 11.1 AssetPlus framework (Youth Justice Board, 2014)

Code C of the Police and Criminal Evidence Act 1984 prescribes what must happen during the detention, treatment and questioning of persons by police officers. It requires the police to have an *Appropriate Adult* present when they detain or question a child or mentally vulnerable adult. Appropriate Adults are intended to be a safeguard against miscarriages of justice by helping people to understand and exercise their rights during detention. They must be present during police interviews with the person. YOTs have a statutory duty to coordinate and arrange Appropriate Adults for all people aged 17 or under who are arrested. No agency is under a statutory duty to arrange this provision for mentally vulnerable adults, therefore practice varies enormously. Often Appropriate Adults will be volunteers or independent sector workers, but in some localities the role is undertaken by child or adult social workers.

The health and social needs of many people in the criminal justice system are often unrecognised or inadequately managed. Liaison and Diversion Services are multi-agency teams (often including social workers) intended to identify people with mental health problems, learning disabilities, substance misuse problems and other vulnerabilities as early as possible when they come into contact with the police and courts (NHS England, 2014). This enables assessment and referral on to appropriate support services, and allows information on their conditions and needs to inform decisions on case management, diversion, charging and sentencing (Figure 11.2).

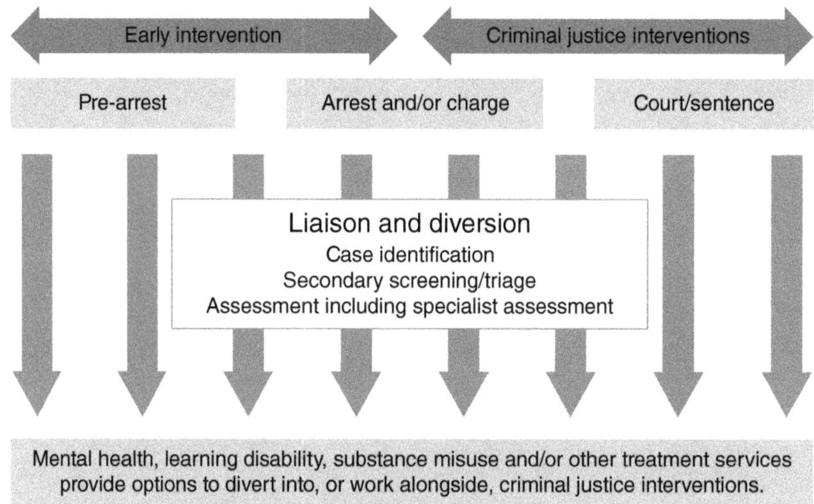

Figure 11.2 Outline of the Liaison and Diversion process (NHS England, 2014)

Care and support needs can continue or develop when people are in prison. Section 76 of the Care Act 2014 places local authorities under a statutory duty to assess the care and support needs of prisoners in their area, and if eligible, provide them with care and support in prison. Prisoners are financially assessed to determine whether they must pay towards the cost of their care, but unlike those in the community, are not entitled to receive direct payments. Local authorities also have a duty to assess care and support needs in preparation for release from prison, and if the person is eligible, provide appropriate services in the community upon release.

Martin – county lines child exploitation

You can read more about these theories and concepts in the following chapters:

- Development; Identity – Chapter 5
- Systemic practice; Attachment; Feedback loops; Grief and loss; Multigenerational transmission process; Continuing bonds; Family therapy – Chapter 6
- Risk; Vulnerability – Chapter 7

Martin is the case manager for Danny, a 14-year-old boy who was charged following his arrest for selling drugs. The pre-sentence report identified Danny as a **vulnerable** victim. Danny had got into a situation where he owed money for cannabis, and members of an organised crime gang forced him to work off his debt (this is known as debt-bondage). Danny was used as part of *county lines*, where vulnerable adults, young people and children move drugs away from urban cities and sell them in smaller towns and rural areas. The term county lines is derived from the dedicated mobile phone lines which are used to make arrangements – the practice is also known as *going country*. Danny's mum and stepdad reported that before his arrest he had been living in fear of the gang, had begun to self-harm and had tried to run away on a number of occasions. The court determined that a Youth Rehabilitation Order (YRO) with a supervision requirement attached would offer the most appropriate means to prevent re-offending.

Danny has been a victim of county lines, a contemporary term to describe a specific practice, but Martin is experienced enough to know at its core this is an age-old issue: exploitation. Martin has to find ways to identify Danny's strengths and any issues that may place him at **risk** of further exploitation or criminal behaviour. Martin passionately believes in **systemic practice**, a key principle of which is that problems are not located within the person, rather they arise in response to the person's relationships with others and their environment. Martin considers the AssetPlus assessment framework (see Figure 11.1) to support his **systemic** approach because it considers the relationship between offending behaviour and personal, family and social factors, and elements of the framework work together in **feedback loops**, rather than in sequential isolation. Martin wonders about Danny's home life and the sort of **attachments** he has with his family. Danny seems to have a supportive mum and stepdad, but his dad died when he was 6.

Martin notices Danny adopts an exaggerated, tough persona. He categorically disputes any suggestion that he has been exploited; he says that it is a load of crap that his mum came up with to keep him from getting a harder sentence. Whenever the opportunity presents, Danny talks proudly about his dad, who came from a locally notorious family and whom Danny refers to as a *gangster*. He is highly critical of his mother. He feels that he lost his links with his dad's family when she got involved with his stepdad. He tells Martin that his relationship with his parents is really bad. When Martin meets with Danny's mum and stepdad, they give an entirely different view. They tell Martin that Danny is so relieved not to have received a custodial sentence and to no longer be involved with the gang that relationships at home have improved significantly. Danny's mum says that she has tried to maintain links with his dad's side of the family, but they are not interested.

Martin tries to think through the implications of these different perspectives, rather than viewing one as wrong and the other as right – he wants to maintain a neutral stance that doesn't align him with any side of this dispute. He realises that whatever the reason, Danny has experienced the **loss** of very significant relationships early in his life. Next time he and Danny meet, Martin says it must have been really difficult for Danny to lose not just his dad, but also his dad's family, and asks who he has talked to about his **grief.** Danny is initially taken aback – he tells Martin that everyone always says he is better off without them, so doesn't get to talk about them, they only come up in the context of arguments. Danny opens up a lot, and Martin is struck by how **vulnerable** he is underneath his persona.

Martin has worked with a lot of young people who have become involved in criminal activity due to social factors and personal circumstances. Many of them gravitated towards crime to gain status and credibility as part of their **developmental** search for **identity**. He certainly feels that this has been a factor with Danny, and that Danny's continuing struggle with his **identity** plays a part in his need to present himself as a tough criminal, rather than a **vulnerable** victim. Martin knows that gangs exploit children and young people because they are less likely to be stopped by police, and if caught are treated more leniently by courts, but he recognises that becoming part of a gang can – at least initially – feel like becoming part of a family. He wonders whether for Danny, getting involved with criminal activities was a way for him to manage his feelings of grief and loss and establish a **continuing bond** with his dad and his dad's family.

Reflective exercise 11.1

Martin is considering trying a **family therapy approach**, where he meets with Danny, his mum and stepdad, and they work through their issues together. What might be the benefits of this approach? What might be problematic?

Judith assesses an offender's needs

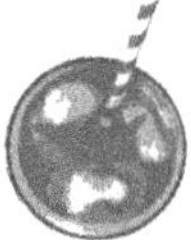

You can read more about these theories and concepts in the following chapters:

- Radical social work; Foucault; Postmodernism; Power (coercion); Anti-discriminatory practice – Chapter 3
- Responsibilisation – Chapter 3
- Identity – Chapter 5
- Loss – Chapter 6
- Risk; Safeguarding; Disability; Stigma – Chapter 7

Jan has very poor physical health as a result of chronic obstructive pulmonary disease. She uses a wheelchair and oxygen and also has an extensive criminal record. Following a raid on her home, she was arrested and charged with selling counterfeit cigarettes. Jan pleaded guilty and it is clear that she will receive a custodial sentence. Liaison and Diversion have referred her for an assessment of her care and support needs to inform her pre-sentence report.

The assessment is allocated to Judith, who telephones Jan. She says Judith can visit if it will help the probation officer to write a more positive pre-sentence report. Judith finds Jan living in squalid conditions. Since she became unable to manage the stairs, she has been sleeping on the sofa, which is heavily soiled. She can't access the upstairs bathroom and looks unkempt and uncomfortable. She is in a lot of pain from her heels dragging along the floor because the foot plates are missing from her wheelchair. There are takeaway cartons and pizza boxes everywhere. Judith is concerned to see overflowing ashtrays and realises that Jan is still smoking whilst using oxygen. She talks to her about this.

Jan tells Judith that she is totally fed up with her life. Her declining health has robbed her of her **identity** and status, and she hates being seen as weak and dependent. Moreover, she is bored and lonely – a steady stream of people used to come to the house to buy cigarettes, but since the police raid, the only contact she has with others is opening the door to delivery drivers. She is ambivalent about the **risk** of smoking near the oxygen cylinder, and says if she blows herself to high heaven it will resolve a lot of problems. However, she does agree not to smoke whilst Judith is there. Jan tells Judith that she has spent time in prison before and views going back as a relief in many ways, at least she will have company.

Judith likes Jan; she is an interesting character who makes no apologies for who she is. Although Judith in no way supports Jan's criminal behaviour, she subscribes to **Foucault's post-modernist** perspective that humanity is characterised by difference, and believes that it is not for her to judge lifestyles that deviate from society's **constructed** expectations. She recognises Jan as a fellow non-conformist and this appeals to her **radical** perspective. Jan is quite taken with Judith too – people from the council never last very long in her house, but Judith doesn't come from an authoritative stance of trying to **coerce** her into anything or exert **power** over her. She seems to genuinely want to help.

Judith completes her assessment and identifies that Jan's needs are eligible for local authority support. In the short-term, Jan agrees to a wheelchair assessment, community nursing referral for the pressure sores on her heels and domestic support to assist with personal care and nutrition. In the long-term, Jan needs to be re-accommodated, but this will be something to revisit in preparation for release from prison. Judith contacts the wheelchair service and Jan is put onto the waiting list. She tries to refer to the community nursing service, but Jan's property is classed as high risk and they are not prepared to visit it. She is told that if Jan gets herself to the surgery, she can be treated there. Judith thinks maybe assistance with this could be incorporated into the package of care, and starts to call around domiciliary care providers. No one is prepared to work with Jan because of the risk of her smoking whilst using oxygen. Judith thinks about **Goffman's three types of stigma** and feels that Jan is being **stigmatised** on the basis of her criminality, but she also recognises that her own negative ideas about physical illness and disability cause her to **self-stigmatise**.

Judith is enormously frustrated by this situation, and tells her colleagues that in her view, the **risks** around attending Jan's property are being inflated because people have made moral judgements about her lifestyle. She did not feel at all at **risk** in Jan's home. The antisocial behaviour is an **historical risk**, not a current one, as people have stopped coming to the house to buy cigarettes, and anyway, Jan was more than happy not to smoke whilst Judith was there. She feels very strongly that Jan is being **discriminated** against. Trish takes an entirely different viewpoint, and argues that Jan's behaviour and choices create risks that others shouldn't be expected to negotiate. She believes that Jan is **responsible** for the negative consequences of her own actions, therefore it is no one's fault but her own that he can't access community nursing or domiciliary care. Karen interjects and asks what about the risk that Jan presents to her neighbours by smoking whilst using oxygen – surely this is a serious **safeguarding** issue? Judith is disappointed to realise that in her eagerness to adopt an **anti-discriminatory** stance with Jan, she has not properly identified and addressed the **risks** she presents to her neighbours.

Reflective exercise 11.2

Do you feel more aligned to Judith's stance, or Trish's? Why?

Do you think that Jan will feel more or less stigmatised once she is in prison? Why?

Akram acts as Appropriate Adult

You can read more about these theories and concepts in the following chapters:

- Religion and spirituality; Social constructionism – Chapter 2
- Austerity; economics – Chapter 3
- Risk; Vulnerability; Safeguarding; Six levels of stigma; Staircase of oppression – Chapter 7
- Reflection and Criticality; Supervision – Chapter 8

Until recently, the council funded a community project which coordinated volunteering opportunities. Amongst many other functions, the project recruited and trained people to act as Appropriate Adults (AA). Project workers coordinated responses when a police request came in, arranging for a trained volunteer to attend the police station to act as AA, and afterwards providing a debriefing opportunity and reimbursing any expenses. **Austerity** has significantly cut the local authority's available social care budget, and councillors voted to reduce funding to the volunteer coordination project. This decision meant that a full-time post was lost, the project had to rationalise the services it provided and could no longer coordinate AA requests from the police. As an interim measure, all AA requests for children and young people are being met within the YOT, and requests in respect of mentally vulnerable adults will be met for anyone currently open to adult services. Ironically, an unanticipated consequence of the council's **economic** decision to reduce funding to the volunteer coordination project has been that a previously voluntary function has been brought in-house, resulting in a cost increase, rather than a saving.

At the start of his placement, Akram identified that he would like an opportunity to undertake AA work if possible, and he has attended training on the role. Today a request has come in for someone to act as AA for Oliver, a 20-year-old who has been charged with sexual assault. Records show that Oliver was referred to adult social care following lengthy involvement with Child and Adolescent Mental Health Services (CAMHS) and now receives a personal budget which is used to purchase social support to enable him to attend university. Dianne tells Akram that this is his opportunity, and advises him to get a drink and a sandwich as he may be hanging around the police station for a long time.

Akram feels anxious. He wanted to be AA, but feels too inexperienced to manage something of this seriousness and he realises that he has instinctively negative feelings towards Oliver. He doesn't want to support someone who has committed a sexual assault. He tells Dianne that he doesn't feel he can do this piece of work because Oliver's behaviour conflicts with his personal values. Dianne asks Akram to consider his *professional* values – social workers don't get to select who they work with; they must uphold *everyone's* rights. She reminds Akram that Oliver has been arrested, but not yet charged, let alone found guilty. Akram reluctantly takes her point, but asserts that this case is too **high risk** for a student. Dianne tells Akram that as Oliver is under arrest in a police station, any **risks** that he may present appear to be very well managed. She tells Akram that she believes that he has all of the skills and knowledge he needs to do this, and reminds him that he is close to qualifying – it's time to lean into discomfort rather than trying to avoid it.

At the police station, Akram is taken to the custody suite and given access to Oliver's custody record. He is told that the duty solicitor has been contacted, and Oliver will not be interviewed until she arrives. Oliver is brought out from his cell and given his rights in Akram's presence, then the two are left to speak alone. Oliver is not at all what Akram expected; he looks very young, and presents as quiet, polite and absolutely terrified. Akram remembers his training and explains his role. He talks Oliver through his rights and tries to give him some sense of what will happen next. Oliver explains that he has never set foot in a police station before and thanks Akram for helping him to better understand the process; he looks a little less terrified. The police return and take Oliver back to his cell to wait for his solicitor to arrive. Akram is escorted to the reception area.

As Akram waits, he eats his sandwich and **reflects** on what has happened. He feels a bit foolish for his initial response to this situation and realises that he instinctively **constructed** notions of **risk** and guilt based upon his emotional response to the alleged offence. As ill-prepared and anxious as he felt, the situation was a hundred times more frightening for Oliver. He recognises that whether innocent or guilty, Oliver is **vulnerable** and will benefit from him being there. He realises that his reluctance to work with Oliver was discriminatory, and resolves to read up on **anti-discriminatory practice** and use it to inform his discussion of this piece of work in his next **supervision**. Akram calls Dianne to update her and let her know that he is pleased she convinced him to do this. Dianne commends Akram for pushing himself out of his comfort zone and tells him she is impressed to hear how he has **critically reflected** and identified his own biases. She thinks that it is great that he is already thinking about using theory to explore this in supervision, and tells him that she has a worksheet they can complete to explore how the **six levels of stigma** informed his instinctive reaction.

Reflective exercise 11.3

Use the **six levels of stigma** (Jones et al., 1984; see Chapter 7) to identify how Akram's initial approach to Oliver's situation stigmatised him.

Use the **staircase of oppression** (Thesen, 2005; see Chapter 7, figure 7.6) to identify how Akram initially objectified Oliver. What changed Akram's approach?

12 PHYSICAL DISABILITIES

Practice context

Globally, over 1 billion people (1 in 7) have disabilities, and although they have the same general health care needs as others, they are three times more likely to be denied health care, and four times more likely to be treated badly within the health care system (World Health Organization, 2011). In the UK, 13 million people have disabilities and 4 million (31%) of them are living in poverty (Joseph Rowntree Foundation, 2020). In 2010, the Coalition government's austerity policy (see Chapter 3) introduced changes to disability benefits with the aim of cutting the Department for Work and Pensions' overall spending by 20%. Between 2010 and 2013, 1.03 million existing disability benefits claimants were reassessed (Barr et al., 2016) and a narrative emerged of disabled people unwilling – rather than unable – to work. Disabled people were presented within the media as either villains or victims (Quarmby, 2013) and increasingly socially stigmatised through categorisation as deserving or undeserving benefit recipients (Garthwaite, 2015). Rather than recognising the suffering people with disabilities were experiencing as a result of austerity, some saw them as responsible for causing it (Healy, 2020). Escaping poverty is an impossible task for a disabled person within a climate where they are both stigmatised by the state welfare system and discriminated against in the employment market. In 2017/18, 50% of working-age disabled people were not working, and those who were employed were likely to work fewer hours and be lower paid than non-disabled peers, regardless of their level of academic attainment (Joseph Rowntree Foundation, 2020).

In 2006, the United Nations General Assembly created an international human rights treaty, the Convention on the Rights of People with Disabilities (UNCRPD), reaffirming that all persons with all types of disabilities must enjoy all human rights and fundamental freedoms. The UK ratified the UNCRPD in 2009, committing to promote and protect the full human rights of disabled people and ensure their full equality. The following year, austerity hit the UK and in

2016, a damning UNCRPD report recognised that it had disproportionately affected disabled people. It strongly suggested that government policy on disability benefits had incited criticism of disabled people which had directly contributed to an increase in disability hate crimes. The UK's progress against the UNCRPD was reviewed again in 2017, resulting in a further highly critical report which identified that severe cuts to health and social care budgets had hit people with disabilities the hardest, and that UK legislation insufficiently addressed and protected disabled people's rights (United Nations Human Rights Office of the High Commissioner, 2017).

The primary piece of legislation governing disabled people's rights in the UK is the Equality Act 2010. The Act makes provisions for people with nine protected characteristics, including disability. In 2016, the House of Lords Equality Act 2010 and Disability Committee scrutinised this legislation and concluded that disabled people's rights had been better protected under the previous Disability Discrimination Acts (1995 and 2005). In their view, 'combining disability with the other protected characteristics in one Act did not in practice benefit disabled people' (House of Lords, 2016, p. 5). The Government Equalities Office (2016) disputed this. Disabled people in the UK live in a hostile environment and face disproportionate disadvantage not as a result of their condition, but through a combination of societal factors. The World Health Organization recognises that disability is a social problem which can only be overcome through social intervention:

> Disabilities is an umbrella term, covering impairments, activity limitations, and participation restrictions. An impairment is a problem in body function or structure; an activity limitation is a difficulty encountered by an individual in executing a task or action; while a participation restriction is a problem experienced by an individual in involvement in life situations. Disability is thus not just a health problem. It is a complex phenomenon, reflecting the interaction between features of a person's body and features of the society in which he or she lives. Overcoming the difficulties faced by people with disabilities requires interventions to remove environmental and social barriers. (World Health Organization, n.d.)

Effective social work can contribute to overcoming these environmental and social barriers firstly by recognising that they exist, and challenging the stigmatisation and discrimination of disabled people, and secondly by ensuring that people with disabilities have the means and support necessary to participate as they wish in education, work and community life. The Children Act 1989 classifies disabled children as in *need* (Section 17: 11), therefore entitled to an assessment from Children's Services, although access to services may be means tested. The Children and Families Act 2014 places further duties on local authorities in relation to disabled children and young people with Special Educational Needs (SEN). It requires them to publicise their local *offer* of services available to SEN children and their families, and introduced Education, Health and Care (EHC) Plans (which replaced Statements of Special Educational Needs). EHC assessments by Children's Services result in EHC Plans which address education, health and care needs from birth to 25 in a single document.

Disabled adults are entitled to assessment under the Care Act 2014 (the process of providing care and support for adults under the Care Act 2014 is set out in Figure 14.1). If assessed needs are eligible (see Figure 12.1), means tested care and support are provided. Depending on the individual person's situation and preference, care and support may be coordinated/arranged by the local authority, they may choose to receive a direct payment and use this to arrange their own care and support, or they may use these two approaches in combination.

Needs

The adult's needs arise from or are related to a physical or mental impairment or illness

Outcomes

As a result of the needs, the adult is unable to achieve two or more of the following:

a) managing and maintaining nutrition
b) maintaining personal hygiene
c) managing toilet needs
d) being appropriately clothed
e) maintaining a habitable home environment
f) being able to make use of the home safely
g) developing and maintaining family or other personal relationships
h) accessing and engaging in work, training, education or volunteering
i) making use of necessary facilities or services in the local community including public transport and recreational facilities or services

Wellbeing

As a consequence, there is or is likely to be a significant impact on the adult's wellbeing, including the following:

a) personal dignity (including treatment of the individual with respect)
b) physical and mental health and emotional wellbeing
c) protection from abuse and neglect
d) control by the individual over day-to-day life (including over care and support provided and the way it is provided)
e) participation in work, education, training or recreation
f) social and economic wellbeing
g) domestic, family and personal relationships
h) suitability of living accommodation
i) the individual's contribution to society

Figure 12.1 Care Act 2014 eligibility decision process

Martin and Akram's Care Act Assessment

You can read more about these theories and concepts in the following chapters:

- Economics; Austerity; Policy; The welfare state – Chapter 3
- Ecological systems theory (macrosystem/microsystem) – Chapter 6
- Poverty; Disability; Vulnerability; Theory of fundamental causes – Chapter 7

Martin and Akram completed an initial home visit in response to concerns around the possible neglect of a 6-year-old girl, Bobbi (see Exercise 7.2, Chapter 7). They discovered that the family was living in extreme **poverty** following the withdrawal of mum Kendra's disability benefit. Kendra has multiple sclerosis (MS), a condition which affects the central nervous system. She has agreed for Martin and Akram to return and complete a Care Act Assessment of her needs. During the assessment, Kendra explains how MS affects her. Her symptoms were fairly mild at first and she enjoyed a period of remission when she was pregnant with Bobbi, but things have been progressing quite rapidly for the past 18 months. She experiences constant fatigue, pain, muscle spasms and tremors, has poor balance and experiences bladder problems. She feels depressed all of the time but doesn't know if that is the MS or a response to the family's situation, or both. Kendra hasn't seen her GP or had her medication reviewed for a long while because you have to ring on the day to request an appointment and wait in a queue until your call is answered. She doesn't often have credit on her phone and when she does, she can't waste it like this. Besides, it takes all of her energy to get herself and Bobbi ready in the morning and get to school – some days she can't even manage this. Kendra is tired and asks if they can leave it there for today. Martin and Akram promise to be in touch very soon.

Martin and Akram are both really affected by this visit. To break the silence as they drive back to the office, Martin asks Akram to consider everything Kendra has told them and apply the Care Act eligibility criteria (see Figure 12.1). Akram identifies that Kendra is eligible to receive care and support because:

1. Her needs are caused by physical illnesses.
2. She is unable to achieve outcomes in respect of her personal hygiene; managing toilet needs; cleaning and maintaining her home; accessing local facilities or services; and accessing work, training or education.
3. This has a significant impact on Kendra's wellbeing in terms of her personal dignity; physical health and emotional wellbeing; participation in work, training or education; and social and economic wellbeing.

Martin agrees; Kendra is eligible for care and support under the Care Act 2014, and Bobbi is a Child in Need under the Care Act 1989, so the family are eligible for services on that basis also. Akram feels enormous relief to know that the family are going to get some help. Martin tells him to get some lunch, then have a think about how theory can help make sense of this situation before they meet up to plan their next moves later on that day.

Akram knows that Martin is a passionate **systemic** practitioner and he remembers **Bronfenbrenner's ecological systems theory** from teaching because of the concentric circle diagram. He thinks about how factors from the **macrosystem** such as the **economic** climate of **austerity** and changing **welfare state policy** on **disability** benefits have affected Kendra and her family at a **micro level,** making them extremely **vulnerable.** He discusses this with Martin, who is really impressed. Akram says that what he doesn't understand is how the family has been left to struggle on for so long before coming to anyone's attention when they are so clearly eligible for support. Martin explains the **theory of fundamental causes** to demonstrate how socioeconomic status creates barriers. The ***system,*** he explains, expects people like Kendra to know how to navigate it, but there are barriers everywhere and poverty makes every hardship harder. If Kendra had had the money to stay on the phone long enough to get a GP appointment, her health may have been better managed, and her GP might well have suggested a referral for social care support much sooner. If GP services weren't so stretched, the appointment system wouldn't have been introduced.

Reflective exercise 12.1

Use the information above and the earlier exercise which introduced Kendra and Bobbi (Exercise 7.2). Apply **Link and Phelan's theory of fundamental causes** (1995) to consider how socioeconomic status has limited Kendra's resources and how this has impacted on the whole family.

Akram's reflective assignment

You can read more about these theories and concepts in the following chapters:

- Feminism; Gender roles; Criticality; Social construction – Chapter 2
- Mentoring – Chapter 5
- Systemic practice; Theory of social action – Chapter 6
- Risk; Vulnerability; Disability – Chapter 7
- Reflection; Supervision; Hypothesising – Chapter 8

Akram is planning for his final summative assignment, a **reflection** on a practice situation. He plans to focus on a needs assessment of Kelvin, a six-year-old wheelchair user, and his family. **Reflecting** on this piece of work helps him to recognise how far he has come: earlier in his placement, he would have been daunted and preoccupied with **risk.** By the time he undertook this assessment, his confidence had grown along with his knowledge and experience, and he understood the need to identify not just **risks**, but also strengths and assets.

Akram **reflects** on how he prepared for the assessment. He reviewed his university learning and remembered being taught that children with **disabilities** are more **vulnerable** to abuse than non-disabled children (Jones et al., 2012). A lecturer had mentioned a charity called Contact provides information for families with disabled children, so he accessed their website (https://contact.org.uk/) and re-read the *Working Together to Safeguard Children* (Department for Education, 2018) guidance. Akram realised families with **disabled** children can face many adversities, not least when having to work with professionals. During **supervision** with Dianne, Akram suggested three visits to the family's house: the first as an introduction, the second to gather information and the third to co-produce the conclusion to the assessment. Akram planned to engage the family using elements of **systemic practice** and diagrammatic tools to help him to explore and understand the family's relationships. He formulated three initial **hypotheses** which he would explore over his three visits:

1 The parent–child relationship is enduring and resilient and Kelvin's needs are being met.
2 The parent–child relationship is breaking down and Kelvin's needs cannot be met.

3 Kelvin's care needs have increased, placing increased strain on the parent–child relationship.

Akram completed an ecomap with Kelvin and his parents, Beth and Harry. This identified that Kelvin had considerable care needs which largely fell onto Beth, who had given up paid employment to better care for him. His assessment concluded that his third hypothesis was met – Kelvin's care needs have increased and though the family's relationships are strong, they are under increased pressure. The conclusion that Akram co-produced with Kelvin, Beth and Harry recommended the family:

1 Be provided with social care support, including access to short-breaks.
2 Seek benefit advice to see if their entitlement has changed.
3 Consider attending a parent support group, where they could benefit from the **mentoring** of other parents.

Akram has learnt that **systemic practice** is a very broad term that covers a lot of different theories. He wants to be specific in his assignment to evidence his ability to apply knowledge and think **critically**. He thinks about **Parsons' social action theory** and its emphasis on assumed **gendered roles**. This doesn't seem relevant as his assessment identified that Beth and Harry had negotiated who cared for Kelvin based on their employment prospects – Harry's job paid more, therefore Beth stayed at home. However, Akram's knowledge of **feminism** helps him to recognise that **socially constructed gender roles** create inequality which leads to women typically earning less than men, whilst at the same time casting women as natural nurturers and automatically allocating caring responsibilities to them. Perhaps Beth and Harry's decision was not as fairly decided as it appeared to be?

Reflective exercise 12.2

Identify three different theories that Akram can use in his assignment to explain the family's situation from Kelvin's perspective first, then Beth's perspective and finally Harry's perspective.

Trish and Karen

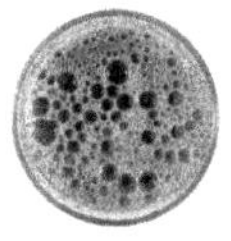

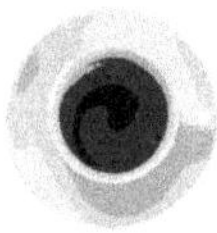

You can read more about these theories and concepts in the following chapters:

- Social construction – Chapter 1
- Psychosocial development (Industry vs Inferiority and Identity vs Confusion); Continuity theory (adaptive strategy) – Chapter 5
- Equilibrium; Grief and loss – Chapter 6
- Disability; Stigma (labelling); Trauma; Social model of disability – Chapter 7

Trish's deafness caused her to consider societal attitudes towards difference very early in life. She was born with hearing loss in both ears and wore hearing aids from just after birth. Her mum was deaf, her dad was not, and she grew up straddling both deaf and mainstream culture and using both British Sign Language and speech. By the time Trish reached her teenage years, her hearing deteriorated, and her hearing aids were less and less effective. She and her family were told that she was a candidate for cochlear implants, and they thought long and hard about whether she should have this surgery. Like any parents, Trish's mum and dad wanted her to have access to the best opportunities in life and they recognised that retaining a level of hearing would enable her to participate in many more situations. But they also strongly felt that deafness was a difference, not a **disability**, and they were proud to be part of the deaf community's rich culture. They worried that having cochlear implants would distort Trish's sense of **identity** by seeming to reject deaf culture and reinforce that hearing was somehow superior. Trish herself wasn't sure that the implants were the right way to go as she generally felt more accepted in the deaf community. Hearing people often ignored her or treated her as if she was making unreasonable demands when she asked for simple communication adjustments like remaining in her line of vision so she could read their lips. She felt stigmatised for her deafness; being mocked for wearing hearing aids and the differences in her speech made her feel **inferior**. On the other hand, she felt an undeniable urge to fit in and be accepted. Eventually, Trish had the implants, but she still proudly identifies as deaf.

Last year Karen was seriously injured in a car accident. She has been off work for a long period of recovery and rehabilitation. She now has walking difficulties and uses a forearm crutch to help her get around, and Ali has arranged for Occupational Health to complete a workplace assessment of her needs so that reasonable adjustments can be made in preparation for her return to work. Karen is well liked, and all of the team are really happy when she comes into the office for the assessment. She catches up with all of her colleagues for a few minutes before the assessor arrives. Karen has a few tears and says she absolutely hates having to go through all this rigmarole, she just wants to get back to normal and for people to stop treating her as **disabled**.

Trish has worked with Karen for a long time and regards her to have excellent values, but her comment about not wanting to be treated as **disabled** conveys an implicit message: **disabled** people are viewed and treated differently, and not in a good way. Trish privately **reflects** on this. Karen is going through a process of **grief and loss** as she adjusts to a major change in her life circumstances following a **traumatic** event. Karen is also aware that others are projecting a **disabled identity** onto her, and this is not an **identity** that she wants for herself. She is not alone – in Trish's experience, very few people who have been reductively **labelled** as disabled see this as the key element of their identity! Disability is an entirely **socially constructed** concept. Trish and Karen have conditions that cause others to regard them as **disabled**, but in line with the **social model of disability**, both feel **disabled** not by their conditions, but by others' attitudes. After a long period of interruption and unpredictability during her recovery, Karen is obviously desperate to come back to work for a return to a state of normality (**equilibrium**). **Continuity theory** characterises this return to work as an **adaptive strategy** which provides Karen with **continuity** between her familiar life before her accident and her unfamiliar life afterwards.

Reflective exercise 12.3

Why is **identity** important? Reflect on your own **identity.** Have you ever had cause to redefine or reconstruct it? How did this feel? Have other people ever described or treated you in a way with which you do not identify? How did this feel?

13 MENTAL DISTRESS

Practice context

Needs relating to mental wellbeing are so prevalent that we encounter them whatever the focus of our social work practice. One in 10 children in the country has a diagnosable mental health condition (NHS Digital, 2018), with children in care four times more likely to have mental health difficulties than children in the general population (Local Government Association, 2017). Over half of all mental health problems start before the age of 14 and by working age, at any given time around one in five of the population has a mental health condition. Suicide rates are rising across all of the countries of the UK (Office for National Statistics, 2019). For over a century, mental health policy and services have been determined by a psychiatric hegemony (see Chapter 4) which conceptualises mental illness as a disorder in the functioning of the brain. In standard psychiatry's neurobiological model, mental illness is either genetically predetermined (faulty genes) or spontaneously occurring (disease) and therefore treatment is medically led, addressing symptoms through predominantly pharmacological interventions. At times, the dominance of psychiatry and discourses premised on medicalised notions of mental *health* have left social work ambiguously placed, but this dominance is beginning to shift. Harnessing the disability rights movement's work on medical and social models of disability (see Chapter 7), mental health service users have brought increased attention to how psychiatry disempowers by disregarding the impact of structural inequality and traumatic life experiences. The growing evidence base of social causation of mental distress now presents an undeniable challenge to the brain disease model. To realise that social factors contribute to mental health difficulties is to realise the need for social responses.

Social models of mental health proceed from the fundamental principle that concepts such as mental health and mental illness, madness and sanity, and diagnostic labels such as schizophrenia, bipolar affective disorder and personality disorder are socially constructed (see Chapter 2). They are premised on perceptions of and deviations from arbitrarily determined social norms. For example, it has been widely decided that it is not normal to hear voices that others don't, and this is a symptom of psychosis. But Maijer et al. (2018) systematically reviewed the existing literature on auditory hallucinations and found that across the world approximately 10% of people have had one or more experience of hearing voices – if one in 10 experience it, can it really be viewed to be abnormal? Transcultural psychiatry recognises that different ways of expressing, understanding and responding to mental distress occur in different cultural contexts. Luhrmann et al.'s 2015 study compared three different populations of people who hear voices. Those in the North American sample were diagnosed as schizophrenic and largely described their voices as intrusive, unreal thoughts; many of those in the South Indian sample felt the voices they heard provided useful guidance; and many in the West African sample viewed their voices as morally good. It seems that social contexts shape whether people view hearing voices as mental illness, or part of the range of human experience.

Rejecting neurobiological notions of brain disease, social models consider how social factors at every level of society produce responses in individuals that are then constructed as mental illness. An ever-growing body of research links increased likelihood of psychiatric diagnosis with factors such as poverty (Wicks et al., 2010), urban environments (Vassos et al., 2012), migration (Cantor-Graae and Selten, 2005), belonging to an ethnic minority (Veling et al., 2008), separation from parents (Varese et al., 2012), and childhood sexual, physical and emotional abuse (Varese et al., 2012). Counter-culture psychiatrist R.D. Laing is famously quoted as saying that insanity is the only sane response to an insane world. Pathologising difficult emotions, behaviours and perceptions as symptoms of disorder suggests that something is wrong with the person. If we try instead to understand what has happened in the person's life, we will very often find that their presentation is a response to trauma (see Chapter 7). Writing in support of an increased social work role in mental health, Goemans argues:

> while we pretend that madness can be cured with pills, we can conveniently ignore all the massive social problems within our communities which directly impact upon mental wellbeing. (2012: 91–2)

The dominant medical narrative has resulted in mental health policy and organisational responses being largely located in the NHS. In her introduction to the Department of Health's strategic statement, *Social Work for Better Mental Health*, Chief Social Worker for Adults Lyn Romeo recognised that the vital role of social work, social care and local government was often overlooked, and asserted that 'social workers are crucial to ensuring people with mental health needs are seen first and foremost as citizens with equal rights, rather than exclusively through a diagnostic or clinical lens' (Allen et al., 2016, p. 4). The statement argues that mental health services must be premised on social models of mental illness, recognise social determinants of health and wellbeing, and address the social trauma that underlies a lot of mental health needs. It establishes that the social work workforce has a great deal to offer people experiencing mental distress through its:

- key skills in tackling stigma, discrimination and exclusion
- legal and statutory knowledge of enablement, care and support systems
- key, cross-agency role in protecting people from harm
- ability to work holistically with people and their social network, helping to strengthen and build sustainable family and social capital

The Local Government Association's report *Being Mindful of Mental Health – The Role of Local Government in Mental Health and Wellbeing* (2017) makes a significant linguistic shift, from mental health/illness, to mental wellbeing/wellness. It argues that rather than treating mental health as a discrete issue, with health-based services targeted at reactively responding to people at times of crisis, communities should be built on principles that encourage mental wellness across the life course:

> With mental health such a fundamentally important issue for the country, and with councils playing such a key role, it is surprising that local government has featured so little in national dialogue about how to improve mental health ... councils influence the mental wellbeing of our communities and ... council services, from social care to parks to open spaces to education to housing, help to make up the fabric of mental health support for the people in our communities. (Local Government Association, 2017, p. 4)

Mental health social work is based on statutory responsibilities drawn from a range of legislation. Children with mental health difficulties will potentially be entitled to assessment and services under Section 17 of the Children Act 1989, and an Education, Health and Care (EHC) Plan under the Children and Families Act 2014. The Mental Capacity Act 2005 applies from the age of 16, and may be relevant if there is reason to believe that the person's mental health is impacting on their capacity to make a specific decision at the time that it needs to be made. Adult needs will be assessed and if eligible, means tested care and support will be provided under the Care Act 2014 (see Figures 12.1 and 14.1). The Mental Health Act 1983 (MHA83) makes provision for the involuntary care and treatment of people of any age. It prescribes the specialist statutory role of the Approved Mental Health Professional (AMHP), responsible for assessing risks related to the person's mental health against their human rights. If the legal criteria are met, AMHPs can apply for their detention under MHA83, which is commonly referred to as 'sectioning'. Although AMHPs may be occupational therapists, nurses or psychologists, 95% of AMHPS are social workers (Office of the Chief Social Worker for Adults, 2019).

Judith supports Kian

You can read more about these theories and concepts in the following chapters:

- Radical social work – Chapter 4
- Non-judgemental stance – Chapter 2
- Social clock (Neugarten's theory); identity – Chapter 5
- Stigma; Trauma; Medical/social models – Chapter 7

Kian is 23, and two years ago he was detained under MHA83 after being removed from a railway line by the transport police. It is believed he was trying to end his life, although he disputes this. Whilst detained, he was diagnosed with schizophrenia and a regime of antipsychotic medication was established. Kian finds the diagnosis of schizophrenia very **stigmatising** and unhelpful.

He also feels very angry that professionals who didn't know him were able to override his human right to liberty and detain him in hospital against his will. Judith started working with Kian in preparation for his discharge. At first it was hard to trust Judith, but her **radical** and **non-judgemental** approach has been very effective in establishing a strong relationship based on Kian's needs, rather than his diagnosis. Judith is a civil libertarian, but she recognises that in the face of the enormous **risk** of Kian ending his life, the AMHP had no choice but to detain him for his own safety. She knows, however, that this is not how Kian views things, and that although the psychiatric detention may have saved his life, he has been **traumatised** by the experience.

Judith understands that the most important thing to Kian is to be able to move on from what has happened and regain a sense of control over his life again. She has supported him to attend the local Recovery College, which offers educational courses designed to help people feel more confident in self-management of their own mental health and wellbeing. This has been really effective: Kian feels more in control and has made friends, which has created opportunities for social connection and interaction. Judith catches up with Kian and he tells her that he wants to stop the medication. Since he started on it, he has gained 3 stones in weight and experiences several unpleasant side effects including constipation, sedation and intermittent lactation. He feels that his medication limits his opportunities for a social life and makes any prospect of a romantic relationship impossible. Judith thinks about this and visualises Kian's **social clock ticking away**. She knows that in **Neugarten's theory**, people who conform to their culture's **social clock** gain acceptance, approval and status; people who do not are viewed with suspicion. Kian feels that his psychiatric admission has interrupted his life and his diagnosis has marked him out as suspicious; it is so important for his sense of **identity** that he is able to demonstrate he can do what other 23-year-olds do – stay out late, socialise, have an intimate relationship. Judith feels proud that Kian has trusted her enough to tell her how he is feeling – he might well just have stopped taking his medication on his own, which could have been **risky**. They agree to request a medical review so that Kian can make an informed decision about withdrawing from the medication or switching to alternative treatments.

Reflective exercise 13.1

If Judith had taken a **medical**, rather than a **social model**, and been led by Kian's diagnosis, rather than his needs, what might her involvement with Kian have looked like?

Lloyd's safeguarding alert

You can read more about these theories and concepts in the following chapters:

- Social construction – Chapter 2
- Responsibilisation – Chapter 3
- Safeguarding; Vulnerability; Risk – Chapter 7
- Reflection – Chapter 8

Lloyd takes a **safeguarding** alert from staff at the local library. They are concerned about a woman called Stella, who has come to the library every day for many years to read, use the computers and print off reams of articles and documents. Staff are concerned that Stella is filthy, and has been wearing the same clothes for a long time. They consider her extremely **vulnerable** as she is frequently subjected to verbal abuse outside the library. Lloyd isn't sure that this meets the threshold for a **safeguarding** enquiry yet, but agrees to look into things.

He reads through Stella's records and finds that she hasn't had any involvement with social care before, but there have been many, many contacts to different council departments about her over recent years. Piecing these bits of information together, he learns that Stella is 54 and lives alone in a terraced house left to her by her parents. Her home is in a very bad state of disrepair; it is filthy and crowded with computer hardware, books and piles of papers. Her hoarding behaviours mean that she can no longer access her bedroom, kitchen or bathroom. As the state of her property has declined, local attitudes towards her have become quite hostile: regular complaints have been made to the council because Stella's house attracts rodents, presents a fire risk and has affected property values and saleability. Stella has always refused to let council officials into her home.

Lloyd **reflects** on what he has read. It strikes him that every contact the council has received about Stella has been a complaint, and this **constructs** a notion of Stella as being problematic. He wishes people had thought more broadly and recognised her as a person with problems, rather than a problematic person; a person at **risk**, as well as a person presenting **risk**. Lloyd suspects Stella is unwell – from what he has read she could meet the criteria for any number of psychiatric diagnoses – however, a label is not needed to see that this is someone whose situation has been deteriorating and has needed help for a long time. **Responsibilising** Stella for her behaviour seems to have resulted in a hostile, rather than a compassionate approach, to the extent that when she has refused to engage, this has been taken as confirmation of her difficult nature, rather than seen as a factor which increases her **vulnerability**. Lloyd thinks about how he can best approach this. He wants to find a way of approaching Stella that will be as non-threatening as possible, so that he will have the best opportunity to engage and assess her. He realises that the library staff did not complain about Stella, they acted out of concern. He decides that Stella may feel less vulnerable and more receptive if he approaches her at the library, and heads off there.

Reflective exercise 13.2

Hoarding is increasingly seen as a form of self-neglect and addressed under safeguarding processes. Should Lloyd **construct** Stella as requiring **safeguarding** from her own actions and therefore begin a Section 42 Safeguarding Enquiry, or as someone with needs requiring care and support and therefore begin a Care Act Assessment? What are the potential benefits and difficulties of each approach?

Lloyd helps Akram prepare for an assessment

You can read more about these theories and concepts in the following chapters:

- Attachment; Grief and loss; Relationships; Systems theory; Social capital – Chapter 6
- Medical/Social model; Pathologising; Stigma – Chapter 7
- Theorising; Hypothesising – Chapter 8

Barry is 44 and worked on building sites from the age of 15 until he sustained a serious back injury 14 months ago. He has not worked since and has become increasingly withdrawn. He lives with his wife and their three children and refuses to claim any benefits, so the family is supported by his wife's income. Six months ago, following the death of his mother, Barry went missing and was eventually found by the police, wandering around in a state of confusion. He was subsequently admitted to a psychiatric hospital, where he was diagnosed with depression and abnormal grief reaction, and started on antidepressant medication. He was followed up in the community by mental health services, but after a while he was discharged as he wouldn't leave the house to come to appointments or therapeutic activities. Barry's GP prescribes his pain medication and antidepressants, but feels that his issues are more **social** than **medical** and manages to persuade him to accept a referral to social care for assessment under the Care Act 2014.

Dianne identifies this as a suitable piece of work for Akram – she can use it as an observation of his practice which she will write up to provide evidence of his performance against the PCFs. She asks him to arrange a home visit and plan for the assessment. Akram wants to get this right, and as Lloyd is recently qualified and has been through the process of having his practice observed, he asks him for advice. Lloyd explains a planning technique that he finds really helpful, and offers to undertake it with Akram. They analyse the referral information carefully, and identify what seem to be the key issues. They write these as headings in one column, with reported information underneath. They then discuss each one in turn, making notes against them to capture their thoughts. The finished plan is shown in Table 13.1.

Table 13.1 Plan for Barry's assessment

Issue	Notes
Mental health • diagnosis of depression and abnormal grief reaction • takes antidepressants	On tablets but still depressed. Does he find tablets helpful? Need to find out what else has been tried/could help. How does Barry see his situation? Does he agree he is depressed? What is an abnormal grief reaction? Can a grief reaction ever be abnormal? Is this **pathologising** of human emotion under a **medical model**? Was he offered support around **grief**? Would he like this?

(Continued)

Table 13.1 (Continued)

Issue	Notes
• hospital admission • didn't engage with mental health team	What ways of understanding grief are there? Need to read up on **theories of grief and loss.** Relationship with mum must have been very important – need to find out more about this and consider **attachment** (does attachment theory cover loss/end of attachment? Read up on this). How does he feel about hospital admission? May have found this **stigmatising** or helpful. How does he feel about mental health team involvement/discharge?
Physical health • back injury 15 months ago • pain medication from GP	How bad is back injury? Is he in pain? Does this contribute to his depression? Could he be over/under medicated? There could be issues with addiction. Are there other physical health issues?
Relationships • wife Helen and 3 children • lost mum 6 months ago	How is Barry's **relationship** with Helen and his children? **Systems theory** identifies that a change in one part of a system affects all other parts – how are Helen and the kids affected by his situation? Helen may be entitled to a carer's assessment/support – does she want this? Kids may also be young carers, how old are they, how are they doing at school, etc? Have **family roles** changed since Barry's injury? What is the impact of this practically and psychologically? What other significant **relationship**s does Barry have? GP made referral – this **relationship** could be a strength.
Money • Helen's wage supports family • Barry has no income and won't claim benefits	How is the family managing? Unless Helen has a very high income it will be very difficult to support a family of 5 on one wage. If they had savings, they may have run out by now. Is **poverty**/debt an issue? Why won't Barry claim benefits? Is this a matter of pride/**stigma**? Can he change his mind?
Occupation • Barry worked in construction from age 15 • he has not worked since back injury 14 months ago	Barry worked on building sites – very physical role. Did this from a young age, a big part of his life/**identity**. Is he struggling to adjust to his new situation? People experience grief and loss in relation to significant life changes as well as bereavement. He may feel he has lost his **identity**. Has lost **social capital** since losing his job. Would have had relationships at work – does anyone keep in touch? Is there a possibility of him returning to work (does he want to?) or retraining? How does he spend his time?

Akram is astonished by how helpful this exercise has been. Not only has he identified lots of points that he will explore during the assessment, but he has also started to **theorise** about Barry's situation and identify a number of **hypotheses** that he can check out through questioning. He needs to go away and read up on some of the theories that he has identified may be helpful, but he actually feels enthusiastic about this, because he will be relating theory to Barry's situation, rather than trying to understand it in an abstract way. He feels that he is resourced to undertake a much more nuanced assessment.

Reflective exercise 13.3

It is not true to say that health professionals follow **medical models** and **social workers** follow social models – Barry's GP has thought about his situation, not just his diagnosis, and recognised the need for social interventions. Reflect on a situation from your experience when a social worker has adopted a medicalised approach, or a health professional has adopted a social model.

14 LEARNING DISABILITIES AND AUTISM

Practice context

In the UK we tend to use the term learning disability; many countries use the term intellectual impairment. Both are umbrella terms for a broad group of conditions that are present before the age of 18 and impact on the way individuals develop in terms of learning and social interaction. Public Health England (2018) separates the causes of learning disability into three distinct periods of development:

1 **Prenatal period (from conception)** – chromosome and genetic anomalies resulting in conditions such as Down's syndrome, Fragile X syndrome, Rhett syndrome; maternal infections such as Rubella; environmental/societal issues such as foetal alcohol syndrome.
2 **Perinatal period (later stages of pregnancy and period immediately after birth)** – cerebral palsy as a result of precipitated or prolonged labour; global developmental delay caused by prematurity or environment factors (for example, abuse, neglect).
3 **Postnatal period (after birth)** – infection such as meningitis, measles, encephalitis; brain injury as a result of abuse or accident trauma; chromosome and genetic anomalies which present during infancy and childhood such as Batten disease, Tay–Sachs disease.

Individuals may share a diagnosis but experience their conditions very differently. Some people will be severely affected and require a very high level of support, whilst others will be very minimally affected and require little or no additional support. Most will fall somewhere between these two extremes.

Autism is a lifelong neurological disorder affecting approximately 1 in 100 children (though some estimates are higher). It can coexist with learning disability, but many autistic people do not have learning disabilities. Although diagnosis often does not come until much later, indicators of autism are usually noticeable by the age of 2 or 3 in the form of particular patterns of behaviour and difficulties in social interactions and communication. Autism is referred to as a spectrum disorder, because it has an extremely broad range of presentations: as Autistic Professor of Special Education Stephen Shore famously says – 'if you've met one person with autism, you've met one person with autism'. Historically, autistic people have not been well served by health and social care services; their needs have tended to be annexed to learning disability or mental health services, although many have neither learning disabilities nor mental health issues.

People with learning disabilities and autism have been subjected to stigma, social exclusion and abuse throughout history and sadly this continues in contemporary times; the following are three examples, but there are countless more:

> **Connor Sparrowhawk** had learning disabilities and was autistic. His assessment in a specialist NHS Assessment and Treatment unit was jointly commissioned by Oxfordshire Clinical Commissioning Group and Oxfordshire County Council at a cost of £3000 per week. Despite having epilepsy, Connor was left to bathe alone with the door closed. On 4 July 2013, Connor drowned in the bath; he was 18 years old. Southern Health, the NHS Trust who operated the unit, recorded his death as natural causes. Connor's family led an astonishingly brave campaign to secure justice. In 2014, an independent review found that Connor's death had been preventable, the outcome of a combination of poor leadership and poor care in the unit. At his inquest in 2015, it emerged that a patient had died in the same bath in 2006. The inquest also revealed that when nursing staff found Connor unconscious in the bath, they had made no attempt to resuscitate him.
>
> **Bethany** (a court order prohibits fully naming Bethany or her father, Jeremey) is autistic and has Pathological Demand Avoidance. She experiences problems with sensory overload and severe anxiety, which can result in her seriously hurting herself and others. When Beth was 15, she was sectioned under the Mental Health Act 1983; she spent the vast majority of the next three years in total seclusion. *The Times* (Purves, 2018) reported:
>
>> A girl lives in a bleak room measuring 12ft by 10ft, with a plastic chair and mattress: meals are passed through a hatch in a steel door. When her father visits, he kneels down to speak through the grille. If he telephones, the handset is held out towards the inmate by a staff member. When she self-harms, shoving part of a pen into her arm, it may be a while before it is removed because of the danger to staff. Is this some murderous psychopath lifer, a Hannibal Lecter? No: Bethany, a girl of 17 with autism. It's a psychiatric unit, privately run, at a hospital in Northampton. And it is four months since a professional assessment accepted, not for the first time, that her needs are not met in this setting – the tiny space poetically called 'seclusion'.
>
> **Whorlton Hall** was a private hospital in a remote part of County Durham. In 2019, undercover filming by the BBC's *Panorama* showed staff routinely intimidating, mocking and unnecessarily restraining patients with learning disabilities and autism. Over the previous year, more than 100 visits had been made to the unit by professionals from the Care Quality Commission (CQC), local authorities and NHS bodies, none of whom picked up on the culture of abuse. It subsequently emerged that the CQC, the independent

regulator of health and social care in England, had suppressed a negative inspection of the service in 2015. Professor Glynis Murphy's independent review of the CQC's handling of Whorlton Hall (2020) found many faults with their approach of regulation. Fundamentally, the report recommended that the CQC simply should not register services like Whorlton Hall, which are in remote places and have out-of-date models of care, as appropriate care provision for people with learning disabilities and autism:

> it can be argued that the real problem, lying behind the events at Whorlton Hall, is the discriminatory attitude of some people towards those with learning disabilities and/or autism, such that they are not treated with the respect due to them as human beings, and are denied their human rights. It can also be argued that, had there been better community-based services, especially for children and young people with learning disabilities and/or autism, then fewer people would need to be admitted to assessment and treatment units. (Murphy, 2020, p. 59)

The neurodiversity movement (generally accepted to have originated from autistic Australian sociologist Judy Singer) argues that just as people are ethnically, culturally and sexually diverse, so are they neurologically diverse. Autism and learning disabilities, therefore, should not be viewed as diseases to be cured, but embraced as naturally occurring differences. But from the examples we have given, it is clear that society rarely takes this stance. The human rights – and indeed the lives – of people with learning disabilities and autism are valued differently. People with learning disabilities have six times the risk of developing mental health problems (Mental Health Foundation, 2015). The *Learning Disabilities Mortality Review* 2018 (University of Bristol, 2018) found that there was a disparity in the age at death of people with learning disabilities and the general population of 23 years for men and 27 years for women. In over half of the deaths reviewed, the person did not receive care which met good practice standards and in 8%, unacceptable care either significantly impacted on their wellbeing, or directly contributed to their death. In 2019, BASW produced a *Capabilities Statement for Social Workers Working with Adults with Learning Disability*, observing that:

> Inadequate and sometimes abusive institutional services are still being experienced by people with learning disability. Confident and effective social work is essential within multidisciplinary services and commissioning to accelerate improvements in the quality of care and support. Social workers need the capabilities to ensure community-based support is planned and provided, maximising people's potential for independence and self-determination, living the lives they want. (BASW, 2019b, p. 2)

Social workers work with people, with autistic people and people who have learning disabilities across a very broad range of services in community, residential and educational settings – sometimes in specialist, dedicated services, but more often in general child and adult services. The 1989 Children Act defines a child as being 'in need' if they are unlikely to achieve or maintain a standard of health and development without intervention of social services or if health or development would be significantly impaired without such intervention or if a child has a disability.

Adults' needs are primarily addressed under the Care Act 2014, but the Mental Capacity Act 2005 and the Mental Health Act 1983 are both relevant to some people with learning disabilities and autism in some situations (see Figure 14.1).

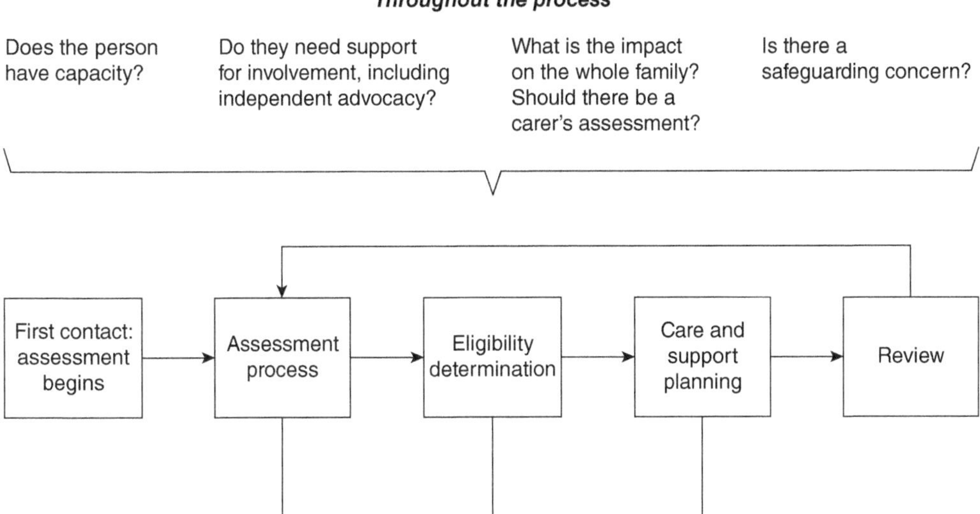

After assessment, the person must be given a record of the assessment. If an elegibility determination is made, the person must also receive a written record of this.
Needs can be met by supporting the person's own strengths, by universal, community or voluntary services, by information and advice, or by a carer.

Figure 14.1 The process of providing care and support for adults under the Care Act 2014

The Autism Act 2009 established the Secretary of State's duty to prepare and publish an autism strategy to improve local authority and NHS provision to meet the needs of autistic adults in England. In 2019, BASW issued a *Capabilities Statement for Social Work with Autistic Adults* advocating for improved practice by focusing on autistic individuals' strengths and abilities rather than their deficits (BASW, 2019c). This statement recognises the importance of neurodiversity as a foundational value in social work with autistic people and practice is underpinned by principles of personalisation, which maintains the person is at the centre of practice to facilitate the (self) identification of their needs.

Karen's duty contact

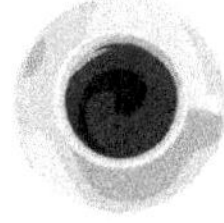

You can read more about these theories and concepts in the following chapters:

- Attachment – Chapter 6
- Pathologising; Medical and social models of disability; Risk; Vulnerability – Chapter 7
- Reflexivity; Critical reflection – Chapter 8

Karen is on duty when Marie self-presents and asks to speak to someone; she takes her into an interview room for a chat. Marie is quite agitated and explains she is autistic and struggling with her daughter, Ellie, who is 13. She finds Ellie's moods and aggression really difficult to manage, particularly when her husband, Mark, is working away from home. Ellie is currently being assessed for attention deficit hyperactivity disorder (ADHD). Karen is a strong supporter of **social,** rather than **medical models of disability**, and thinks that this all sounds very **pathologising**; however, she knows that some people find diagnosis helpful.

While talking with Marie, Karen notices her becoming more uneasy and agitated. The interview room has a flickering light and there is an audible low hum from the office heating system; Marie keeps getting distracted and moving her gaze from the light to the heater and back again. Karen has a cousin with autism and considers how this room would affect him. She likes her cousin but can't imagine him as a parent caring for a child. She thinks about how she adapts her communication for him and tries the same approach with Marie, speaking slowly and precisely. In line with a **social, rather than a medical model**, Karen tries not to overemphasise Marie's diagnosis, and focuses instead on asking questions that can help her gain a better understanding of the relationship between mother and daughter. She can't help feeling uneasy about how Marie talks about Ellie and feels she needs to consider their **attachment** and Marie's parenting capacity in order to identify any issues relating to Ellie's welfare.

Karen asks Marie about her feelings towards Ellie and how she shows her emotional warmth. Marie replies that Ellie is always well fed and the house is warm. Karen probes a little more and is surprised when Marie tells her that actually, she doesn't have to *like* Ellie, just because she is her daughter. Marie explains that Ellie often hits her and sometimes she has to hold her to stop her from hurting herself or others. She says she finds emotions very difficult – Mark is much better at that type of thing but he works away a lot. Marie finds Karen patronising with her very slow voice. She just wants some practical help about how to cheer Ellie up when she is upset and to find whether she can access any additional support when Mark is away. Marie is increasingly agitated by the flickering light and low hum, and Karen's approach is not helping.

Karen is beginning to feel threatened by Marie; she can see that she is increasingly irritated, and her responses are becoming more and more hostile. She is concerned by her lack of empathy for her child and whilst desperately not wanting to **pathologise** her, she keeps returning to the idea that being autistic negatively affects her parenting capacity. Ellie may be at emotional or even physical risk too. On the other hand, Marie is regularly experiencing violence from Ellie, so both mother and daughter are **vulnerable** and at **risk** in this situation. Karen decides that the best thing to do is to draw things to a close for now and let Marie leave the room. She explains she will talk the situation through with a colleague and get back to her.

Karen asks Judith if she has time to discuss this with her; Judith listens as Karen explains what has just unfolded. Karen acknowledges that she found the situation challenging and Marie's behaviour a little threatening. Judith validates Karen's feelings, but encourages her to be more **reflexive** and think about how *she* may have affected Marie. Judith points out that Karen appears to have been really aware of how difficult Marie was finding the environment, so why didn't she take her out of it? Simply acknowledging that the environment was poor and switching rooms may well have reduced Marie's stress and enabled Karen to better engage with her. Not wanting to adopt a medicalised approach led her to avoid directly discussing autism, but didn't stop her from generalising an approach her autistic cousin finds beneficial to Marie. That in itself was very pathologising, rather than person-centred. Similarly, the fact that someone is suggesting that Ellie has ADHD – even if Karen does not subscribe to this diagnosis – surely indicates that Ellie must be experiencing and presenting a lot of challenges?

Critically reflecting with Judith helps Karen to realise that she has taken an overly simplistic view of the **social** and **medical models**: in trying not to **pathologise** through medical diagnosis, she ended up **pathologising** Marie's parenting instead. Marie was asking for support and Karen didn't listen to her or try to better understand how Ellie's behaviour affected her. Karen decides that she will call Marie later on in the day and start the whole conversation over – perhaps she will feel more comfortable talking over the phone.

Reflective exercise 14.1

Reflect on how Marie's contact with Karen might have played out if Marie had not mentioned that she was autistic.

How do cultural normative assumptions about parenting disadvantage parents like Marie, who are not neurotypical?

Martin's visit

You can read more about these theories and concepts in the following chapters:

- Social construction – Chapter 2
- Anti-oppressive practice; Critical consciousness – Chapter 4
- Conditioning – Chapter 5
- Risk (culture of fear, risk society); Vulnerability; Staircase of oppression (objectification, stereotyping); Social role valorisation – Chapter 7

Jean had a fall and was taken to A&E. She has a broken hip and is admitted to a ward. Her son, George, who has Down's syndrome, stays until she is settled and then leaves her to get some rest. Later on that night, Jean is restless and tells a nurse she is worried about George. The next day the ward contacts social care to explain what has happened to Jean and highlight that George is vulnerable and unsupported. As Martin is on duty, he agrees to look into things. There is no recent information on the system about George; he has not had any involvement from services for a number of years. From what Martin can establish, it looks as though it has always been just Jean and George, and without his mum or a package of care, George might be at significant risk. Martin rings the landline, but no one picks up, so he decides to call round to the house. He knocks and knocks, but there is no answer. He feels uneasy. Maybe George is cowering inside, too afraid to answer the door, or maybe someone has taken advantage of him whilst his mum hasn't been there to protect him – he could be hurt. A woman is coming down the path to the house next door, so Martin asks her if she has seen George. 'Not today', she replies, 'but he usually leaves for work quite early'. She points down the road to a small supermarket.

As he walks down the road, Martin feels annoyed with himself. He values equality and strives very hard for his practice to be **anti-oppressive**, but he recognises that he has made a lot of automatic negative assumptions about George based on very little information. He realises how **conditioned** he is by notions of **risk** in **society**, and how **fear culture** often drives social workers to think of the worst-case scenario. Using his internal **reflection** as a process of **critical consciousness**, Martin realises that he had automatically **objectified** George, rather than seeing him as a person. From here he had rapidly progressed up the **staircase of oppression**, **constructing** George as **vulnerable** and applying **stereotypes** about people with learning disabilities: it never occurred to him that the reason he couldn't get hold of George was that he was at work, because he automatically assumed that someone with a learning disability wouldn't work.

At the supermarket, Martin asks the man on the checkout about George and he gives him a shout. George comes through from the back of the store and Martin explains that he has come to talk to him about his mum. George looks shocked and asks what has happened. Martin explains that Jean is in hospital with a broken hip. 'I know that', George says, 'I called the ambulance and went in with her. Has something *else* happened? Martin explains that he just wanted to check that George was ok and will be able to manage without Jean. George thanks him, but says he really has to get back to work, he's in the middle of receiving a delivery. He writes down his mobile number and tells Martin to give him a ring after his shift finishes at 4pm. George has a **valued social role**, and his time is as important as Martin's.

Reflective exercise 14.2

George's mum, Jean, said she was worried about him managing on his own, but this is not the same as saying that he *couldn't* manage on his own. How could nursing staff have responded to this situation differently? How did their assumptions influence Martin's **construction** of George as **vulnerable** and at **risk**?

Lloyd's blog

You can read more about these theories and concepts in the following chapters:

- Power – Chapter 4
- Normalisation; Stigma; Social role valorisation – Chapter 7
- Critical reflection – Chapter 8

Deciding if someone can decide

Today I was asked to decide if someone could decide, and it made me think a lot. Paul is 25 and he wants to move in with his girlfriend Julie. What's that got to do with me? Well, because Paul has a learning disability, the housing agency questioned whether he had the mental capacity – the ability to make a decision at the time that it needs to be made – to enter into a tenancy agreement. The Mental Capacity Act (MCA) Code of Practice says that 'A person's capacity must not be judged simply on the basis of their age, appearance, condition or an aspect of their behaviour' (Department of Constitutional Affairs, 2007, p. 40), but as soon as the housing agency discovered that Paul had a learning disability they did the reverse, and rang me, his social worker.

I first met Paul a year ago, but since long before then, everyone in Paul's life has been working to help him achieve his aim of having a '**normal**' life. It says something about our society when **normalcy** is an aspiration. Paul doesn't want to achieve anything remarkable; he just wants to be able to go through life without automatically being **stigmatised,** discriminated against and excluded. Wolf Wolfensberger (1983) and other proponents of **social role valorisation theory** called for action to enable people with learning disabilities (and other marginalised groups) to undertake **socially valued roles** which would make them more visible and change the negative way in which they are valued. Paul has worked hard to conform to society's expectations and change its view of him. He moved out of his mum and dad's house to his own flat in a supported living scheme. With support he learnt how to budget, shop, make meals, pay bills and keep his flat clean and tidy. He went to college to learn how to use computers and there he met Julie, and fell in love. They've been together for four years now. He got a job as a porter at a local hotel and he's never had a single day off sick. Paul plays by the rules of society – he participates, he contributes, he conforms; he's a real team player, an excellent friend and partner, a good son and a caring neighbour. But society doesn't treat him equally. The test of capacity set out by Section 2 of the MCA has two parts:

Does the person have an impairment of the mind or brain, or is there some sort of disturbance affecting the way their mind or brain works?

Well yes, Paul has a learning disability, that is not in dispute.

If so, does that impairment or disturbance mean that the person is unable to make the decision in question at the time it needs to be made?

Having had the privilege of knowing Paul for the last year I can categorically answer no, his learning disability doesn't prevent him from making a decision about entering into a tenancy agreement. When my partner and I got our first place together fresh out of university, we signed a tenancy agreement without any problems or intrusions. No one asked if we knew how to budget or pay bills (we didn't), no one asked anything other than did we have the required deposit. We benefited from the positive assumption that we were responsible adults, but no one *tested* this. Paul and Julie have spent years proving themselves to other people. They are *more* than ready for this. But that broad diagnostic label of learning disability – which means something different for each person who has it –

is enough for every decision that Paul and Julie try to take to be subject to scrutiny. And although it gave me great pleasure to tell the housing officer that Paul absolutely had the mental capacity to enter into a tenancy agreement, it felt wrong that I was given the **power** to decide whether he could decide.

Reflective exercise 14.3

As social workers, we try to address inequality. Some of the legislation we work under – for example, the Mental Health Act 1983 and the Mental Capacity Act 2005 – directly infringe people's rights on the basis of neurological difference. Is this acceptable? Why?

15 OLDER PEOPLE

Practice context

A global demographic shift is taking place as people live longer than ever before. In the UK, we can expect to live an average of 10 years longer than our parents' generation, and almost two decades longer than our grandparents (Centre for Ageing Better, 2020). One in three children born in the UK today can expect to live to 100 (Government Office for Science, 2016). The fact that many of us are living longer is the direct result of universal access to health care, better housing, improved access to food, water and sanitation, economic security and social support. It is arguably the greatest achievement of the welfare state, and yet as we highlighted in Chapter 5, it is rarely portrayed positively. We are alarmed and depressed by news and media reports which present our *ageing population* as a *demographic time bomb* which will create an *unmanageable economic burden*. Such views are far from new. Smith and Pelling (1991, p. 47) cite an American law dating back to 1772 which, 'required the Justices of Peace to search arriving ships for old persons, as well as other undesirables, and to send them away in order to prevent the growth of pauperism'. Bytheway and Johnson (1990, cited in Bytheway, 1995, p. 14) identify these pervasive, negative characterisations of older people as ageism:

(a) Ageism generates and reinforces a fear and denigration of the ageing process, and stereotyping presumptions regarding competence and the need for protection
(b) In particular, ageism legitimates the use of chronological age to mark out classes of people who are systematically denied resources and opportunities that others enjoy, and who suffer the consequences of such denigration, ranging from well-meaning patronage to unambiguous vilification

The Centre for Ageing Better's 2020 report, *Doddery but Dear*, identifies that rather than being recognised as diverse people with unique, individual biographies (Ray and Phillips,

2012) older people are homogenised through stereotypes. Discrimination is present in both active negative constructions of older people as burdensome and more passive dismissal through attitudes of 'benign indifference' (Abrams et al., 2015). Older people often internalise this negativity and develop a negative sense of self, which ironically can result in them performing in line with – and therefore inadvertently validating – limiting stereotypes (Swift and Steeden, 2020). Challenging ageism as social workers requires us to recognise that many unhelpful narratives about older people emanate from within health and social care. Of course, older people experience ill health, but that is not to say that all older people should be *presumed* to be in poor health (Nelson, 2005). When we normalise pain and ill health as an expectation of getting older, there is a risk that older people receive a poorer standard of treatment and support (Abrams et al., 2016). Martens et al. (2005) suggest that in some cases the association of ageing with ill health and death results in care professionals preferring not to work with older people so as not to be confronted with their own inevitable ageing and mortality.

That our population is ageing is undeniable, but we must not accept the dominant discourse that this is a disaster. People acquire a tremendous range of knowledge and skills over the course of their lives and although many will develop needs as a result of ageing, this does not negate their assets. Stereotypes can be challenged and changed by policies, services and practices which value older people and represent their true diversity. The World Health Organization's *Global Strategy and Action Plan on Ageing and Health* (2017) proceeds from an assumption that ageing is valuable, it is good to get old and society is better off for having older populations. It calls for action to address:

- older people's human rights, including their right to the best possible health
- gender equality amongst older people
- older people's equality and non-discrimination, particularly on the basis of age
- older people's equity
- intergenerational solidarity which enables social cohesion between generations

Historically, people's social capital and the value with which they are held has been perceived to reduce once they reach retirement, and continually decline the older they get. But in 25 years' time, one in five people will be over 60 (World Health Organization, 2017). This increasing longevity requires us to recognise and harness the value of older people, aspire for people of all ages to live full, active and satisfying lives, and remove existing structural barriers to older citizens' participation. Existing models of work, retirement, housing, care and support were designed for a different demographic. Typically, in later life declining income coincides with increased care costs, making poverty a significant issue for many older people. In the March 2017 budget, Theresa May's Conservative government committed to publishing a Green Paper on social care which would enable a public consultation on how people pay for their social care. Although our ageing society is recognised as one of the UK's four 'Grand Challenges' in HM Government's *Industrial Strategy: Building a Britain Fit for the Future* (2017), the Green Paper on social care has been repeatedly delayed and at the time of writing has still not been published.

Social work with older people is sometimes delivered through specialist teams which may be integrated or collocated with health and other disciplines, but quite often takes place in generic teams working with people of all ages. In either case, care and support needs are addressed under the Care Act 2014 (see Figures 12.1 and 14.1), and may arise from the person's own situation, their caring role for another, or both. BASW's *Capabilities Statement for Social Workers in England who Work with Older People* (2018b) recognises that older people are a large and varied group and therefore have varied experiences of ageing and the life course. It defines social work with older people (sometimes called gerontological social work) as:

> concerned with maintaining and enhancing the quality of life and well-being of older people and people close to them, and with promoting dignity, choice, independence and interdependence. (BASW, 2018b, p. 6)

Trish's safeguarding enquiry

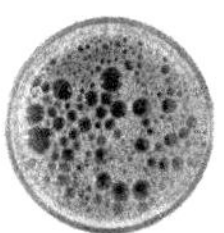

You can read more about these theories and concepts in the following chapters:

- Ageism; Activity theory; Continuity theory – Chapter 5
- Grief and loss – Chapter 6
- Safeguarding; Vulnerability; Risk – Chapter 7

Geri is an 82-year-old woman who lives in a housing with care community. She has been admitted to hospital three times recently following falls and hospital staff suspect that she may be in the early stages of dementia, as she often seems confused. She will be followed up in the outpatient clinic to assess this. More pressingly, Geri is extremely thin and seems undernourished, her clothes are stained, and her personal and oral hygiene is poor. Nursing staff raise a **safeguarding** alert on the basis that staff at the housing scheme are neglecting her. Trish is asked to gather some further information to see if a **safeguarding** enquiry under Section 42 of the Care Act 2014 needs to take place.

Trish rings Geri and finds her quite a character. She says that there is no problem at all with the care staff, and Trish is very welcome to come round to her apartment and see how lovely it is. Trish asks Geri if it is ok for her to speak to the staff, and Geri says, 'of course, dear, you have a job to do – do whatever you feel you must!' She is very happy to keep talking and in no rush to get off the phone. Trish contacts the care provider. The manager explains that her care company is privately contracted to provide care to residents who own properties at a retirement community. Geri bought an apartment a couple of years ago, downsizing from a very large property after her husband's death. She is not surprised by the hospital's concerns, but has a different view. She attributes Geri's apparent confusion and her unkempt appearance to her drinking, which has steadily increased since she moved in, and can regularly exceed four bottles of wine a day. Although care staff try to discourage Geri from drinking so much, they are quite sure that she has full mental capacity to make this choice. Trish decides that she will take up Geri's offer and visit the apartment.

Most of the people that Trish works with are affected by **poverty**, and she is quite shocked by the contrast of Geri's situation. Her apartment is in a gated community with immaculately kept grounds, and when Geri welcomes her in, she sees that it is indeed lovely; spacious and beautifully furnished. Geri asks Trish if she would like a glass of rosé – Trish thanks her but says she'd rather have a coffee. As the two women talk, Geri explains how terribly she misses her husband and how she bitterly regrets selling the home that they had shared for more than 40 years. She feels that she was pressured by her children who felt that the house and garden were too big for her to manage on her own, and she would be safer living somewhere with support. She knows their intentions were good, but she misses her neighbours and her big garden. There is nothing to do here – her apartment is cleaned and maintained for her, a gardener attends to the grounds and she has little in common with her neighbours. She knows she drinks too much, but the day passes more pleasantly with a bottle or two of rosé.

Trish feels really sad as she reflects on the **ageist** assumptions that have been made about Geri. Her children have identified their mother as **vulnerable** and in need of protection, but this is not how she sees herself. They saw the family home as a source of **risk**, but to Geri it was an asset, and a point of **continuity** with her life before bereavement. Trish thinks about **activity theory**, and recognises that giving up her home has caused Geri to lose her social connections and her sense of purpose. This has affected her self-esteem and because she has not found any meaningful way to replace what she has lost, she is using alcohol to get through. Rather than screening her for alcohol/substance misuse as they might a younger person, the hospital has made an age-based assumption that Geri has dementia. This is not a **safeguarding** situation, but Geri will benefit from an assessment of her needs to identify support which may help her with her **grief**, alcohol use and loneliness.

Reflective exercise 15.1

Consider how class and wealth/**poverty** impact on people's situations and social work's responses.

What options does Geri have available to her to improve her situation and reduce her loneliness that someone living on a basic state pension would not?

If Geri's care was arranged by the state, rather than privately, would her drinking be approached the same way?

Ali investigates a complaint

You can read more about these theories and concepts in the following chapters:

- Feminism – Chapter 2
- Age stratification; Ageism; Psychosocial development (generativity); Disengagement theory – Chapter 5
- Activity theory; Social capital – Chapter 6

Ali reads through a complaint that he has been asked to investigate about work undertaken by the hospital discharge team. The complainant, Andrew, is 65 and his 89-year-old father, Samuel, has dementia. Last year, Samuel's needs escalated suddenly, and he was admitted to hospital. Samuel was very distressed and unsettled, and ward staff found his behaviour difficult to manage. He was always calmer and less distressed when Andrew was there, so Andrew took unpaid leave from work to support his dad's assessment on the ward and throughout his subsequent admission into intermediate care. Samuel was assessed as needing a permanent placement, and Andrew took more time off work to be part of pre-admission assessments with residential care providers. Samuel eventually moved into a registered care home, but was re-admitted into hospital after two days because they were unable to manage his needs. Andrew's employer refused to allow him any more time off, and so reluctantly, he handed in his notice.

On the ward it was determined that Samuel was eligible for NHS funded care and he was discharged to a dementia nursing care placement. Specialist nursing staff were able to respond well to Samuel's needs; his distress subsided, and he soon settled very well. Andrew felt that he had put his life on hold to prioritise his dad's needs, and this came at the very high cost of giving up his job. His complaint was that the hospital social work team was wrong to have placed Samuel into intermediate care. If discharge planning during the first admission had identified that he needed nursing care, he would have gone somewhere where his needs were appropriately met, avoided a great deal of disruption and upset, and Andrew would have retained his job.

Ali thinks all of this through. He doesn't know if the hospital discharge team were at any fault – he will come to a conclusion on that after he has investigated. However, he does know that Andrew has had a raw deal. He thinks about his own father and knows he would want to be there for him exactly as Andrew was for Samuel. He also thinks about how much he loves his job, and how difficult it would be if he had to make the choice that Andrew was faced with. **Age stratification** hierarchically ranks citizens into age groups. At the age of 65, Andrew meets the demographic of an older person, and yet his father who is also in this demographic relies on his care. Ali knows that the ageing population means that this is becoming a very common situation, and thinks that society needs to rethink the arbitrary markers it puts down about when someone is old. Erikson's **psychosocial developmental** task between the ages of 40 and 65 is **Generativity vs Stagnation**, but can people in modern society really be expected to be ready to pass over to the next generation by 65? **Disengagement theory** suggested that as people got older, they naturally withdrew from society, but Andrew did not want to give up his job; this was a situation he was forced into by circumstance. Having given it up, however, **ageist** attitudes about older people in the employment market make it highly unlikely that he will get another job of an equivalent status. Andrew had **social capital** as both an employee and a son, but society currently makes it very difficult for people in his situation to be both.

Reflective exercise 15.2

As a result of increased life expectancy, many people find themselves in Andrew's situation of having to choose between their career and caring for their elderly parents. This has obvious parallels with the traditional expectation that women would be primary caregivers and sacrifice their careers in order to become mothers. How can **feminism** inform how society responds to our ageing population?

Dianne's carer assessment

You can read more about these theories and concepts in the following chapters:

- Critical consciousness – Chapter 3
- Psychosocial development (Integrity vs Despair); Activity theory; Ageism – Chapter 5
- Intersectionality – Chapter 6
- Personhood – Chapter 7

Dianne visits Matthew, who has requested a carer's assessment. Matthew is 76 and his husband Gregory has dementia. She can see how Matthew dotes on Gregory; he settles him down with a jigsaw and takes Dianne into the next room so that he can speak frankly. Matthew explains that he is worried about Gregory's long-term care. At the moment, he can look after all of his needs, but he knows that things will get worse. Dianne explains that this is a very normal concern, and assures Matthew that his and Gregory's needs will be regularly reassessed to make sure that the correct level of support is provided. Matthew says perhaps Dianne doesn't understand what he is saying – Gregory is a gay man, and dementia care services are not designed for gay men. He will not entertain the thought of Gregory going into a care home where people don't respect his **identity**. He and Gregory have fought against discrimination all of their lives, and there is no way that he will allow his husband to be desexualised or expected to conform to heteronormative assumptions.

Dianne pauses for thought. She has not come across this particular situation before, and realises that a lot of people with dementia must be faced with it. If she is honest, sexuality is just not something that she thinks about when she is working with older people, so she too is guilty of ageist desexualisation and heteronormativity. **Reflecting** on this now, she can clearly see how the **intersection** of inequality that Gregory faces as a gay man with dementia significantly increases the risk of his **personhood** being undermined. Now that she is **critically conscious** of this issue, she needs to go away and do some research so that she can support Matthew to make appropriate future plans for himself and his husband.

Reflective exercise 15.3

Society increasingly embraces diversity in younger people, but fails to recognise – or even consider – that older people may have diverse genders or sexualities. How does ageism at structural, cultural and personal levels reinforce this?

SUMMARY AND FINAL THOUGHTS

In our practice and as social work educators, we have often encountered fantastic students and social workers who are unconfident, reluctant, or avoidant when it comes to applying theory. Perhaps theory has been introduced in an inaccessible way, leaving the person feeling confused, or maybe they received an unhelpfully critical response to an early attempt to apply theory. Negative formative experiences such as these can result in *theory fright*. We believe that theory fright arises not because of problems with the student, but because of problems with the academic or practice education approach. We set ourselves the ambitious task of writing an accessible, practice-based book that would demystify theory, and support readers to embrace it, rather than fear it!

In Part I we focused on demystification. The recognition that theorising is a constant and universal human instinct is liberating and empowering – it means that no one is a theory novice, everyone has existing theory skills from which they can draw. Similarly, recognising that theory shapes the way in which we understand and structure our world helps us to see social work itself is a theoretical construct which is practiced in a theoretical context, and involves the application of theory to make sense of people's situations. We know that people often struggle to engage with literature on theory, and to make this task less daunting we introduced a range of theories which can support social work practice across the life course in a simple and straightforward way. We hope that this has provided you with the confidence to explore more in-depth texts and develop more nuanced understandings.

In Part II we focused on the why, when, and how of applying theory in practice. We were very cautious not to give the impression that there is a *right* way to apply theory; people's situations are unique, as are practitioner's approaches. We used the practice experiences of fictional characters with different backgrounds, at different points of their professional social work journeys to model different approaches. These scenarios demonstrate that there are as many problems and advantages inherent in being an experienced practitioner as there are in being a student. The key message that we wanted to convey was that social work is a profession *practiced by people, with people*, and theory is what helps us transcend from a *helpful person*, to a *helping professional*.

Social work is, at its very core, about working with vulnerable people during times of crisis. As we were finalising the draft of this book, the world changed. The Covid-19 pandemic brought terrible levels of illness, suffering and death. The vital nature of social care suddenly became clear to those who had never had cause to consider it before, exposing disparities of funding, organisation, and esteem. We are enormously proud of how our students on placement and our colleagues in practice creatively adapted their ways of working in order to meet people's social needs in the face of unprecedented challenge. The impact of the pandemic will continue as both physical and economic situations gradually unfold. The full extent of social consequences will take time and much research to realise. Existing theory will be used, and new theory will be developed to make sense and form an understanding of both people's experiences and social work's response.

REFERENCES

Abrams, D., Swift, H.J., Lamont, R.A. and Drury, L. (2015) *The Barriers to and Enablers of Positive Attitudes to Ageing and Older People, at the Societal and Individual Level.* Technical report. Government Office for Science, Kent, UK.

Abrams, D., Swift, H.J. and Mahmood, L. (2016) *Prejudice and Unlawful Behaviour: Exploring Levers for Change.* Research Report 101, Equality and Human Rights Commission. Available at: www.equalityhumanrights.com/sites/default/files/research-report-101-prejudiceand-unlawful-behaviour.pdf (accessed 18 September 2020).

Adams, R., Dominelli, L. and Payne, M. (2009) *Practising Social Work in a Complex World.* Basingstoke: Palgrave Macmillan.

Ahmed-Mohamed, K. (2011) Social work practice and contextual systemic intervention: Improbability of communication between social work and sociology. *Journal of Social Work Practice*, 25(1), pp. 5–15.

Allen, R., Carr, S., Linde, K. and Sewell, H. (2016) *Social Work for Better Mental Health: A Strategic Statement.* Available at: https://assets.publishing.service.gov.uk/government/uploads/system/uploads/attachment_data/file/495500/Strategic_statement_-_social_work_adult_mental_health_A.pdf (accessed 18 September 2020).

Alston, P. (2018) *Statement on Visit to the United Kingdom, by Professor Philip Alston, United Nations Special Rapporteur on extreme poverty and human rights.* Available at: www.ohchr.org/Documents/Issues/Poverty/EOM_GB_16Nov2018.pdf (accessed 1 December 2019).

Althusser, L. (2007) *Politics and History.* London: Verso.

Archer, M.S. (2003) *Structure, Agency and the Internal Conversation.* Cambridge: Cambridge University Press.

Archer, M.S. (2007) *Making Our Way Through the World: Human Reflexivity and Social Mobility.* Cambridge: Cambridge University Press.

Ash, A. (2013) A cognitive mask? Camouflaging dilemmas in street-level policy implementation to safeguard older people from abuse. *The British Journal of Social Work*, 43(1), pp. 99–115.

Atchley, R.C. (1989) A continuity theory of normal aging. *The Gerontologist*, 29(2), pp. 183–90.

Aziz, R., Roth, D. and Lindley, B. (2012) *Understanding Family and Friends Care: The Largest UK Survey.* London: Family Rights Group. Available at: https://www.frg.org.uk/images/e-publications/ffc-report-3.pdf (accessed 18 September 2020).

Baginsky, M., Moriarty, J., Manthorpe, J., Stevens, M., MacInnes, T. and Nagendran, T. (2010) *Social Workers' Workload Survey Messages from the Frontline: Findings from the 2009 Survey and Interviews with Senior Managers.* Leeds: Children's Workforce Development Council and King's College London.

Baginsky, M., Ixer, G. and Manthorpe, J. (2020) Practice frameworks in children's services in England: An attempt to steer social work back on course? *Practice: Social Work in Action*, Available at https://www.tandfonline.com/doi/abs/10.1080/09503153.2019.1709634?journalCode=cpra20 (accessed 4 July 2020).

Bailey, R. and Brake, M. (1980) *Radical Social Work and Practice*. London: Edward Arnold.

Baldwin, M. (2004) Critical reflection: Opportunities and threats to professional learning and service development in social work organizations in social work. In N. Gould and M. Baldwin (eds), *Critical Reflection and the Learning Organization*. Aldershot: Ashgate, pp. 41–56.

Bandura, A. (1965) Influence of model's reinforcement contingencies on the acquisition of imitative responses. *Journal of Personality and Social Psychology*, 1(6), pp. 589–95.

Bandura, A. (1969) Social learning of moral judgments. *Journal of Personality and Social Psychology*, 11(3), pp. 275–9.

Bandura, A. (1973) *Aggression: A Social Learning Analysis*. Englewood Cliffs, NJ: Prentice-Hall.

Bandura, A. (1977) Self-efficacy: Toward a unifying theory of behavioral change. *Psychological Review*, 84(2), pp. 191–215.

Bandura, A. (1978) Social learning theory of aggression. *Journal of Communication*, 28(3), pp. 12–29.

Bandura, A. (1994) Self-efficacy. In V. Ramachaudran (ed.), *Encyclopaedia of Human Behavior* (Vol. 4). New York: Academic Press, pp. 71–81.

Barak, A. (2016) Critical consciousness in critical social work: Learning from the theatre of the oppressed. *British Journal of Social Work*, 46(6), pp. 1776–92.

Barkan, S. and Rocque, M. (2018) Socioeconomic status and racism as fundamental causes of street criminality. *Critical Criminology*, 26, pp. 211–31.

Barnett, P. et al. (2019) Ethnic variations in compulsory detention under the Mental Health Act: A systematic review and meta-analysis of international data. *Lancet Psychiatry*, 6(4), pp. 305–17.

Barr, B., Taylor-Robinson, D., Stuckler, D., Loopstra, R., Reeves, A. and Whitehead, M. (2016) 'First, do no harm': Are disability assessments associated with adverse trends in mental health? A longitudinal ecological study. *Journal of Epidemiology and Community Health*, 70(4), pp. 339–45.

BASW (2011) *BASW UK Supervision Policy*. Available at: https://www.basw.co.uk/system/files/resources/basw_73346-6_0.pdf (accessed 18 September 2020).

BASW (2014) *Code of Ethics*. Available at: www.basw.co.uk/system/files/resources/Code%20of%20Ethics%20Aug18.pdf (accessed 8 November 2019).

BASW (2018a) *Professional Capabilities Framework for Social Work in England: Guidance on Using the 2018 Refreshed PCF*. Available at: https://www.basw.co.uk/system/files/resources/PCF%20Final%20Documents%20Overview%2011%20June%202018.pdf (accessed 8 November 2019).

BASW (2018b) *Capabilities Statement for Social Workers in England who Work with Older People*. Available at: www.basw.co.uk/resources/capabilities-statement-social-workers-england-who-work-older-people (accessed 18 September 2020).

BASW (2019a) *Anti-Poverty Practice Guide for Social Work*. Available at https://www.basw.co.uk/resources/anti-poverty-practice-guide-social-work (accessed 1 June 2020).

BASW (2019b) *Capabilities Statement for Social Workers Working with Adults with Learning Disability*. Available at: www.basw.co.uk/system/files/resources/181064%20Learning%20Disability%20Capability%20Statement%2019.06.19.pdf (accessed 19 February 2020).

BASW (2019c) *The capabilities statement for social work with autistic adults*. Available at https://www.basw.co.uk/the-capabilities-statement-social-work-autistic-adults (accessed 1 March 2020).

Beckett, C. and Horner, N. (2016) *Essential Theory for Social Work Practice* (2nd edn). London: Sage.

Beddoe, L. (2010) Surveillance or reflection: Professional supervision in 'the Risk Society'. *British Journal of Social Work*, 40(4), pp. 1279–96.
Berger, P.L. and Luckmann, T. (1966) *The Social Construction of Reality: A Treatise in the Sociology of Knowledge*. New York: Anchor Books.
Bernstein, R. (1983) *Beyond Objectivism and Relativism: Science, Hermeneutics, and Praxis*, Philadelphia: The University of Pennsylvania Press.
Bertalanffy, L. von (1968) *General System Theory: Foundations, Development, Applications*. New York: George Braziller.
Bibby, J., Grace, E. and Abbs, I. (2020). *Will COVID-19 be a watershed moment for health inequalities?* The Health Foundation, Available at: https://www.health.org.uk/publications/long-reads/will-covid-19-be-a-watershed-moment-for-health-inequalities (accessed 20 September 2020).
Bourdieu, P. (1986) The forms of capital. *Handbook of Theory and Research for the Sociology of Education*, ed. J. Richardson. Westport, CT: Greenwood, pp. 241–58.
Bourdieu, P. (1996) On the family as a realized category. *Theory, Culture & Society*, 13(3), pp. 19–26.
Bowen, M. (1990) *Family Therapy in Clinical Practice*. Lanham, MD: Rowman & Littlefield.
Bowlby, J. (1997) *Attachment and Loss: Volume I, Attachment*. London: Random House
Bowlby, J. (1998) *Attachment and Loss: Vol. 2, Separation, anxiety and anger*. London: Pimlico.
Bowlby, J. (1981) *Attachment and Loss: Vol. 3, Loss: sadness and depression*. Harmondsworth: Penguin.
Bowlby, J. and Parkes, C.M. (1970) Separation and loss within the family. In E.J. Anthony (ed.), *The Child in his Family*. New York: Wiley, pp. 197–216.
Bray, R., De Laat, M., Godinot, X., Ugarte, A. and Walker, R. (2019) *The Hidden Dimensions of Poverty*. Pierrelaye: International Movement ATD Fourth World. Available at: www.atd-fourthworld.org/wp-content/uploads/sites/5/2019/05/Dim_Pauvr_eng_FINAL_July.pdf
Brenner, J. and Fraser, N. (2017) What is progressive neoliberalism? A debate. *Dissent*, 64(2), p. 130.
British Humanist Association (2011) *Religion and Belief: Census Results 2011*. Available at: https://humanism.org.uk/campaigns/religion-and-belief-some-surveys-and-statistics/census-2011-results/ (accessed 24 February 2019).
Brodsky, B., Cloitre, M. and Dulit, R. (1995) Relationship of dissociation to self-mutilation and childhood abuse in borderline personality disorder. *American Journal of Psychiatry*, 152(12), pp. 1788–92.
Bronfenbrenner, U. (1977) Toward an experimental ecology of human development. *American Psychologist*, 32(7), pp. 513–31.
Bronfenbrenner, U. (1979) *The Ecology of Human Development*. Cambridge, MA: Harvard University Press.
Brown, H. (2011) The role of emotion in decision making. *Journal of Adult Protection*, 13(4), pp. 194–202.
Bruner, J.S. (1978) The role of dialogue in language acquisition. In A. Sinclair, R.J. Jarvelle and W.J.M. Levelt (eds), *The Child's Concept of Language*. New York: Springer-Verlag, pp. 241–255.
Brydon, K. (2012) Promoting diversity or confirming hegemony? In search of new insights for social work. *International Social Work*, 55(2), pp. 155–67.
Burke, C. (2012) Social workers putting in longer hours, survey finds. *The Guardian*. Available at: www.theguardian.com/social-care-network/2012/sep/25/social-workers-longer-hours-survey (accessed 20 September 2020).
Butler, E., Egloff, B., Wilhelm, F., Smith, N., Erickson, E. and Gross, J. (2003) The social consequences of expressive suppression. *Emotion*, 3(1), pp. 48–67.

Butler, J. (1990) *Gender Trouble: Feminism and the Subversion of Identity*. New York: Routledge.

Byng-Hall, J. (1985) The family script: A useful bridge between theory and practice. *Journal of Family Therapy*, 7(3), pp. 301–5.

Bytheway, W.R. (1995) *Ageism*. Buckingham: Open University Press.

Cairns, K. (2004) *Attachment, Trauma and Resilience: Therapeutic Caring for Children*. London: BAAF.

Calder, M. and Hackett, S. (2003) *Assessment in Child Care: Understanding and Developing Frameworks for Practice*. Lyme Regis: Russell House Publishing.

Cann, R. and Lawson, K. (2016) *Cuts: The View from Foster Carers (England). The Impact of Austerity Measures on Fostered Children and the Families that Care for Them*. London: The Fostering Network.

Cannon, W.B. (1932) *The Wisdom of the Body*. New York: W.W. Norton & Co.

Cantor-Graae, E. and Selten, J. (2005) Schizophrenia and migration: a meta-analysis and review, *American Journal of Psychiatry*, 162(1), pp. 12–24.

Carey, M. and Foster, V. (2011) Introducing 'deviant' social work: Contextualising the limits of radical social work whilst understanding (fragmented) resistance within the social work labour process. *British Journal of Social Work*, 41(1), pp. 576–93.

Carpenter, J., Webb, C., Bostock, L. and Coomber, C. (2012) *Effective Supervision in Social Work and Social Care: SCIE Research Briefing* 43. London: Social Care Institute for Excellence. Available at: www.scie.org.uk/publications/briefings/briefing43/ (accessed 18 September 2020).

Casey, L. (2012) *Listening to Troubled Families*. London: Department for Communities and Local Government.

D'Cruz, H., Gillingham, P. and Melende, S. (2007) Reflexivity, its meanings and relevance for social work: A critical review of the literature, *British Journal of Social Work*, 37(1), pp. 73–90.

CDC (Centers for Disease Control and Prevention) (2019) *Preventing Adverse Childhood Experiences: Leveraging the Best Available Evidence*. Atlanta, GA: National Center for Injury Prevention and Control, Centers for Disease Control and Prevention.

Centre for Ageing Better (2020) *Doddery but Dear? Examining Age-related Stereotypes*. Available at: www.ageing-better.org.uk/publications/doddery-dear-examining-age-related-stereotypes (accessed 18 September 2020).

Chapman, R. (2019) *Undertaking a Fostering Assessment in England*. London: CoramBAAF.

Clarke, J., Gewirtz, S. and McLaughlin, E. (2000) Reinventing the welfare state. In J. Clarke, S. Gewirtz and E. McLaughlin (eds), *New Managerialism, New Welfare*. London: Sage, pp. 1–26.

Cocker, C. and Hafford-Letchfield, T. (2014) *Rethinking Anti-Oppressive Theories for Social Work Practice*. London: Palgrave Macmillan.

Cohen, I. (1989) *Structuration Theory, Anthony Giddens and the Constitution of Social Life*. Basingstoke: Macmillan.

Collins, D., Jordan, C. and Coleman, H. (2010) *An Introduction to Family Social Work*. Andover: Cengage Learning.

Connell, R. (1995) *Masculinities*. Cambridge: Polity Press.

Connell, R. (2002) On hegemonic masculinity and violence: Response to Jefferson and Hall. *Theoretical Criminology*, 6(1), pp. 89–99.

Connolly, M. and Harms, L. (2012) *Social Work Theory and Practice*. Melbourne: Cambridge University Press.

Cook, S. (2020) If social work knowledge is still based on western values, can practice really be anti-oppressive? *Community Care*. Available at: https://www.communitycare.co.uk/2020/02/03/social-work-knowledge-still-based-western-values-can-practice-really-anti-oppressive/?utm_ (accessed 20 September 2020).

CoramBAAF (2018) Statistics: England – Looked after children, adoption and fostering statistics for England. Available at: https://corambaaf.org.uk/fostering-adoption/looked-after-children-adoption-fostering-statistics/statistics-england (accessed 12 December 2019).

Corby, B. (2006) *Applying Research in Social Work Practice*. Maidenhead: Open University Press.

Corby Peters, S. (2018) Defining social work leadership: A theoretical and conceptual framework. *Journal of Social Work Practice*, 32(1), pp. 31–44.

Corker, M. and Shakespeare, T. (2002) *Disability/Postmodernity: Embodying Disability Theory*. London: Continuum.

Cornell University (2005) Urie Bronfenbrenner, father of Head Start program and pre-eminent 'human ecologist', dies at age 88. Available at:www.news.cornell.edu/stories/Sept05/Bronfenbrenner.ssl.html (accessed 22 July 2009).

Cranny-Francis, A., Waring, W., Stavropoulos, P. and Kirkby, J. (2003) *Gender Studies: Terms and Debates*. Basingstoke: Palgrave Macmillan.

Crenshaw, K. (1989) Demarginalizing the intersection of race and sex: A black feminist critique of antidiscrimination doctrine, feminist theory and antiracist politics. *University of Chicago Legal Forum*, Vol. 1989, Article 8. Available at: https://chicagounbound.uchicago.edu/uclf/vol1989/iss1/8/ (accessed 20 September 2020).

Crittenden, P. (2000) A dynamic-maturational approach to continuity and change in patterns of attachment. In P. Crittenden and A. Claussen (eds), *The Organization of Attachment Relationships*. Cambridge: Cambridge University Press, pp. 348–357.

Crown Prosecution Service (2010) *Guidance on the Distinction between Vulnerability and Hostility in the Context of Crimes Committed against Disabled People*. London: The Stationery Office.

Croisdale-Appleby, D. (2014) *Re-visioning Social Work Education*. London: Department of Health and Social Care.

Cumming, E. and Henry, W. (1961; Reprint 1979) *Growing Old: The process of disengagement*. New York: Basic Books.

Cummins, I. (2020) Using Fraser's model of 'progressive neoliberalism' to analyse deinstitutionalisation and community care. *Critical and Radical Social Work*, 8(1), pp. 77–93.

Cunningham, J. and Cunningham, S. (2014) *Sociology and Social Work* (2nd edn). London: Learning Matters, Sage.

Darwin, C. (1839) *Voyages of the Adventure and Beagle Vol 3*. Available at: https://books.google.co.uk/books?id=yvovNUgBk4sC&pg=PA468&lpg=PA468&dq#v=onepage&q&f=false (accessed 2 February 2020).

David, M. (2008) Social inequalities, gender and lifelong learning – a feminist sociological review of work, family and education. *International Journal of Sociology and Social Policy*, 28(7/8), pp. 260–72.

Deming, W.E. (1993) '4'.*The New Economics for Industry, Government, and Education*. Boston: MIT Press.

Deacon, L. and MacDonald, S. (2017) *Social Work Theory and Practice*. London: Sage.

Department for Constitutional Affairs (2007) *Mental Capacity Act 2005 Code of Practice*. London: HMSO.

Department for Education (2011a) *The Children Act 2011 Guidance and Regulations Volume 4: Fostering Services*. London: HM Government.

Department for Education (2011b) *Fostering Services: National Minimum Standards*. London: HM Government.

Department for Education (2014) *Knowledge and Skills for Child and Family Social Work*. Available at: https://assets.publishing.service.gov.uk/government/uploads/system/uploads/attachment_data/

file/338718/140730_Knowledge_and_skills_statement_final_version_AS_RH_Checked.pdf (accessed 20 September 2020).

Department for Education (2015) *The Children Act 1989 Guidance and Regulations, Volume 2: Care Planning, Placement and Case Review*. Available at: www.gov.uk/government/uploads/system/uploads/attachment_data/file/441643/Children_Act_Guidance_2015.pdf (accessed 8 November 2019).

Department for Education (2017) *Children Looked After in England (including Adoption), year ending 31 March 2017*. Available at: https://assets.publishing.service.gov.uk/government/uploads/system/uploads/attachment_data/file/664995/SFR50_2017-Children_looked_after_in_England.pdf (accessed 8 November 2019).

Department for Education (2018) *Working Together to Safeguard Children*. Available at: https://assets.publishing.service.gov.uk/government/uploads/system/uploads/attachment_data/file/729914/Working_Together_to_Safeguard_Children-2018.pdf (accessed 13 February 2020).

Department for Education (2019) *Children Looked After in England (including adoption) year ending 31st March 2019*. Available at: https://assets.publishing.service.gov.uk/government/uploads/system/uploads/attachment_data/file/850306/Children_looked_after_in_England_2019_Text.pdf (accessed 15 December 2019).

Department of Health (2015) *Knowledge and Skills Statement for Social Workers in Adult Services*. Available at: https//assets.publishing.service.gov.uk/government/uploads/system/uploads/attachment_data/file/411957/KSS.pdf (accessed 4 July 2020).

Derrida, J. and Bass, A. (1995) *Writing and Difference*. London: Routledge.

Diamond, L. (2008) *Sexual Fluidity: Understanding Women's Love and Desire*. Cambridge, MA: Harvard University Press.

Dix, H., Hollinrake, S. and Meade, J. (2018) *Relationship-based Social Work with Adults*. Northwich: Critical Publishing.

Doel, M. (2012) *Social Work: The Basics*. Abingdon: Routledge.

Doel, M. and Shardlow, S. (1998) *The New Social Work Practice*. Aldershot: Ashgate.

Dominelli, L. (1996) Deprofessionalizing social work: Anti-oppressive practice, competencies and postmodernism. *British Journal of Social Work*, 26(2), pp. 153–75.

Dominelli, L. (2002a) *Anti-oppressive Social Work Theory and Practice*. Basingstoke: Palgrave Macmillan.

Dominelli, L. (2002b) *Feminist Social Work Theory and Practice*. Basingstoke: Palgrave.

Dominelli, L. (2008) *Anti-Racist Social Work* (3rd edn). London: Palgrave.

Donnellan, H. and Jack, G. (2008) *The Survival Guide for Newly Qualified Child and Family Social Workers: Hitting the Ground Running*. London: Jessica Kingsley.

Doran, G. (1981) There's a S.M.A.R.T. way to write management's goals and objectives. *Management Review*, 70(11), pp. 35–6.

Dunleavy, P. and Hood, C. (1994) From old public administration to new public management. *Public Money and Management*, 14(3), pp. 9–16.

Engels, F. and Barrett, M.L. (1986 edn) *The Origin of the Family, Private Property and the State*. London and New York: Penguin Books.

Erikson, E.H. (1963) *Childhood and Society* (2nd edn.) New York: Norton.

Erikson, E.H. (1966) Eight ages of man. *International Journal of Psychiatry*, 2(3), pp. 281–307.

Erikson, E.H. (1970) Autobiographic notes on the identity crisis. *Daedalus*, 99(4), pp. 730–59.

Erikson, E.H. (1994) *Identity: Youth and Crisis*. New York: W.W. Norton & Co.

Fairclough, N. (1992) *Discourse and Social Change*. Cambridge: Cambridge University Press.

Family Action (n.d.) Our work with troubled families. Available at: www.family-action.org.uk/troubled-families/ (accessed 4 February 2020).

Farrell, D. (2008) Psychological trauma. In R. Tummey and T. Turner (eds), *Critical Issues in Mental Health*. Basingstoke: Palgrave Macmillan, pp. 142–60.

Featherstone, M. and Hepworth, M. (1991) The mask of ageing and the postmodern life course. In M. Featherstone, M. Hepworth and B.S. Turner (eds), *The Body: Social Process and Cultural Theory*. London: Sage, pp. 371–89.

Felitti, V.J., Anda, R.F., Nordenberg, D., Williamson, D.F., Spitz, A.M., Edwards, V., Koss, M.P., and Marks, J.S. (1998) Relationship of childhood abuse and household dysfunction to many of the leading causes of death in adults: The Adverse Childhood Experiences (ACE) Study. *Aces*, 14(4), pp. 245–58.

Fenton, J. (2019) *Social Work for Lazy Radicals*. London: Red Globe Press.

Ferguson, H. (2018) How social workers reflect in action and when and why they don't: The possibilities and limits to reflective practice in social work. *Social Work Education: The International Journal*, 37(4), pp. 415–27.

Ferguson, I. and Woodward, R. (2009) *Radical Social Work in Practice: Making a Difference*. Bristol: Polity Press.

Finch, J. (2007) Displaying families. *Sociology*, 41(1), pp. 65–81.

Fineman, M.A. (2005) *The Autonomy Myth: A Theory of Dependency*. New Press.

Fineman, M. (2008) The vulnerable subject: Anchoring equality in the human condition. *Yale Journal of Law and Feminism*, 20(1), pp. 9–15.

Fineman, M. (2017) Vulnerability and inevitable inequality. *Oslo Law Review*, 4, pp. 133–49.

Firmin, C. (2018) *Abuse between Young People: A Contextual Account*. Abingdon: Routledge.

Fish, S. and Hardy, M. (2015) Complex issues, complex solutions: Applying complexity theory in social work practice. *Nordic Social Work Research*, 5(1), pp. 98–114.

Fook, J. (2000) Deconstructing and reconstructing professional expertise. In B. Fawcett, B. Featherstone, J. Fook and A. Rossiter (eds), *Practice and Research in Social Work: Postmodern Feminist Perspectives*. London: Routledge, pp. 105–20.

Fook, J. (2002) *Social Work: Critical Theory and Practice*. London: Sage.

Fook, J. (2016) *Social Work: A Critical Approach to Practice* (3rd edn). London: Sage.

Fook, J. and Gardner, F. (2007) *Practising Critical Reflection: A Handbook*. Maidenhead: Open University Press.

Foucault, M. (1982) The subject and power. *Critical Inquiry*, 8(4), pp. 777–95.

Foucault, M. (2001) *Madness and Civilization: A History of Insanity in the Age of Reason*. London: Routledge.

Foyle, J. (2015) *Placement Disruption: A Review of Cases of Children in Care in England and Wales where Stable Placements are Threatened for Financial Reasons*. London: Nationwide Association of Fostering Providers.

Fraiberg, S., Adelson, E. and Shapiro, V. (1975) Ghosts in the Nursery: A Psychoanalytic Approach to the Problems of Impaired Infant-Mother Relationships. *Journal of American Academy of Child Psychiatry*, 14(3), pp. 387–421.

Freire, P. (1998) *Teachers as Cultural Workers: Letters to Those Who Dare Teach*. Boulder, CO: Westview Press.

Freire, P. (2006) *Pedagogy of the Oppressed 30th Anniversary Edition*. New York: Continuum.

Freire, P. and Moch, M. (1987) A critical understanding of social work. *Journal of Progressive Human Services*, 1(1), pp. 3–9.

Freud, S. (1962) *The Ego and the Id*. London: Hogarth Press and the Institute of Psychoanalysis.

Freud, S. (1890, 1954 Print) *The Interpretation of Dreams*. London: Allen & Unwin.

Freud, S. and Strachey, J. (1949 edition: 2011 print) *Three Essays on the Theory of Sexuality*. London: Martino Fine Books.

Furedi, F. (2018) *How Fear Works: Culture of Fear in the 21st Century*. London: Bloomsbury Continuum.

Furstenberg, F. and Kaplan, B. (2007) Social capital and the family. In J. Scott, J. Treas and M. Richards (eds), *The Blackwell Companion to the Sociology of Families*. Oxford: Blackwell Publishing, pp. 218–32.

Galpin, D., Maksymluk, A. and Whiteford, A. (2019) Is anyone asking why social workers are 'failing' to be resilient? *Community Care*. Available at: https://www.communitycare.co.uk/2019/04/10/is-anyone-asking-social-workers-failing-resilience/ (accessed 4 July 2020).

Garrett, P.M. (2018) *Social Work and Social Theory: Making Connections*. Bristol: Policy Press.

Garthwaite, K. (2015) 'Keeping meself to meself' – How social networks can influence narratives of stigma and identity for long-term sickness benefit recipients. *Social Policy and Administration*, 49(2), pp. 199–212.

Gautier, A. and Wellard, S. (2014) Disadvantage, discrimination, resilience: The lives of kinship carers. Available at: https://www.bl.uk/collection-items/disadvantage-discrimination-resilience-the-lives-of-kinship-families (accessed 7th July 2020).

Giddens, A. (1976) *New Rules of Sociological Method*. London: Hutchinson.

Giddens, A. (1992) *The Transformation of Intimacy: Sexuality, Love and Eroticism in Modern Societies*. Cambridge: Polity.

Giddens, A. (1994) Living in a post-traditional society. In U. Beck, A. Giddens and S. Lash (eds), *Reflexive Modernization: Politics, Tradition and Aesthetics in the Modern Social Order*. Cambridge: Polity, pp. 56–109.

Giddens, A. and Pierson, C. (1998) *Conversations with Anthony Giddens: Making Sense of Modernity*. Stanford, CA: Stanford University Press.

Gilbert, T. and Powell, J. (2010) Power and social work in the United Kingdom. *Journal of Social Work*, 10(1), pp. 3–22.

Gill, O. and Jack, G. (2007) *The Child and Family in Context: Developing Ecology Practice in Disadvantaged Communities*. Lyme Regis: Russell House Publishing.

Gitterman, A. (2014) Social work: A profession in search of its identity. *Journal of Social Work Education*, 50(4), pp. 599–607.

Goemans, R. (2012) A consideration of the nature and purpose of mental health social work. *Mental Health and Social Inclusion*, 16(2), pp. 90–6.

Goffman, E. (1963) *Stigma: Notes on the Management of Spoiled Identity*. New York: Simon & Schuster.

Goldstein, H. (1973) *Social Work Practice: A Unitary Approach*. Columbia: University of South Carolina Press.

Government Equalities Office (2016) *Government Response to the House of Lords Select Committee Report on the Equality Act 2010: The Impact on Disabled People*. Available at: https://assets.publishing.service.gov.uk/government/uploads/system/uploads/attachment_data/file/535441/Government_response_to_the_LSC_report_on_disability.pdf (accessed 20 September 2020).

Government Office for Science (2016) *Future of an Ageing Population*. Available at: https://assets.publishing.service.gov.uk/government/uploads/system/uploads/attachment_data/file/816458/future-of-an-ageing-population.pdf (accessed 20 September 2020).

Gramsci, A. (2003 edn) *Selections from the Prison Notebooks*. London: Lawrence and Wishart.

Grant, C. and Osanloo, A. (2014) Understanding, selecting and integrating a theoretical framework in dissertation research: Creating the blueprint for your 'house'. *Administrative Issues Journal: Connecting Education, Practice and Research*, 4(2), pp. 12–26.

Gray, M. and Lovat, T. (2008) Practical mysticism, Habermas, and social work praxis. *Journal of Social Work*, 8(2), pp. 149–62.

Hall, S. (1999) The question of cultural identity. In S. Hall, D. Held and T. McGrew (eds), *Modernity and its Futures*. Cambridge: Polity Press, pp. 273–326.

Hardy, M. (2016) Discretion in the history and development of social work. In T. Evans and F. Keating (eds), *Policy and Social Work Practice*. London: Sage, pp. 11–30.

Hari, J. (2018) *Lost Connections: Why You're Depressed and How to Find Hope*. London: Bloomsbury.

Harlow, E. (2003) New managerialism, social service departments and social work practice today. *Practice*, 15(2), pp. 29–44.

Harris, J. (1998) Scientific management, bureau-professionalism, new managerialism: The Labour process of state social work. *British Journal of Social Work*, 28(6), pp. 839–62.

Harris, J. (2003) *The Social Work Business*. London: Routledge.

Harvey, L.H. and Reed, M. (1996) Social sciences as the study of complex systems. In D. Kiel and E. Elliott (eds), *Chaos Theory in the Social Sciences: Foundations and Applications*. Ann Arbor: The University of Michigan Press, pp. 295–324.

Hatton, K. (2015) *New Directions in Social Work Practice* (2nd edn). London: Learning Matters, Sage.

Havighurst, R.J. (1961) Successful ageing. *The Gerontologist*, 1(1), pp. 8–13.

Hawkins, R. and Maurer, K. (2012) Unravelling social capital: Disentangling a concept for social work. *British Journal of Social Work*, 42(2), pp. 353–70.

Healy, K. (2005) *Social Work Theories in Context*. Basingstoke: Palgrave Macmillan.

Healy, K. (2012). *Social Work Methods and Skills*. Basingstoke: Palgrave MacMillan.

Healy, K. (2014) *Social Work Theories in Context* (2nd edn). Basingstoke: Palgrave Macmillan.

Healy, J. (2020) 'It spreads like a creeping disease': Experiences of victims of disability hate crimes in austerity Britain. *Disability & Society*, 35(2), pp. 176–200.

Hearn, J., Edwards, J. and Popay, J. (1998) *Men, Gender Divisions and Welfare*. London: Routledge.

Helm, D. (2011) Judgements or assumptions? The role of analysis in assessing children and young people's needs. *British Journal of Social Work*, 41(5), pp. 894–911.

Herman, J. (1992) *Trauma and Recovery: The Aftermath of Violence – From Domestic Abuse to Political Terror*. New York: Basic Books.

Heron, G. (2004) Evidencing anti-racism in student assignments: Where has all the racism gone? *Qualitative Social Work*, 3(3), pp. 277–95.

Heslop, P. and Meredith, C. (2019) *Social Work: From Assessment to Intervention*. London: Sage.

Hills, J. (2012) *Introduction to Systemic and Family Therapy*. Basingstoke: Palgrave Macmillan.

Hingley-Jones, H. and Ruch, G. (2016) 'Stumbling through'? Relationship-based social work practice in austere times. *Journal of Social Work Practice*, 30(3), pp. 235–48.

HM Government (2017) *Industrial Strategy: Building a Britain Fit for the Future*. Available at: https://assets.publishing.service.gov.uk/government/uploads/system/uploads/attachment_data/file/730048/industrial-strategy-white-paper-web-ready-a4-version.pdf (accessed 20 September 2020).

Hodge, D. (2015) *Spiritual Assessment in Social Work and Mental Health Practice*. New York: Columbia University Press.

Hoffman, E. (1988) *The Right to be Human: A Biography of Abraham Maslow*. New York: St. Martin's Press.

Hollomotz, A. (2007) Disability, oppression and violence: Towards a sociological explanation. *Sociology*, 47(3), pp. 477–93.

Hollomotz, A. (2009) Beyond 'vulnerability': An ecological model approach to conceptualizing risk of sexual violence against people with learning difficulties. *British Journal of Social Work*, 39(1), pp. 99–112.

Hood, C. (1995) The 'new public management' in the 1980s: variations on a theme. *Accounting, Organisations and Society*, 20(2/3), pp. 93–109.

Hothersall, D. (2003) *History of psychology* (4th edn). McGraw-Hill Education.

Hothersall, S. and Maas-Lowit, M. (2010) *Need, Risk and Protection in Social Work Practice*. London: Learning Matters.

Hough, R.E. (2012) Adult protection and 'intimate citizenship' for people with learning difficulties: Empowering and protecting in light of the No Secrets review. *Disability and Society*, 27(1), pp. 131–44.

House of Lords Equality Act 2010 and Disability Committee, Equality Act 2010: The Impact on Disabled People, 24 March 2016, HL Paper 117 of session 2015–16, p. 5. Available at: https://publications.parliament.uk/pa/ld201516/ldselect/ldeqact/117/117.pdf (accessed 20 September 2020).

Howe, D. (1994) Modernity, postmodernity and social work. *British Journal of Social Work*, 24(5), pp. 513–32.

Howe, D. (1999) *Attachment Theory, Child Maltreatment and Family Support: A Practice and Assessment Model*. Basingstoke: Macmillan.

Howe, D. (2009) *A Brief Introduction to Social Work Theory*. Basingstoke: Palgrave Macmillan.

Howell, E. (2005) *The Dissociative Mind*. London: Analytic Press.

Humanists UK (2011) *The Census Campaign 2011*. Available at: https://humanism.org.uk/campaigns/successful-campaigns/census-2011/ (accessed 4 July 2020).

Ingleby, E. (2010) *Applied Psychology for Social Work*. London: Learning Matters, Sage.

Innes, H. and Innes, P. (2013) *Personal, Situational and Incidental Vulnerabilities to ASB Harm: A Follow Up Study*. Cardiff: Universities Police Science Institute, Cardiff University.

James, A. and Curtis, P. (2010) Family displays and personal lives. *Sociology*, 44(6), pp. 1163–80.

Johnson, G. and Puplampu, K. (2008) Internet use during childhood and the ecological techno-subsystem. *Canadian Journal of Learning and Technology*, 34 (1). DOI: 10.21432/T2CP4T

Jones, C. (1996) Anti-intellectualism and the peculiarities of British social work education. In N. Parton (ed.), *Social Theory, Social Change and Social Work*. London: Routledge, pp. 190–210.

Jones, C. (1999) Social Work: Regulation and Managerialism. In Hexworthy, M. and Halford, S. (eds), *Professionals and the New Managerialism in the Public Sector*. Buckingham: Open University Press, pp. 37–49

Jones, C. and Hackett, S. (2011) The role of 'family practices' and 'displays of family' in the creation of adoptive kinship. *British Journal of Social Work*, 41(1), pp. 40–56.

Jones, E., Farina, A., Hastorf, A., Markus, H., Miller, D. and Scott, R. (1984) *Social Stigma: The Psychology of Marked Relationships*. New York: Freeman.

Jones, L., Bellis, M., Wood, S., Hughes, K., McCoy, E., Eckley, L., Bates, G., Mikton, C., pp. 37–49 Shakespeare, T., and Officer, A. (2012) Prevalence and risk of violence against children with disabilities: a systematic review and meta-analysis of observational studies. *The Lancet*, 380(9845), pp. 899–907.

Jones, S., McWade, P. and Toogood, S. (2016) CAPBS Practice Paper 5: Normalisation and social role valorisation. British Institute Learning Disabilities. Available at: https://docplayer.net/90094910-Normalisation-and-social-role-valorisation.html (accessed 20 September 2020).

Joseph Rowntree Foundation (2020) *UK Poverty 2019/20*. Available at: www.jrf.org.uk/report/uk-poverty-2019-20 (accessed 20 September 2020).

Kahneman, D. (2011) *Thinking, Fast and Slow*. London: Penguin.

Keating, F. (2016) Concluding thought: The interface between social policy and social work. In T. Evans and F. Keating (eds), *Policy and Social Work Practice*. London: Sage, pp. 172–5.

Kemshall, H. (2013) *Working with Risk*. Cambridge: Polity Press.

Kerr, M.E. and Bowen, M. (1988) *Family Evaluation: An Approach Based on Bowen Theory*. New York: Norton & Company.

Kerr, M.E. (2000) *One Family's Story: A Primer on Bowen Theory*. The Bowen Center for the Study of the Family. Available at http://www.thebowencenter.org (accessed 4 July 2020).

Khan, M., Ilcisin, M. and Saxton, K. (2017) Multifactorial discrimination as a fundamental cause of mental health inequities. *International Journal for Equity in Health*, 16(1), p 43

Kitwood, T. (1993) Towards a theory of dementia care: The interpersonal process. *Ageing and Society*, 13(1), pp. 51–67.

Kitwood, T. (1997) *Dementia Reconsidered: The Person Comes First*. Buckingham: Open University Press.

Klass, D., Silverman, P.R. and Nickman, S.L. (Eds) (1996) *Continuing Bonds: New Understandings of Grief*. Philadelphia: Taylor and Francis.

Krumer-Nevo, M. and Komem, M. (2015) Intersectionality and critical social work with girls: Theory and practice. *British Journal of Social Work*, 45(4), pp. 1190–206.

Kubler-Ross, E. (1969) *On Death and Dying*. New York: Macmillan.

Kuhn, T.S. (1970) *The Structure of Scientific Revolutions* (enlarged, 2nd edn). Chicago: University of Chicago Press.

Lamb, M. and Tamis-Lemonda, C. (2004) The role of the father: An introduction. In M. Lamb (ed.), *The Role of Father in Child Development* (4th edn). Chichester: Wiley and Sons.

Lambert, M. and Crossley, S. (2017) Getting with the (troubled families) programme: A review. *Social Policy & Society*, 16(1), pp. 87–97.

Lawler, J. and Bilson, A. (2010) *Social Work Management and Leadership: Managing Complexity with Creativity*. Abingdon: Routledge.

Lee, C. (2014) Conservative comforts: Some philosophical crumbs for social work. *British Journal of Social Work*, 44(8), pp. 2135–44.

Lenin, I.V. (1977 edn) *Selected Works*. Moscow: Progress Publishers.

Liebenberg, L., Ungar, M. and Ikeda, J. (2015) Neo-liberalism and responsibilisation in the discourse of social service workers. *British Journal of Social Work*, 45(3), pp. 1006–21.

Link, B. and Phelan, J. (1995) Social conditions as fundamental causes of disease. *Journal of Health and Social Behavior* 35(Extra Issue), pp. 80–94.

Link, B. and Phelan, J. (2001) Conceptualizing stigma. *Annual Review of Sociology*, 27, pp. 363–85.

Lishman, J. (2018) Evaluation. In J. Lishman, C. Yuill, J. Brannan and A. Gibson (eds), *Social Work: An Introduction* (2nd edn). London: Sage, pp. 533–43.

Local Government Association (2017) *Being Mindful of Mental Health – The Role of Local Government in Mental Health and Wellbeing*. Available at: www.local.gov.uk/being-mindful-mental-health-role-local-government-mental-health-and-wellbeing (accessed 20 September 2020).

Luhmann, N. (1995) *Social Systems*. Stanford, CA: Stanford University Press.

Luhrmann, T., Padmavati, R., Tharoor, H. and Oseic, A. (2015) Hearing voices in different cultures: A social kindling hypothesis. *Topics in Cognitive Science*, 7(4), pp. 646–63.

Lyotard, J.F. (1984/2005) *The Postmodern Condition: A Report on Knowledge*. Manchester: Manchester University Press.

Maas-Lowit, M. (2018) Politics and social policy. In J. Lishman, C. Yuill, J. Brannan and A. Gibson (eds), *Social Work: An Introduction* (2nd edn). London: Sage, pp. 46–60.

Maclean, S. and Harrison, R. (2015) *Theory and Practice: A Straightforward Guide for Social Work Students* (3rd edn). Lichfield: Kirwin MacClean Associates.

MacDermott, F. (2014) Complexity theory, trans-disciplinary working and reflective practice. In A. Pycroft and C. Bartollas (eds), *Applying Complexity Theory*. Bristol: Policy Press, pp. 181–98.

Macdonald, G. and Macdonald, K. (2010) Safeguarding: A case for intelligent risk management. *The British Journal of Social Work*, 40(4), pp. 1174–91.

Macvarish, J. and Lee, E. (2019) Constructions of parents in adverse childhood experiences discourse. *Social Policy & Society*, 18(3), pp. 467–77.

Maercker, A., Michael, T., Fehm, L., Becker, E. and Margraf, J. (2004) Age of traumatisation as a predictor of post-traumatic stress disorder or major depression in young women. *British Journal of Psychiatry*, 184, pp. 482–7.

Maijer, K., Begemann, M.J.H., Palmen, S.J.M.C., Leucht, S. and Sommer, I.E.C. (2018) Auditory hallucinations across the lifespan: A systematic review and meta-analysis. *Psychological Medicine*, 48(6), pp. 879–88.

Main, M. and Solomon, J. (1990) Procedures for identifying infants as disorganized-disorientated during the strange situation. In M. Greenberg, D. Cicchetti and E.M. Cummings (eds), *Attachment in the Pre-school Years: Theory Research and Intervention*. London: Guildford Press, pp. 121–60.

Manthorpe, J., Moriarty, J., Hussein, S., Stevens, M. and Sharpe, E. (2015) Content and purpose of supervision in social work practice in England: Views of newly qualified social workers, managers and directors. *British Journal of Social Work*, 45(1), pp. 52–68.

Marcuse, H. (1964/2002) *One-Dimensional Man*. London: Routledge.

Marmot, M. (2010) *Fair society, healthy lives. The Marmot Review: strategic review of health inequalities in England post-2010*. Available at: http://www.instituteofhealthequity.org/resources-reports/fair-society-healthy-lives-the-marmot-review (accessed 6 July 2020).

Marmot, M., Allen, J., Boyce, T., Goldblatt, P. and Morrison, J. (2020) *Health Equity in England – The Marmot Review. 10 Years On*. Available at: www.health.org.uk/publications/reports/the-marmot-review-10-years-on (accessed 6 July 2020).

Martens, A., Goldenberg, J.L. and Greenberg, J. (2005) A terror management perspective on ageism. *Journal of Social Issues*, 61(2), pp. 223–39.

Marx, K. (1983 edn) *Capital, Volume 1*. London: Lawrence and Wishart.

Mattsson, T. (2014) Intersectionality as a useful tool: Anti-oppressive social work and critical reflection. *Qualitative Social Work*, 29(1), pp. 8–17.

Mayo, E. (1933) *The Human Problems of an Industrial Civilization*. New York: The Macmillan Company.

McGoldrick, M., Gerson, R. and Petry, S. (2008) *Genograms: Assessment and Intervention* (3rd edn). New York: Norton.

McNeece, C.A. and Thyer, B.A. (2004) Evidence-based practice and social work. *Journal of Evidence-Based Social Work*, 1(1), pp. 7–25.

Mead, M. (1963) *Sex and Temperament in Three Primitive Societies*. New York: William Morrow.

Mental Health Foundation (2015) A new way forward. Available at: https://www.mentalhealth.org.uk/sites/default/files/a-new-way-forward-5.pdf (accessed 18 September 2020).

Miller, A. (1990) *Thou Shalt Not Be Aware: Society's Betrayal of the Child*. London: Pluto Press.

Ministry of Housing, Communities and Local Government (2019) *National Evaluation of the Troubled Families Programme 2015–2020: Findings*. Available at: https://assets.publishing.service.gov.uk/government/uploads/system/uploads/attachment_data/file/786889/National_evaluation_of_the_Troubled_Families_Programme_2015_to_2020_evaluation_overview_policy_report.pdf (accessed 4 February 2020).

Ministry of Justice (2019) *Standards for Children in the Youth Justice System*. Available at: https://assets.publishing.service.gov.uk/government/uploads/system/uploads/attachment_data/file/780504/Standards_for_children_in_youth_justice_services_2019.doc.pdf (accessed 19 February 2020).

Mitchell, G. and Agnelli, J. (2015) Person-centred care for people with dementia: Kitwood reconsidered. *Nursing Standard*, 30(7), pp. 46–50.

Morgan, D.H.J. (1996) *Family Connections*. Cambridge: Polity Press.

Mullaly, R. (1997) *Structural Social Work: Ideology*, Theory and Practice (2nd edn).Toronto: McClelland Stewart.

Munro, E. (2011) *The Munro Review of Child Protection: Final Report A Child-centred System*. London: Department for Education.

Murphy, G. (2020) *CQC Inspections and Regulation of Whorlton Hall 2015–2019: An Independent Review*. Available at: www.cqc.org.uk/sites/default/files/20020218_glynis-murphy-review.pdf (accessed 21 September 2020).

Narey, M. (2014) *Making the Education of Social Workers Consistently Effective*. London: Department for Education.

Nelson, T.D. (2005) Ageism: Prejudice against our feared future self. *Journal of Social Issues*, 61(2), pp. 207–21.

Newman, D.M. (1999) *Sociology of Families*. California: Pine Forge Press.

Newman, J. and Clarke, J. (2009) *Publics, Politics and Power: Remaking the Public in Public Services*. London: Sage.

NHS Digital (2018) Mental health of children and young people in England, 2017. Available at: https://digital.nhs.uk/data-and-information/publications/statistical/mental-health-of-children-and-young-people-in-england/2017/2017 (accessed 21 September 2020).

NHS England (2014) *Liaison and Diversion Process*. Available at: www.england.nhs.uk/wp-content/uploads/2014/04/ld-op-mod-1314.pdf (accessed 19 February 2020).

Nirje, B. (1992) *The Normalization Principle Papers*. Uppsala: Centre for Handicap Research, Uppsala University.

Noble, C. and Irwin, J. (2009) Social work supervision: An exploration of the current challenges in a rapidly changing social, economic and political environment. *Journal of Social Work*, 9(3), pp. 345–58.

Noddings, N. (2002) *Starting at Home: Caring and Social Policy*. Berkeley: University of California Press.

Office for National Statistics (2019) *Suicides in the UK: 2018 registrations*. Available at: https://www.ons.gov.uk/peoplepopulationandcommunity/birthsdeathsandmarriages/deaths/bulletins/suicidesintheunitedkingdom/2018registrations (accessed 6 July 2020).

Office of the Chief Social Worker for Adults (2019) *National Workforce Plan for Approved Mental Health Professionals (AMHPs)*. Available at: https://assets.publishing.service.gov.uk/government/uploads/system/uploads/attachment_data/file/843539/AMHP_Workforce_Plan_Oct19__3_.pdf (accessed 6 July 2020).

Oko, J. (2011) *Understanding and Using Theory in Social Work* (2nd edn). Exeter: Learning Matters.

Osburn, J. (2006) An overview of social role valorization theory. *The SRV Journal*. Available at: https://socialrolevalorization.com/wp-content/uploads/2019/03/srv_theory_joe_osburn.pdf

Oxford Dictionary (2019) https://en.oxforddictionaries.com/definition/theory (accessed 9 February 2019).

Parsons, T. (1951) *The Social System*. Glencoe, IL: Free Press.

Parton, N. (1996/2000) Social theory, social change and social work: An introduction. In N. Parton (ed.), *Social Theory, Social Change and Social Work*. Abingdon: Routledge, pp. 4–18.

Pastorelli, C., Vittorio, C., Barbaranelli, C., Rola, J., Rozsa, S. and Bandura, A. (2001) A structure of children's perceived self-efficacy: A cross national study. *European Journal of Psychological Assessment*, 17(2), pp. 87–97.

Payne, M. (2014) *Modern Social Work Theory* (4th edn). Basingstoke: Palgrave Macmillan.

Peas, B. (2009) From radical to critical social work: Progressive transformation or mainstream incorporation. In P. Adams, L. Dominelli and M. Payne (eds), *Critical Practice in Social Work* (2nd edn). Basingstoke: Palgrave Macmillan.
Pew Research Center (2017) *The Changing Global Religious Landscape*. Available at: www.pewforum.org/2017/04/05/ (accessed 9 July 2019).
Piaget, J. (1953) *The Origin of Intelligence in the Child*. London: Routledge & Kegan Paul.
Piaget, J. (1955/1976) *The Child's Construction of Reality* (M. Cook, trans.). London: Routledge & Kegan Paul.
Piaget, J. (2001) *The Psychology of Intelligence*. London: Routledge.
Piaget, J. and Gruber, H.E. (1977) *The Essential Piaget*. London: Routledge & Kegan Paul.
Piaget, J. and Inhelder, B. (2000) *The Psychology of the Child*. New York: Basic Books.
Pincus, A. and Minahan, A. (1973) *Social Work Practice: Model and Method*. Itasca, IL: Peacock.
Pinkney, C., Robinson-Edwards, S., Glynn, M. (2018) *England's Gun Crime Capital. Youth and Policy*. Available at: https://www.youthandpolicy.org/articles/on-road-youth-work/ (accessed 25 January 2020).
Price, V. and Simpson, G. (2007) *Transforming Society? Social Work and Sociology*. Bristol: The Policy Press.
Prochaska, F. (2006) *Christianity and Social Service in Modern Britain: The Disinherited Spirit*. Oxford: Oxford University Press.
Public Health England (2017) *Health Profile for England*. Available at: https://www.gov.uk/government/publications/health-profile-for-england (accessed 1 June 2020).
Public Health England (2018) *Learning Disability: Applying All Our Health*. Available at: https://www.gov.uk/government/publications/learning-disability-applying-all-our-health (accessed 4 July 2020).
Public Health Wales NHS (2015) *The Welsh Adverse Childhood Experiences (ACE) Study*. Available at: www2.nphs.wales.nhs.uk:8080/PRIDDocs.nsf/7c21215d6d0c613e80256f490030c05a/d488a3852491bc1d80257f370038919e/$FILE/ACE%20Report%20FINAL%20(E).pdf (accessed 4 July 2020).
Purves, L. (2018) Bethany's case revives our worst fears about asylums. *The Times*, 15 October. Available at: www.thetimes.co.uk/article/bethany-case-revives-worst-fears-about-asylums-bt66kfb9z (accessed 5 July 2020).
Putnam, R. (1995) Bowling Alone: America's Declining Social Capital. *Journal of Democracy*, 6(1), pp. 65–78.
Putman, R. (2000) *Bowling Alone: The Collapse and Revival of American Community*. New York: Simon & Schuster.
Quarmby, K. (2013) *Why We Are Failing Disabled People?* London: Portobello Books.
Raitakari, S., Juhila, K. and Räsänen, J. (2019) Responsibilisation, social work and inclusive social security in Finland. *European Journal of Social Work*, 22(2), pp. 264–76.
Ralston, K. and Gayle, V. (2017) *Exploring 'Generations and Cultures of Worklessness' in Contemporary Britain*. Available at: https://www.youthandpolicy.org/articles/generations-of-worklessness/ (accessed 4 July 2020).
Ray, M. and Phillips, J. (2012) *Social Work with Older People*. Basingstoke: Palgrave Macmillan.
Raynor, P. and Vanstone, M. (2016) Moving away from social work and halfway back again: New research on skills in probation. *British Journal of Social Work*, 46(4), pp. 1131–47.
Rees, A., Holland, S. and Pithouse, A. (2012) Food in foster families: Care, communication and conflict. *Children and Society*, 26(2), pp. 100–11.
Reijman, S., Foster, S. and Duschinsky, R. (2018) The infant disorganised attachment classification: Patterning within the disturbance of coherence. *Social Science and Medicine*, 200, pp. 52–8.

Reisch, M. and Andrews, J. (2001) *The Road not Taken: A History of Radical Social Work in the United States*. Philadelphia: Brunner-Routledge.
Ribbens, J., McCarthy, J. and Edwards, R. (2011) *Key Concepts in Family Studies*. London: Sage.
Riley, M.W., Johnson, M.E. and Foner, A. (1972) *Aging and Society: A Sociology of Age Stratification*. New York: Russell Sage Foundation.
Rogers, C. (1951) *Client-centred Therapy*. London: Constable and Company.
Rogowski, S. (2011a) Managers, managerialism and social work with children and families: The deformation of a profession? *Practice*, 23(3), pp. 157–67.
Rogowski, S. (2011b) Relationships versus managerialism. *Professional Social Work*, February, pp. 24–5.
Roulstone, A. and Mason-Bish, H. (eds) (2012) *Disability, Hate Crime and Violence*. Abingdon: Routledge.
Rubin, M., Konrad, S., Nimmagadda, J., Scheyett, A. and Dunn, K. (2018) Social work and interprofessional education: Integration, intersectionality, and institutional leadership. *Social Work Education*, 37(1), pp. 17–33.
Ruch, G., Turney, D. and Ward, A. (2010) *Relationship-based Social Work: Getting to the Heart of Practice*. London: Jessica Kingsley.
Russell, M. (2019) PSWs cannot fulfil Munro's vision within closed leadership systems. *Community Care*. Available at: www.communitycare.co.uk/2019/01/30/psws-cannot-fulfil-munros-vision-within-closed-leadership-systems/ (accessed 1 February 2020).
Sakamoto, I. and Pitner, R. (2005) Use of critical consciousness in anti-oppressive social work practice: Disentangling power dynamics at personal and structural levels. *British Journal of Social Work*, 35(4), pp. 435–52.
Sayce, L. (1998) Stigma, discrimination and social exclusion: What's in a word? *Journal of Mental Health*, 7(4), pp. 331–43.
Schechter, D., Coots, T., Zeanah, C., Davies, M., Coates, S., Trabka, K., Marshall, R., Liebowitz, M. and Myers, M. (2005) Maternal mental representations of the child in an inner-city clinical sample: Violence-related posttraumatic stress and reflective functioning, *Attachment & Human Development*, 7(3), pp. 313–31.
Schofield, G. and Beek, M. (2014) *The Secure Base Model*. London: BAAF.
Schön, D.A. (1983) *The Reflective Practitioner: How Professionals Think in Action*. New York: Basic Books.
Scottish Government (2018) *Delivering for Today, Investing for Tomorrow: The Government's Programme for Scotland 2018–2019*. Available at: www.gov.scot/publications/adverse-childhood-experiences/ (accessed 21 September 2020).
Scourfield, P. (2018) *Putting Professional Leadership into Social Work Practice*. London: Sage.
Scragg, T. and Mantell, A. (2011) *Safeguarding Adults in Social Work*. London: Learning Matters.
Shack, L., Jordan, C., Thomson, C.S. et al. (2008) Variation in incidence of breast, lung and cervical cancer and malignant melanoma of skin by socioeconomic group in England. *BMC Cancer*, 8, p. 271.
Shakespeare, T. (2012) Disability in developing countries. In N. Watson, A. Roulstone and C. Thomas (eds), *Routledge Handbook of Disability Studies*. Abingdon: Routledge.
Shakespeare, T. and Watson, N. (2002) The social model of disability: an outdated ideology? *Research in Social Science and Disability*, 2, pp. 9–28.
Shaw, I. (2007) Is social work research distinctive? *Social Work Education*, 26(7), pp. 659–69.
Shildrick, T., MacDonald, R., Webster, C. and Garthwaite, K. (2010) *The Low-pay, No-pay Cycle: Understanding recurrent poverty*. Joseph Rowntree Foundation. Available at: https://www.jrf.org.uk/sites/default/files/jrf/migrated/files/unemployment-pay-poverty-full.pdf (accessed 21 September 2020).

Shildrick, T., MacDonald, R., Furlong, A., Roden, J. and Crow, R. (2012) *Are 'Cultures of Worklessness' Passed Down the Generations?* Joseph Rowntree Foundation. Available at: https://www.jrf.org.uk/sites/default/files/jrf/migrated/files/worklessness-families-employment-full.pdf (accessed 6 July 2020).

Shildrick, T. (2018) *Poverty Propaganda: Exploring the Myths*. Bristol: The Policy Press.

Silverman, D. (2005) *Doing Qualitative Research: A Practical Handbook* (2nd edn). London: Sage.

Siporin, M. (1980) Ecological systems theory in social work. *Journal of Sociology and Social Welfare*, 7(4), pp. 507–32.

Skinner, B.F., Catania, A.C. and Harnad, S. (1988) *The Selection of Behavior: The Operant Behaviorism of B. F. Skinner: Comments and Consequences*. Cambridge: Cambridge University Press.

Smith, E. (2011) Teaching critical reflection. *Teaching in Higher Education*, 16(2), pp. 211–23.

Smith, R. (2012) Segmenting an audience into the own, the wise, and normals: A latent class analysis of stigma-related categories. *Communication Research Reports*, 29(4), pp. 257–65.

Smith, R.M. and Pelling, M. (1991) *Life, Death and the Elderly: Historical Perspectives*. London: Routledge.

Social Work Reform Board (2012) Building a safe and confident future: Maintaining momentum progress report from the Social Work Reform Board. Available at: https://assets.publishing.service.gov.uk/government/uploads/system/uploads/attachment_data/file/175947/SWRB_progress_report_-_June_2012.pdf (accessed 1 April 2020).

Stanley, T. and Russell, M. (2014) The Principal Child and Family Social Worker: A Munro recommendation in practice. *Practice: Social Work in Action*, 26(2), pp. 81–96.

Strehler, B.L. (1962) *Time, Cells, and Aging*. New York: Academic Press.

Swift, H. and Steeden, B. (2020) *Exploring Representations of Old Age and Ageing: Literature Review*. Available at: www.ageing-better.org.uk/sites/default/files/2020-03/Exploring-representations-of-old-age.pdf (accessed 21 September 2020).

Tafvelin, S., Hyvonen, U. and Westerberg, K. (2014) Transformational leadership in the social work context: The importance of leader continuity and co-worker support. *British Journal of Social Work*, 44(4), pp. 886–904.

Taylor, C. and White, S. (2000) *Practising Reflexivity in Health and Welfare: Making Knowledge*. Buckingham: Open University Press.

Teater, B. (2014) *An Introduction to Applying Social Work Theory and Methods*, Maidenhead: The Open University.

The Spectator (1869) No title. Available at: http://archive.spectator.co.uk/article/27th-november-1869/2/mr-goschen-has-published-an-able-minute-on-the-nec (accessed 20 June 2017).

Thesen, J. (2005) From oppression towards empowerment in clinical practice – offering doctors a model for reflection. *Scandinavian Journal of Public Health*, 33(Suppl 66), pp. 47–52.

Thomas, G. (ed.) (2010) *Origin and Development of Social Work in India*. New Delhi: Indira Gandhi National Open University.

Thomas, S. (1999) Historical background and evolution of normalization-related and social role valorization related training. In R.J. Flynn and R. Lemay (eds), *A Quarter-century of Normalization and Social Role Valorization: Evolution and Impact*. Ottawa: University of Ottawa Press, pp. 353–74.

Thompson, N. (1992/2016) *Anti Discriminatory Practice* (6th edn). Basingstoke: Palgrave Macmillan.

Thompson, N. (2010) *Theorizing Social Work Practice*, Basingstoke: Palgrave Macmillan.

Thompson, P. (2010) Theory Fright – Part1. Available at: https://patthomson.net/2018/11/12/theory-fright-part-one/ (accessed 2 July 2020).

Tong, R. (1989) *Feminist Thought: A Comprehensive Introduction*. Boulder, CO: Westview Press.

Trevithick, P. (2003) Effective relationship-based practice: A theoretical exploration. *Journal of Social Work Practice*, 17(2), pp. 173–86.

Tulle, E. and Lynch, E. (2011) Later life. In C. Yuill and A. Gibson (eds), *Sociology for Social Work: An Introduction*. London: Sage, pp. 116–37.

Turbett, C. (2014) *Doing Radical Social Work*. Basingstoke: Palgrave MacMillan.

Turnell, A. (2012) *The Signs of Safety: Comprehensive Briefing Paper*. Perth: Australia: Resolutions Consultancy Pty Ltd.

Turnell, A. and Edwards, S. (1999) *Signs of Safety: A Solution and Safety Oriented Approach to Child Protection Casework*. New York: Norton.

Turner, A. (2019) *Academics voice concerns over What Works Centre's family group conferences study*. Available at: www.communitycare.co.uk/2019/06/03/academics-voice-concerns-works-centres-family-group-conferences-study/ (accessed 1 December 2019).

Turner, J.R. and Baker, R.M. (2019) Complexity theory: An overview with potential applications for the social sciences. *Systems*, 7(1). Available at: file:///C:/Users/djrw7/Downloads/systems-07-00004-v2.pdf (accessed 2 December 2019).

Unger, M. (2004) Surviving as a postmodern social worker: Two Ps and three Rs of direct practice. *Social Work*, 49(3), pp. 488–96.

UNICEF (1989) *What is the Convention on the Rights of the Child?* Available at: www.unicef.org/child-rights-convention/what-is-the-convention (accessed 1 December 2019).

United Nations (2006) *Convention on the Rights of Persons with Disabilities* (CRPD). Available at: www.un.org/development/desa/disabilities/convention-on-the-rights-of-persons-with-disabilities.html (accessed 2 March 2020).

United Nations Human Rights Office of the High Commissioner (2017) *Committee on the Rights of Persons with Disabilities Reviews Report of the United Kingdom*. Available at: www.ohchr.org/EN/NewsEvents/Pages/DisplayNews.aspx?NewsID=21993&LangID=E (accessed 2 March 2020).

University of Bristol (2018) *Learning Disability Mortality Review (LeDeR) Annual Report 2018*. Available at: https://www.bristol.ac.uk/media-library/sites/sps/leder/LeDeR_Annual_Report_2018%20published%20May%202019.pdf (accessed 5 July 2020).

Van der Kolk, B., Perry, C. and Herman, J. (1991) Childhood origins self-destructive behaviour. *American Journal of Psychiatry*, 148(12), pp. 1665–71.

Van Dijk, T. (2011) Introduction: The study of discourse. In T. Van Dijk (ed.), *Discourse Studies: A Multidisciplinary Introduction*. London: Sage, pp. 1–8.

Valentine, G. and Harris, C. (2014) Strivers vs skivers: Class prejudice and the demonisation of dependency in everyday life. *Geoforum*, 53, pp. 84–92.

Varese, F., Smeets, F., Drukker, M., Lieverse, R., Lataster, T., Viechtbauer, W., Read, J., van Os, J. and Bentall, P. (2012) Childhood adversities increase the risk of psychosis: A meta-analysis of patient-control, prospective- and cross-sectional cohort studies. *Schizophrenia Bulletin*, 38(4), pp. 661–71.

Vassos, E., Pedersen, C.B., Murray, R.M., Collier, D.A. and Lewis, C.M. (2012) Meta-analysis of the association of urbanicity with schizophrenia, *Schizophrenia Bulletin*, 38(6), pp. 1118–23.

Veling, W., Susser, E., van Os, J., Mackenbach, J.P., Selten, J.P. and Hoek, H.W. (2008) Ethnic density of neighborhoods and incidence of psychotic disorders among immigrants, *American Journal of Psychiatry*, 165(1), pp. 66–73.

Vibeke, S. and Turney, D. (2017) The role of professional judgement in social work assessment: A comparison between Norway and England. *European Journal of Social Work*, 20(1), pp. 112–24.

Vuletic, M. (2018) What is philosophy? *Ninewells*, 2 February. Available at: https://ninewells.vuletic.com/philosophy/what-is-philosophy/ (accessed 29 August 2019).

Vygotsky, L. (1931) The development of thinking and concept formation in adolescence. Available at: www.marxists.org/archive/vygotsky/works/1931/adolescent/ch10.htm (accessed 1 December 2019).

Vygotsky, L. (1967) Play and its role in the mental development of the child. *Soviet Psychology*, 5(3), pp. 6–18.

Vygotsky, L. (1978) *Mind and Society*. Cambridge, MA: Harvard University Press.

Vygotsky, L. and Luria, A. (1930) Tool and symbol in child development. Available at: www.marxists.org/archive/vygotsky/works/1934/tool-symbol.htm (accessed 1 December 2019).

Wadsworth, B.J. (1978) *Piaget for the Classroom Teacher*. New York and London: Longman.

Wadsworth, B.J. (2004) *Piaget's Theory of Cognitive and Affective Development*. Boston: Pearson Education.

Walby, S. (1997) *Gender Transformations*. London: Routledge.

Walby, S. (2007) Complexity theory, systems theory, and multiple intersecting social inequalities. *Philosophy of the Social Sciences*, 37(4), pp. 449–70.

Walby, S., Armstrong, J. and Strid, S. (2012) Intersectionality: Multiple inequalities in social theory. *Sociology*, 46(2), pp. 224–40.

Walsh, G. (2018) The ACEs campaign: Cause for worry or celebration? *Times Educational Supplement*, 11 November. Available at: www.tes.com/news/aces-campaign-cause-worry-or-celebration (accessed 21 September 2020).

Webb, S. (2006) *Social Work in a Risk Society: Social and Political Perspectives*. Basingstoke: Palgrave Macmillan.

Webster-Stratton, C. (2003) *The Incredible Years: A Trouble-shooting Guide for Parents of Children Aged 3–8*. Toronto: Umbrella Press.

Weeks, J., Heapy, B. and Donovan, C. (2007) The lesbian and gay family. In J. Scott, J. Treas and M. Richards (eds), *The Blackwell Companion to the Sociology of Families*. Oxford: Blackwell Publishing, pp. 340–355.

West, C. and Zimmerman, D. (1987) Doing gender. *Gender and Society*, 1(2), pp. 125–51.

Weston, K. (1991) *We Choose: Lesbians, Gays, Kinship*. New York: Columbia University Press.

Wicks, S., Hjern, A. and Dalman, C. (2010) Social risk or genetic liability for psychosis? A study of children born in Sweden and reared by adoptive parents, *American Journal of Psychiatry*, 167(10), 1240–6.

Wijedasa, D. (2015) *The Prevalence and Characteristics of Children Growing up with Relatives in the UK*. Briefing paper 001. Bristol: Hadley Research Centre for Adoption and Foster Studies.

Williams, S. and Rutter, L. (2015) *The Practice Educator's Handbook* (Post-Qualifying Social Work Practice Series). London: Learning Matters.

Wilson, K., Ruch, G., Lymbery, M. and Cooper, A. (2011) *Social Work: An Introduction to Contemporary Practice* (2nd edn). Harlow: Pearson Education.

Winnett, R. and Kirkup, J. (2012) Problem Families Have Too Many Children. *Daily Telegraph* 20th July 2012. Available at: https://www.telegraph.co.uk/news/politics/9416535/Problem-families-have-too-many-children.html (accessed 6 July 2020).

Worden, W. (2009) *Grief Counseling and Grief Therapy: A Handbook for the Mental Health Practitioner* (4th edn). Hove: Routledge.

Wolfensberger, W. (1972) *Normalization: The Principle of Normalization in Human Services*. Available at: https://digitalcommons.unmc.edu/wolf_books/1/ (accessed 6 July 2020).

Wolfensberger, W. (1983) Social role valorization: A proposed new term for the principle of normalization. *Mental Retardation*, 21(6), pp. 234–9.

Wolfensberger, W. (1998) *A brief introduction to Social Role Valorization: A high-order concept for addressing the plight of societally devalued people, and for structuring human services* (3rd edn). New York: Syracuse University.

Wolfensberger, W. (2000) A brief overview of Social Role Valorization. *Mental Retardation*, 38(2), 105–23.

World Health Organization (1997) *The World Health Report 1997: Conquering Suffering, Enriching Humanity*. Available at: www.who.int/whr/1997/en/ (accessed 27 November 2019).

World Health Organization (2011) *World Report on Disability*. Available at: www.who.int/disabilities/world_report/2011/en/ (accessed 27 November 2019).

World Health Organization (2017) *Global Strategy and Action Plan on Ageing and Health*. Available at: www.who.int/ageing/WHO-GSAP-2017.pdf?ua=1 (accessed 27 November 2019).

World Health Organization (n.d.) Disabilities. Available at: www.who.int/topics/disabilities/en/ (accessed 1 March 2020).

Youth Justice Board (2014) AssetPlus framework diagram. Available at: https://assets.publishing.service.gov.uk/government/uploads/system/uploads/attachment_data/file/362278/AssetPlus_framework_diagram.pdf (accessed 20 February 2020).

Yuill, C. and Gibson, A. (2011) *Sociology for Social Work: An Introduction*. Los Angeles: Sage.

Yuval-Davis, N. (2006) Intersectionality and feminist politics. *European Journal of Women's Studies*, 13(3), pp. 193–209.

INDEX